DISABILITY, POLITICS & THE STRUGGLE FOR CHANGE

EDITED BY LEN BARTON

David Fulton Publishers
London

To Rachel and Sarai

David Fulton Publishers Ltd
Ormond House, 26–27 Boswell Street, London WC1N 3JZ

www.fultonpublishers.co.uk

First published in Great Britain by David Fulton Publishers 2001.

Note: The rights of Len Barton to be identified as the author of this work has been asserted by him in accordance with the Copyright, Designs and Patents Act 1988.

British Library Cataloguing in Publication Data
A catalogue record for this book is available from the British Library.

ISBN 1–85346-809-6

Typeset by Book Production Services, London
Printed and bound in Great Britain by The Cromwell Press Ltd, Trowbridge, Wilts.

Contents

Contributors

Simone Aspis is a disabled woman labelled by the standardised psychological tests as having learning difficulties and is a special school survivor. Simone is the People First Inclusive Education contact and has supported young disabled people with learning difficulties to participate in Special Educational Needs Tribunal Proceedings when appealing for a supported mainstream school placement. She is the author of two inclusive education papers, 'Disabled Children with Learning Difficulties Fight For Inclusive Education' and 'Why Exams And Tests Do Not Help and Non Disabled Children Learn Together in A Mainstream School'. A third paper due to be published in 2001 will be 'Developing A More Inclusive Assessment Model For All Children'.

Colin Barnes is Professor of Disability Studies at the University of Leeds. He is a disabled writer and researcher, and the Director of the University's internationally renowned Centre for Disability Studies. He has conducted research on a whole range of disability issues and published widely.

Len Barton is Professor of Inclusive Education at the Institute of Education, University of London and is the Director of an Inclusive Education Research Centre. He is the founder and editor of *Disability and Society* and has published extensively on issues relating to socio political perspectives on disability and inclusive education. He is particularly committed to both teaching and supervision of research degrees. One of his key interests is in developing an informed understanding and appreciation of the fundamental importance of cross-cultural ideas and links.

Anne-Marie Callus works with older students with intellectual disabilities who attend special schools in Malta, preparing them for the transition to adult services and life after school. She also carries out training programmes for careworkers. She obtained a MEd from the University of Wales, Swansea, in 1998, specialising in the education of students with severe intellectual disabilities. She worked with children and adults with intellectual disabilities in Cardiff, through *Cardiff University Social Services* and *Opportunity Housing Trust*.

Joseph M. Camilleri, National Commission for Persons with Disabilities, Malta attended a mainstream school and the University of Malta. He trained as a teacher at the then Malta College of Arts, Science and Technology. Between 1977–89 he taught English at secondary level in a Church school. Between 1989 and 1994 he was in involved in the development of distance education packages with the University of Malta's Centre for Distance Learning. In April 1994, he assumed the position of Chairman of the National Commission Persons with Disability. He is heavily committed to raising public awareness regarding disability issues, in this respect he has made many appearances on radio and television, and written articles in newspapers and journals. He is a member of various committees and boards and he organises a variety of disability-related lectures at tertiary and other levels. Joe has a mobility impairment.

Harlan Hahn is a tenured, full professor at a large university in Los Angeles. He is also a spokesperson for Disability Forum in Santa Monica. He has published more than 100 articles in professional journals and seven books.

Bill Hughes is Head of the Division of Sociology and Social Policy at Glasgow Caledonian University. He has published in the *Body and Society* and *Disability and Society* and his research interests in the body, medicine and disability are reflected in his co-authorship of a book recently published by the Open University Press entitled *The Body, Culture and Society: An Introduction*.

Geoffrey Mercer is a Senior Lecturer in the Department of Sociology and Social Policy and a member of the Centre for Disability Studies at the University of Leeds. He is co-author of a book published by the Polity Press entitled Barnes, *Exploring Disability: A sociological introduction*.

Mike Oliver is Professor of Disability Studies at the University of Greenwich. He has written many books and articles on disability issues and is currently rewriting "The Politics of Disablement". He is Chair of the Research Sub-committee of the British Council of Disabled People, an Executive Editor of *Disability and Society* and a member of the Social Research Committee of the National Lottery Charities Board.

Richard Rieser, London, UK is a disabled person, parent, writer, activist and has been a teacher working in all phases for 25 years. Positions held include Chair of The Alliance for Inclusive Education, Director of Disability Equality in Education and a member of the UK Government National Advisory Group on Special Educational Needs, Vice-Chair of the NUT disability working group for 11 years and Vice-Chair of the Council for Disabled Children.

Marcia Rioux is Professor and Chair, School of Health Policy and Management, York University, Toronto, Canada. She has been involved in international human rights work in disability for 25 years in Canada, India, the Caribbean, Latin America and Europe. In Canada she has headed the Roeher Institute and worked at the Canadian Human Rights Commission, the Law Reform Commission, and the Royal Commission on Employment Equity. She is widely published in the field. She holds a PhD in Jurisprudence and Social Policy from Boalt Hall Law School, University of California, Berkeley.

Martin Sullivan is a lecturer in Social Policy and Disability Studies at Massey University, Palmerston North, Aotearoa New Zealand. His research interests focus on the implications the interrelationships between body, self and society have for disabled people in terms of subject position and subjectivity. He is currently planning a book on masculinity and disability.

Carol Thomas is a Senior Lecturer in Applied Social Science at Lancaster University, UK. She is the author of *Female Forms: experiencing and understanding disability*. Her work in disability studies has also resulted in a wide range of journal articles and book chapters, mainly exploring different aspects of women's disability experiences. Carol is also undertaking research in the fields of cancer studies and health inequality.

Anastasia Vlachou-Balafouti is a Lecturer at the Department of Special Education at the University of Thessaly in Greece. She has worked in both comprehensive and special secondary schools and has been involved in national and cross-national teaching and research projects in the areas of special/inclusive education. She is particularly interested in promoting inclusive educational policies and practices and inclusive curricula and pedagogy. She is the author of the book *Struggles for Inclusive Education*.

Introduction

After careful consideration I have decided to break with tradition and not provide an editor's condensed overview of the main points of each chapter. The last chapter of the book has provided some details of this nature. Instead, I will offer some insights into the reason for the chosen themes of the book, why these particular authors were invited to contribute, what subjects they were asked to address and some final thoughts on the publication.

The contributors are disabled and non-disabled and represent a range of perspectives on the issues under examination. They were asked to address the theme of the book in a critical and informative manner. In particular, they were encouraged to engage with this task through illustrations about themselves, and/or, the particular country and context they were writing from. Friendships, and/or awareness of their work and of the particular stage of policy development that their societies were currently experiencing, influenced the decision making. Finally, the limited number of publications dealing with these issues in some societies was also an important factor that influenced the invitations.

This book is concerned with attempting to revisit some important ideas and questions including the conceptualisation and understanding of disability, the nature of politics and political action, the question of change, the position and role of the disability movement and the contribution of cross-cultural insights to such issues. Existing ideas and understandings are discussed from within various historical, socio-political and cultural contexts. The authors are at different stages of understanding and interpretation and are not homogeneous with regard to their relations to structural forms of discrimination and oppression, their approaches or their plans of action.

The authors do share some points of commonality in terms of values and commitment. They support a social model of disability and thus are critical of theoretical, practical and policy approaches that pathologise, individualise, sentimentalise and legitimate deficit, blame-the-victim and tragedy models of disability. They also recognise the importance of thinking about disability in relation to other forms of inequality and institutionalised forms of discrimination, including racism, gender, sexuality and ageism. This form of relational thinking provides a basis for seeking collective support and a shared conviction of the fundamental seriousness of the demand for change, the magnitude of the task and the complexity of the issues, for example, in terms of the reality of simultaneous forms of oppression. Finally, they see themselves as learners and thus recognise the vital importance of engaging in debate and dialogue in which points of difference can be recognised and viewed as part of a creative tension. Through this developmental and disturbing process alternative ideas, insights and questions emerge. The chapters in this book do not provide blueprints for how to deal with the conceptual, political and practical issues that they raise. Nor are they to be viewed as final authoritative statements on the issues under examination. Each of the contributors recognises the challenge of grappling with the contentious nature of the ideas and the difficulties of making connections between historical, situational, biographical and structural factors.

No apology is being offered for the use of the language of struggle in relation to both the theme and form of writing in which contributors have approached their work. It is used as an indication of the seriousness with which the issues and ideas are perceived and the degree of commitment including the depth of feelings and emotionality involved. The writers feel passionate about these matters. They do not underestimate the task involved in establishing a non-discriminatory and inclusive society. Nor are they complacent over their own work and the more collective developments that need to increasingly emerge. The struggles over principles, values, priorities, political awareness, intentions and forms of action is both a fertile ground and a conflictual process in which there are no easy, quick, slick answers. Learning with and from one another especially in terms of cross-cultural conditions, relations and practices is an essential, difficult and exciting feature of the change process.

All the contributions need to be critically engaged with and any identified limitations should not be viewed as an attack on the basic principle of pursuing such explorations in creative and imaginative ways, but rather as an indication of the urgent need for much more sustained work. Thus, the book will hopefully stimulate debate and raise new questions and topics for research. The concern is not to close down critical analysis and discussion but to encourage a dialogue with interested parties.

At the end of each chapter the authors have provided two questions. I appreciate that the value of including questions is debatable but at least they provide the reader with some insights into the thinking of the authors with regard to some of the issues they believe need to be urgently and seriously discussed. Hopefully, as you read these papers you will be able to identify other questions and insights that need to be engaged with.

Len Barton
September 2001

Acknowledgements

I am grateful to Helen Oliver for all her help with the preparation of this manuscript.

My thanks to all the contributors for their responses to my requests and comments and for keeping to very tight deadlines.

CHAPTER 1

Disability, struggle and the politics of hope

Len Barton

Introduction

In this chapter the context in which change is viewed as a necessity with regard to the position and experience of disabled people will be briefly examined. The centrality of the issue of politics will also be explored in terms of its meaning and function in contributing to the development of change. Finally, the question of hope will be discussed in relation to its motivating and unifying possibilities.

Politics

Whenever the term 'politics' is used it reflects a variety of possible meanings. In popular discourse, especially as expressed in the tabloid press, it is often understood in relation to particular politicians or parties and their questionable behaviour or misleading, fictitious claims or statements. Politics in this sense is viewed in terms of sleaze, corruption and as a term of abuse. The impact of these accounts have perhaps contributed to a much more common and increasing attitude among the general populace. This position views politics as being of little concern to people's everyday lives and interests except as a topic of contempt or a source of jokes and amusement. This more general indifference is most vividly demonstrated in the declining interest in membership of political parties and the numbers who do not even exercise their vote during elections (Dean 2001; Gamble 2000). At best politics is seen as boring, and at worst irrelevant or trivial.

This disenchantment with politics in the West is for some political analysts like Gamble (2000) part of a deeper pessimism and fatalism which:

> … reflects the disillusion of political hopes in liberal and socialist utopias in the Twentieth Century and a wide-spread disenchantment with the grand narratives of the Enlightenment about reason and progress, and with modernity itself. Its most characteristic expression is in the endless discourses on endism – the end of history, the end of ideology, the end of the nation state, the end of the public domain, the end of politics itself – all have been proclaimed in recent years. Our contemporary fate is to live in the iron cages erected by vast impersonal forces arising from globalisation and technology, a society which is both anti

political and unpolitical, a society without hope or the means either to imagine or promote an alternative future. (Preface)

In his critical analysis of both the nature and validity of the claims relating to what he terms the various 'endisms' that are currently being promoted, Gamble seeks to re-examine the importance of politics and argues for its necessity at both an individual and societal level. In confronting the complexity of the social conditions and relations of the contemporary world, he contends, that politics is an activity, a means of creating a space in which the fundamental questions of '… who are we, what should we get, how shall we live' and 'what should be conserved, and what reformed, what should be public and what private and the rules by which societies should be governed' (p. 1) can be seriously explored. Through this means a conception of human agency as central to the change process and of the belief in and importance of being able to create alternative visions and future possibilities are reinforced.

In an attempt to resist the dangers of extremism with regard to optimism and pessimism in relation to human agency and structural constraints, he recognises the

… inescapable tension between agency and constraint and therefore between politics and fate. (p. 17)

This is part of a more creative perspective in which:

Understood in this way fate both constrains and enables, it sets the limits but also provides opportunities. (p. 18)

So in seeking to critique the discrediting, debunking tendencies with regard to the meaning and value of politics, both in popular and academic discourses, Gamble powerfully maintains:

The political realm which is constituted by the three dimensions of the political – politics as power, politics as identity and politics as order – remains a crucial component of human experience and human capacity. (p. 6)

Each of these dimensions allows for the exploration of particular questions including; who gets what, when and how?; who are we?; how should we live?

Conflict is an integral feature of each of these spaces and involves struggles over, for example,

… who takes decisions as to how resources are allocated, and what these decisions are; conflict over identities of meaning different things and how these are expressed and represented, conflict over the constitutive principles of different political, economic and social orders. (p. 8)

Understanding the nature of and relationship between these dimensions is absolutely crucial. This is an essential feature of political activity. Its significance is particularly manifest in relation to individuals and groups who are experiencing institutionalised forms of inequality and discrimination. Addressing internal and external forms of oppression, endeavouring to identify, understand and challenge disabling barriers and seeking individual and collective empowerment and solidarity reinforce the political nature of these engagements. Disabled people are not only involved in struggles over attitudes but also over the realisation of citizenship, social justice, equity and protection through anti-discrimination legislation based on human rights.

The reduction of the space for the imagination and realisation of alternative possibilities to the present system and relations, will only be prevented by the active pursuit of the political dimensions integral to human experience. Without politics a sense of helplessness and hope-lessness becomes a more ominous possibility.

Hope

A fundamental argument of this chapter is that there is now an urgency about the need for further attention being given to the development of a political analysis which is inspired by a desire for transformative change and that constitutes hope at the centre of the struggles for inclusivity. The perspective both recognises the profundity of the forms of discrimination and inequalities that need to be addressed and that this ultimately requires a collective response. *Ad hoc*, piecemeal or minimalist approaches to reform will be ineffectual in realising the sorts of changes required. At both an individual and collective level a crucial task is to develop a theory of political action which also involves the generation of tactics or strategies for its implemen-tation. This is a difficult but essential agenda.

In the opening to her recent book, bell hooks (2000), the Afro-American feminist, describes an incident in her life during a period in which she was experiencing being 'often overwhelmed by grief so profound it seemed as though an immense sea of pain was washing my heart and soul away' (p. xv). On her way to her work at Yale University she had to pass a construction site and on one of the walls painted in bright colours was the statement: 'The search for love continues even in the face of great odds' (p. xv). Whenever she passed this site this affirmation of love's possibility gave her hope.

The struggle for inclusion and more democratic forms of relationships and processes within society often seems like an impossible task. This experience often includes feelings of frustration, exhaustion and demoralisation. This is why hope is a fundamental prerequisite for the effective realisation of the struggle for transformative change.

Hope is essential in the struggle for change. It involves a recognition of the unacceptable nature of the present conditions and relations, a desire to be in a different situation and a conviction that this is possible. It involves a belief that the possibilities of change of the current situation are not foreclosed. Without hope the kind of social transformation that is being advocated will not be realised. Hope is based on critical analyses of the past and present social conditions and relations (Allman 1999). Writing on the role of pedagogy in providing serious critiques of dominant ideologies and encouraging ways of learning that are empow-ering, Freire (1998) contends that:

> … the attempt to do without hope in the struggle to improve the world, as if that struggle could be reduced to calculated acts alone, or a purely scientific approach is a frivolous illu-sion… Without a minimum of hope, we cannot so much as start the struggle. (pp. 8 and 9)

This perspective is based on a vision of human agency and history as always in a process of becoming.

In terms of the approach being advocated in this chapter, hope reminds us of the importance of understanding the world in order to change it. It is based on a strong conviction that current conditions and relations are not natural, proper or eternal. They can be changed. Hope therefore, can mobilise, galvanise and inspire. It arises from within a social context characterised by unacceptable inequalities and discrimination.

It is of paramount importance that hope is grounded in an informed understanding of the social conditions and relations of the past; as Apple (1986) reminds us, we 'need to recapture the past to see what is possible' (p. 177). This historical understanding will alert us to the dangers which Simon (1987) so perceptively warns against. We must not:

> ... romanticise all dreams about the future. Not all fantasy is benign. The basis of what many people view as a 'better tomorrow' sometimes includes the unjust and oppressive disparagement or control over others. Not all dreams are dreams of hope. (p. 382)

Hope does not provide a foolproof blueprint with regard to the future, nor is it a wishful fantasy about how good the future will be. It does entail overlapping states of mind in which doubt will be a factor and as Lazarus (1999) maintains:

> It provides the grounds for our continuing engagement in life, even when there is only a slender thread of hope on which to rely. (p. 675)

No matter how slender, it does provide a coping strategy and grounds for continuing the struggle.

While hope is deeply personal, within a social and political context in which grand narratives about the world are being discouraged and excessive individualism reinforced, there is a real danger of hope being privatised. Thus, there is a need to encourage collective hope and this is why the organisations of disabled people are so important in the struggle for personal and collective empowerment.

Social movements

Part of the struggle of groups that have been constituted as 'other' or negatively different, is to develop a voice in which positive images of identity are created and maintained. Social movements have specific characteristics which arise from within particular historical and socio-economic conditions. They are concerned with the pursuit of change and their forms and priorities are directed towards the realisation of a more democratic and inclusive society. Such movements are examples of forms of cultural and political opposition to those socio-economic conditions and relations that have generated and legitimated discriminatory and exclusionary policies and practices. Thus, the women's movement, gay and lesbian movements are organisations that have been created in order to offer support and encouragement for their members as well as providing an external function, that of educating and critiquing those outside the movement.

These movements are visionary and provide resources of hope and as Taylor (1997) so perceptively maintains:

> The strength of social movements lies in the types of issue that people are mobilised around; identifying the vacuum, the gaps that are not being addressed and what impact these have on the specific group to be targeted. (p. 258)

Thus they offer alternative ways of thinking and engaging with particular issues and questions, such as, identity, difference and community. They provide as Crowther and Shaw (1997) contend:

> ... the impetus, energy and resources which mobilise people for collective action. (p. 266)

This may encourage a strong involvement in the formal political system in the struggle for change or contribute to the generation of new forms of political activity.

Social movements are involved in challenging the status quo, in making more transparent the ways in which knowledge and power come together in relation to specific issues; they are concerned with what might yet be rather than uncritically accepting the way things are; they create spaces for new knowledge and forms of action to emerge; and finally they transform desires and raise expectations (Touraine, 1981; Scott, 1990; Crowther and Shaw, 1997).

In their insider account of the rise of the British disability movement, Campbell and Oliver (1996) highlight the four criteria derived from Marx and McAdam (1994) against which any social movement must be judged:

> These are whether any new political or economic changes have resulted from its activities, whether any specific legislation has resulted, what changes in public opinion and behaviour have been produced, and whether any new organisations or institutions have been created. (p. 168)

However, Campbell and Oliver also maintain that in relation to the disability movement there are three further criteria against which the movement should be evaluated. These are:

> ... the extent of the consciousness raising and empowerment amongst disabled people, the extent to which disability issues are raised internationally, and the promotion of disability as a human and civil rights issue. (p. 168)

The disability movement is both a national and international development. In Britain factors such as, the increasing recognition by disabled people of the failure of party politics, charitable and voluntary organisations to meet their needs, the emergence of the civil rights movement and the feminist movement both acted as role models in the struggle for social justice, equity and anti-discrimination legislation and they all contributed to the development of the movement (Shakespeare 1993; Campbell and Oliver 1996; Oliver 1997).

According to Morris (1992a) the disability movement faces several challenges:

> As with other social and political movements, the first task of the disability movement is concerned with raising our own consciousness about the way society disables us. Through that awareness we can join with other disabled people to form our own organisations. These organisations support us, helping to break down the isolation many of us experience and also attempt to change the way that non-disabled people respond to impairment. (p. 27)

This is part of the struggle for recognition on the part of disabled people and their organisations that their lives have value and that they have a valuable contribution to make to the communities in which they live. This is in stark contrast to those organisations *for* disabled people that have legitimated a charitable approach to disability and who through their publicity and campaigns have evoked images of pity and guilt and devalued the position and interests of disabled people. This issue is of fundamental importance, for as Morris (1992a) so forcefully argues, it is about who has the *right* to say what disabled people need, or how disabled people should be represented to the public and how monies raised in their name should be spent.

In all social movements the process of involvement changes the participants. They become different in terms of their self-awareness and identity. This can have significant consequences for how other people view them, as Beresford and Campbell (1994) indicate in relation to involvement in the disability movement:

> We became 'unrepresentative' in ways some service providers do not want. We became confident, experienced, informed and effective. (p. 317)

Personal and collective support, skills, knowledge and experience acquired from participation in the movement, are all significant factors in the process of empowerment.

In the struggle for change a perennial issue concerns the position of the movement over relationships with government. This question raises some serious dilemmas as Campbell and Oliver (1996) so forcefully remind us:

> As other social movements have found to their cost, to get too close is to risk incorporation, while to remain too aloof is to risk marginalisation and a slow death because of resource starvation. (p. 148)

This issue highlights the complexity of the task that organisations which simultaneously both provide a critical stance and seek constructive relationships with governments continually face.

Efforts to understand exclusionary and disabling barriers and especially their institutionalised forms, to develop an agenda and strategies for change, to establish alternative values and priorities will involve conflicts and can never be a smooth and untroubled process. It is a learning experience that will entail creative, constructive, disturbing, conflictual and emotionally draining elements.

So, for example, the position and function of the British Council of Disabled People is currently the subject of critical review by members of the organisation. Some members like Penny Germon (2000) argue, that things are going wrong and the foundations of the movement are fragmenting. Part of the reason for this she maintains, is a lack of leadership:

In my view there is a leadership vacuum. The 'highly organised disabled people's movement' is fragmenting. We are losing the very thing that gave us power, our organisation and solidarity. If we allow this to continue, we will pay a heavy price – the price will be our movement.

We need somewhere we can come together, debate the urgent issues, combine our energy and resources and decide on our collective priorities – we need clear leadership. (p. 18)

While agreeing with the need for change within the movement Ann Rae (2000) believes that one of the fundamental reasons why this has become a priority is because of 'barriers to dialogue and debate' and the dangers of appeasement and compromise by individuals and key post holders within the organisation. In a powerful plea she asks several important questions including:

Why should we keep quiet when individual disabled people publicly voice a view implying it is a representative view, that we individually or organisationally disagree with? Why should we not challenge Disabled People who are in a representative role, but clearly following an individualistic/careerist position. (p. 6)

Adding to these concerns Finkelstein (2000), one of the founders of the disability movement in Britain, argues that for the movement to deal constructively with its difficulties serious consideration needs to be given to strategies and tactics for change in volatile socio-economic contexts. He also maintains that these strategies and tactics can and do benefit from an informed historical understanding of past mistakes and successes. This is a crucial issue because, he contends, we are witnessing within the movement the emergence of 'creeping apathy'. Part of this re-examination also includes a re-assessment of the nature and value of the social model of disability.

In seeking to understand and discuss the developments and experiences of organisations of disabled people we do need to resist the danger of overly romantic, idealised, historical conceptions of the relations and practices involved. Membership of such organisations entails the development of critical reflection that focuses on both *internal* and external divisive and exclusionary barriers. This is why the establishment and maintenance of an infrastructure that supports debate and dialogue is of fundamental importance.

A crucially important aspect of the struggle that disabled people and their organisations have been engaged in concerns the question of the politics of representation. This involves challenging disablist, negative conceptions and encouraging positive images and understandings of disability. Particular slogans such as 'Piss on Pity', 'It's choices and rights not charity that we want', reflect both a recognition of the offensiveness of disabling barriers on the one hand, and the desire to identify and challenge them on the other. Underpinning this approach is a public affirmation of a positive view of difference.

In a booklet published by Jigsaw Partnerships (1995) a group of young disabled people concerned with the question of a positive view of difference establish some clear reasons as to why positive image posters are necessary. They include:

- There are not enough positive images of disabled people by disabled people.
- There is a need to challenge the stereotyped images of disabled people that have been created by non-disabled people through the media and especially in charity advertising.
- It is important to raise awareness of the rights of disabled people to equality of access and opportunity….(p. 1)

The challenge of how to create a society in which all citizens experience full participation including the maximum development of their abilities is an urgent and fundamental task. A serious engagement with the complexity of these difficulties will require a recognition of the necessity of understanding the interrelationship between history, biography, context and structural factors.

Thus, the challenges we face at the level of global markets and the inequalities and dependency creating conditions and relations between different regional and geographical spheres as well as the issue of the dangerous destruction of the ecology of the earth are unprecedented. Within this more global context the question of the politics of identity, difference and community need to be addressed (Gamble 2000). The necessity of political analysis has never been more urgent. Nor will this be an easy linear form of progress. It will involve setbacks, conflicts and serious disputes. These challenges cannot be effectively addressed except through politics. Thus, the undermining and dismissal of politics needs to be viewed as a reactionary and dangerous perspective. This is because as Gamble (2000) so importantly and perceptively notes:

> Politics as an activity is not just part of our experience but *constitutive* of it (p. 98 – my emphasis).

From this perspective, the question of disability in terms of who and how it is defined, represented and engaged with in terms of policy and practice, are fundamentally political issues.

Issues of definition and understanding in relation to the position of subordinate groups are explored by Young (2000) within a wider debate about questions of democratic equality, civil society and inclusion. Part of her analysis is about a critical exploration of the politics of identity in favour of one which gives support to relational understanding of subordinate groups. Young (2000) argues that:

> A democratic process is inclusive not simply by formally including all particularly affected individuals in the same way, but by attending to the social relations that differentially position people and condition their experiences, opportunities and knowledge of the society. (p. 83)

Structural relations are viewed as impacting on individuals and groups thereby positioning them in unequal terms in relation, for example, to issues of power, knowledge, resource allocation and opportunities. This has serious implications for as Young maintains:

> Claims of justice made from specific social groups positions exposes the consequence of such notions of power and opportunity. (pp. 86–7)

This approach raises objections to conceptions of subordinate groups as an undifferentiated unity and gives emphasis to the centrality of a positive view of difference. Engaging with these issues of definition and understanding is part of the struggle to establish a politics of hope. This process is complex, contentious and demanding intellectually, emotionally and interpersonally.

Conclusion

Fundamental to a politics of hope is the recognition that hopelessness is a disempowering, restrictive and demoralising experience. It involves an assault upon a person's identity, self-worth and their psycho-emotional and social well-being. From within the context and experience of discriminatory and unequal social conditions and relations hope arises. Understanding the barriers to self- and collective actualisation is part of the process of regeneration that the politics of hope entails. Any attempt to minimise or trivialise the offensive and fundamental seriousness of oppression and marginalisation in the lives of disabled people is a reactionary and counterproductive influence that needs to be critiqued and ruthlessly challenged.

In her book on *Justice and the Politics of Difference,* Young (1990) maintains, that while a notion of justice in terms of distribution is important, it tends to obscure issues of domination and oppression. This perspective recognises the centrality of social structure and relations and the decision-making procedures involved, especially in terms of their influence in sustaining and legitimating social inequalities. In order to develop an adequate understanding of the multiple factors involved in this process we need, according to Young, a family of concepts. They are 'exploitation, marginalisation, powerlessness, cultural imperialism and violence' (p. 9). The concepts of oppression and domination are fundamentally important if we are to understand injustice. While recognising the contentious nature of her arguments, Young outlines the assumptions that have influenced her thinking and working. They are:

> ...that basic equality in life situations for all persons is a moral value; that there are deep injustices in our society that can be rectified only by basic institutional changes; that the groups I have named are oppressed; that structures of domination wrongfully pervade our society. (p. 14)

These are some of the key assumptions that have influenced the writing of this chapter.

The question of disability provides us with an opportunity for raising serious questions about the nature of the existing society we live in and the kind of society we desire or hope for. Why and how a society excludes particular individuals and groups involves processes of categorisation in which the inferior, unacceptable aspects of a person's makeup are highlighted and legitimated. How we understand this activity will be influenced by the values we are committed to. Which definition is seen as significant, why and with what consequences, must therefore, be the subject of serious critical scrutiny. Removing ignorance, stereotypes and fear is thus a task which will have reciprocal benefits for disabled and non-disabled people. We need a public confirmation that discrimination in its varied forms is not acceptable and must be challenged.

The testimony to the profoundly serious nature of this situation can be found in the voices of disabled people and the accounts of their experiences and position. For example:

> It is clear that most of us have found that other people's reactions are a very important part of the experience of disability. It's almost as if our disability grants unwritten permission for people to pry or stare or offer solutions when none were asked for. It's a form of stress that is very seldom recognised. Each intrusion proves yet again that we are seen as different and separate and no longer part of the general stream of life. (Morris 1989: 78)

Against the realities of these experiences and the conditions that sustain them, disabled people are demanding changes. They are not arguing for sameness, or to become as normal as possible, nor are they seeking an independence without assistance. Their vision is of a world in which discrimination and injustice are removed. They are desirous of the establishment of alternative definitions and perceptions based on a dignified view of difference. The struggle for inclusion is thus disturbing, demanding and developmental. It involves the experience of exercising choices and rights and, for example, in relation to independence, having assistance when and how they require it (Morris 1993a).

In a powerful manner, Oliver and Barnes (1998) outline their hope of a better world. It is ...

> ... a world in which all human beings, regardless of impairment, age, gender, social class or minority ethnic status, can coexist as equal members of the community, secure in the knowledge that their needs will be met and that their views will be recognised, respected and valued. It will be a very different world from the one in which we now live. It will be a world which is truly democratic, characterised by genuine and meaningful equality of opportunity, with far greater equity in terms of wealth and income, with enhanced choice and freedom, and with a proper regard for environmental and social continuity. The creation of such a world will be a long and difficult process. (p. 102)

This takes us beyond the issue of disablement to an inclusive society for all. It will require political action. Hence the necessity for a politics of hope.

Questions

- How far is the question of hope an important aspect of your own thinking and practice?
- Is the conception of a 'politics of hope' helpful with regard to the issue of disability?

CHAPTER 2

The politics of disability and the struggle for change

Colin Barnes and Geof Mercer

Introduction

There is little doubt that during the last two decades or so our understanding of disability has been transformed. Although the traditional individualistic medical approach remains prevalent, many people across the world, including politicians and policy makers, now recognise that 'disability' is an equal opportunities/human rights issue on a par with sexism, heterosexism, racism and other forms of social exclusion. Since 1981, the United Nations (UN) International Year of Disabled People, the UN has promoted various initiatives on the equalisation of opportunities for disabled persons for member states. Nations as diverse as America and China now have anti-discrimination laws designed to combat discrimination against this increasingly large section of the world's population (Stone 1999). There is general agreement too that these remarkable and unprecedented achievements are due, almost exclusively, to the politicisation of disability by disabled people and their organisations in various nations throughout the world (Driedger 1989; Campbell and Oliver 1996).

This chapter centres on this process of politicisation. The analysis will address both macro and micro sociological concerns, although the emphasis will be on the former, including disabled people's relationship to 'conventional' politics, self-organisation, and the emergence of a positive 'disabled' identity. The discussion examines: orthodox political structures and processes and the various barriers to disabled people's participation, the emergence of the disabled people's movement, the struggle for rights and the limits of the law. Claims that the disabled people's movement exemplifies a 'new' social movement and an evaluation of these developments indicate that key challenges and dilemmas threaten to undermine recent gains and the ongoing struggle for change.

Politics and power

For sociologists the concept of 'power' refers to any aspect of social life where there is inequality between two or more people and there are attempts to maintain or transform the situation. (Marconis and Plummer 1995). This extends to the main political institutions and those responsible for the organisation and regulation of society. In western-style liberal democracies, such as Britain and the United States of America (USA), these include Parliament and Congress, Prime Minister and President, local and state governments, the civil service and sponsored bureaucracies, political parties, pressure groups and the courts. These exercise varying degrees of power and influence, which affect every aspect of our daily lives. Further-more, feminists stress that even the closest personal relationships involve inequalities of power and a constant process of negotiation and change. Thus, the full range of relations between disabled and non-disabled people in one way or another demonstrate power and political dimensions (Oliver 1990).

In most 'western' type societies power is legitimated through the democratic process. Although democracy implies that power is exercised by the people as a whole, it is generally considered impractical for everyone to participate directly in the decision-making process. Instead, a system of 'representative democracy' has evolved whereby elected leaders are peri-odically accountable to the people. However, the political life of the West is shaped largely by the free market economic principles of capitalism. Individuals are 'free' to vote for the leader of their choice and to pursue their own personal self-interests. But most western democracies are characterised by stark inequalities in wealth and influence. Such disparity gives far more choices and opportunities to some than others.

All of which has particular resonance for people with impairments. For the overwhelming majority of disabled people, everyday interaction is a constant struggle for equality and change (Coleridge 1993; Campbell and Oliver 1996; Drake 1999; Sayce 2000). Government determines social policy in terms of health, education, employment and welfare and government-spon-sored bureaucracies of one form or another. Poverty is disproportionately high among the disabled population in both the minority world of the West and the majority world of the rest (LaPlant *et al.* 1997; Charlton 1998; Stone 1999; Burchardt 2000). Most importantly, disabled people encounter various obstacles when attempting to influence the political process.

Voting in national and local elections is one of the most basic rights of a democratic society. Yet disabled people around the world face many barriers when exercising their right to vote (Charlton, 1998). For example, in Britain, one of the world's oldest representative democracies, disabled people designated with 'mental illness' or 'learning difficulties' are often excluded from the electoral register. All too often the right to vote is dependent on the awareness and integrity of others. But low expectations and the mistaken assumption among the general public that people so labelled are not entitled to vote, mean that many go unregistered (Enticott and Graham 1992; Sayce 2000).

Physical access also poses major problems for disabled people wishing to vote in elections. In Britain several studies have documented the negative experiences of disabled people when voting. These include transport difficulties in getting to the polling station, and access problems in entering the polling station, the polling booth and when marking the ballot paper. In the 1997 British General Election 94 per cent of polling stations had one or more access problems (Christie 1999). As a result disabled people's dependence on others: relatives, friends and/or professional helpers, are reinforced if they wish to vote. Many disabled people are simply unable to vote because they have no one to help them.

Of course disabled people voting by post or by proxy may overcome these difficulties. But this is a long drawn-out process that many find unnecessarily bureaucratic and daunting. Postal ballots also mean voting before the election campaign is over. Hence, postal and proxy voting are poor substitutes for proper access facilities. Furthermore, relevant political information is rarely produced in accessible formats such as Braille, tape, video or symbols, for different sections of the disabled community (Christie 1999; Disability Rights Task Force 1999). Since access issues pose major problems for disabled people throughout the democratic world it is likely that those living outside Britain encounter similar difficulties when exercising their political rights.

Disabled people wishing to enter party politics encounter similar problems. Historically, some disabled Britons were actually barred from entering politics. Since the 18th century electoral agents and returning officers were guided by various publications including: Whitlocke's *Notes upon the King's Writs for Choosing Members of Parliament* and *Parker's Conduct of Parliamentary Elections*. The former excludes 'those rendered incapable by physical or mental disability' (Whitelocke 1766: 461). The latter provides three grounds for the exclusion of candidates: incapacity by reason of (a) mental or physical disability; (b) circumstance, character or conduct; (c) certain offices or positions (Wollaston 1970 cited in Drake 1999: 90). As recently as 1955 'deaf and dumb persons' were declared 'ineligible for Parliament' (Schofield 1955: 83).

It remains the case that disabled people are rarely encouraged to enter party politics. This contrasts dramatically with recent initiatives by all Britain's political parties to increase the numbers of candidates from hitherto excluded groups such as women and minority ethnic communities. Nevertheless, the number of members of parliament with impairments rose slightly following the 1997 General Election. However, none is primarily concerned with disability issues. This is unsurprising since in Britain, as in most representative democracies, the main political parties claim to represent the interests of society as a whole rather than one particular group no matter how large or diverse it may be. Consequently, in the 1997 British General Election:

> neither of the (main) parties, the candidates, election material nor the media paid significant attention to issues that may effect disabled people. (Christie 1999: 67)

Alternatively, single-issue pressure group lobbying and campaigns provided a further avenue for political action by disabled people. This form of political involvement increased significantly in the latter half of the 20th century. There are now hundreds of such organisations, varying widely in membership, operating at both local and national levels.

But pressure groups vary in their access to, and influence on, the policy-making process. In a capitalist society those with the most political clout are the more established 'corporate groups' that play a crucial role in the economy. Examples include employer's federations and large trades unions. There is also another, more pluralistic world of 'competing interest groups', associated with voluntary action. But, since they have a less pivotal role in economic activity, they have considerably less influence (Cawson 1982). Groups concerned with disability tend to be located in the latter category.

Moreover, there are significant differences between 'disability' and 'disabled people's' organisations in their objectives, their membership and their leadership. The former includes those organisations that adhere to a more traditional individualistic deficit approach to disability. They are usually, but not always, controlled and run exclusively by non-disabled people. They are mainly concerned with service provision for disabled people, their families and professionals, and often represent the interests of a particular group of disabled people. Examples include the Royal Association for Disablement and Rehabilitation (RADAR) and The Royal Commonwealth Society for the Blind.

In Britain, as in other wealthy nations, there are economic advantages such as tax concessions for organisations with charitable status. They are, however, prohibited from overt political action. It is also illegal for 'beneficiaries' of these agencies to be members of their management boards or committees. Hence, it is difficult for disabled people to effectively control such organisations or for charities to engage openly in political activity (Lloyd 1993). Yet many established disability organisations have, historically, acted as both disability charities and pressure groups. In doing so they have built up close working relationships with politicians and policy makers which 'gives them a degree of credibility but relatively little power' (Barnes 1991: 218).

Moreover, until recently, it was not thought important that disability charities should 'represent' as much as 'look after' disabled people's interests. Historically, the key decision makers in organisations *for* disabled people were salaried professionals who put forward their own 'expert' views about the needs of their particular 'client group'. When coupled with their fund-raising strategies and dependency creating services, this overtly paternalistic approach serves only to undermine disabled people's efforts to empower themselves (Oliver and Barnes 1998). However, in recent years some of these agencies have engaged in parliamentary or lobbying activity along with similarly inclined organisations controlled and run by disabled people themselves.

These organisations tend to favour a more proactive self-help or activist approach to disability politics. These include grassroots self-help and advocacy agencies such as Britain's Derbyshire Coalition for Inclusive Living and America's Berkeley Centre for Independent Living. Other organisations *of* disabled people are concerned solely with collective action and consciousness raising. Examples include Britain's Disability, Direct Action Network (DAN) and Americans with Disabilities for Accessible Public Transport (subsequently renamed, American Disabled for Attendant Programs Today) (ADAPT). These groups are often members of umbrella/coordinating bodies such as the British Council of Disabled People (BCODP), the American Coalition of Citizens with Disabilities (ACCD) and the Disabled People's International (DPI).

Radicalism and rights

Since the 1960s, disabled people, their organisations and allies around the world have increasingly campaigned for equal rights and opportunities. The economic and political upheavals of the period, especially in the USA, provided the inspiration for this phenomenon. The combination of conventional lobbying tactics and mass political action as adopted by black civil rights activists and the women's movement provided a catalyst for change for the emergent American 'disability rights movement' (Shapiro 1993; Charlton 1998). Until the 1970s American disability politics was characterised by a loosely structured farrago of grassroots groups and organisations. A disabled activist, Judy Heumann, formed a notable example, Disabled in Action (DIA), to campaign exclusively for disabled people's rights in New York in 1970. Swelled by the growing numbers of disabled Vietnam War veterans, the movement grew in stature and confidence. Demonstrations, sit-ins and other protests became more prominent. For instance, during the closing stages of the presidential election in 1972, the DIA joined with a group of disabled Vietnam veterans to occupy President Richard Nixon's re-election headquarters in

New York to demand, albeit unsuccessfully, a televised debate on the question of disability rights (Shapiro 1993).

This type of activity impacted on American politicians up for re-election and sympathetic Congressmen began to insert disability-related clauses into the 1973 Rehabilitation Act. Section 504 is particularly important because, for the first time, it prohibited discrimination against disabled people in federally funded programmes. The 1973 Act also enhanced environmental access, first addressed in the United States by the 1968 Architectural Barriers Act, and encouraged more comprehensive services, employment opportunities, and an increase in the numbers of Centres for Independent Living (CILs). Furthermore:

> The enactment of section 504 was brought about largely by the activism of disabled people themselves. A number of sit-ins took place before the appropriate regulations were finally issued. The militancy of these sit-ins … vividly contradicted the stereotype of the disabled person as powerless. (Zola 1983: 56)

Notwithstanding, it took several years and much more campaigning to translate section 504 into meaningful policy regulations. A key player in these activities was the American Coalition of Citizens with Disabilities (ACCD). Formed in 1974, from an existing network of self-help groups the ACCD boasted over 60 local and national affiliated organisations. But around this time a tension emerged between those favouring advocacy within the federal or state systems and those 'outsiders' engaged in grassroots campaigns (Scotch 1989).

Moreover, during the 1980s direct political action gradually gave way to lengthy judicial battles involving disabled individuals seeking redress through the American courts, all of which attracted considerable media attention and helped raise the profile of the disability rights campaign. The intensifying pressure on politicians and policy makers led eventually to the passing of the 1990 Americans with Disabilities Act (ADA), its primary aim being the integration of disabled Americans into the mainstream. The ADA outlawed discrimination on the grounds of 'disability' in employment, environmental access, transportation, state and local government and telecommunications systems. Its passage through Congress symbolised a major shift in perceptions of disability rights in the USA. Although not all disabled people's demands were achieved, it remains undoubtedly the most comprehensive anti-discrimination law anywhere in the world (Charlton 1998).

Subsequently, concerns have been raised about the implementation of the ADA and how far its original goals have been met. Early estimates suggested that the financial outlay on 'accommodations' for disabled people within the workplace would be relatively low. Additionally, these costs could be spread across different levels of government, private businesses and consumers. Unfortunately, this has yet to be translated into meaningful improvements in the economic situation of the majority of disabled Americans. The actual proportion of disabled Americans in full- or part-time work declined from 33 per cent in 1986 to 31 per cent in 1994 (Charlton 1998). Furthermore, there are growing concerns about the ADA's monitoring and enforcement procedures and whether it is reaching adequately minority groups within the disabled population (NCD 2000).

Since the 1970s British organisations controlled and run by disabled people have shared similar goals to their American contemporaries. The first steps to getting an anti-discrimination law on to the statute books were taken by the Committee on Restrictions Against Disabled People (CORAD). The Committee was appointed by the Labour government in 1978 and chaired by a disabled person, Peter Large. By focusing on a range of issues including access to public buildings, transport systems, education, employment and entertainment, CORAD located the problem of discrimination within a structural or institutional context. It recommended several policy initiatives including the introduction of legislation to address the restrictions encountered by disabled people (CORAD 1982). However, the Thatcher government of the 1980s was unsympathetic. Consequently, Jack Ashley, a deaf Labour MP, introduced a private member's anti-discrimination bill in July 1982 but this was defeated. It was only after 14 subsequent attempts, and 13 years later, that the 1995 Disability Discrimination Act (DDA) was passed.

Britain's campaign for anti-discrimination legislation gathered momentum in 1985 with the setting up of the Voluntary Organizations for Anti-Discrimination Legislation (VOADL) Committee, renamed Rights Now, in 1992. This heralded an uneasy alliance between organisations controlled by disabled people, such as the BCODP, and the more traditional organisations for disabled people like RADAR. Hitherto, the latter had been reluctant to support the campaign for disability rights legislation. The late 1980s was also a period when the influence of a radical new method of consciousness raising, based on the social model of disability and known as Disability Equality Training (DET), became evident. It promoted the politicisation and radicalisation of increasingly large sectors of disabled people. Subsequently, political activity both within and outside the conventional corridors of power intensified. While parliamentary lobbying continued, the DAN was formed in 1993 and several high-profile demonstrations followed. Taken together these initiatives heightened public attention to the demand for civil rights legislation for disabled people. The Conservative government responded with the introduction of the 1995 Disability Discrimination Act (DDA) (Oliver and Barnes 1998).

At the international level, the European Commission adopted a communication on equal opportunities for disabled people in 1996. Although member states are not required to take specific action they are encouraged to abandon segregated facilities in favour of mainstreaming for disabled people. Also, a clause to counter discrimination against various groups including disabled people was written into the revised Treaty of the European Union in 1997 (Sayce 2000: 182). Member nations are also encouraged to promote the UN's 'Standard Rules on the Equalization of Opportunity for Persons with Disabilities' (UN 1993), widely regarded as the most far-reaching official document to date on disability rights. The Standard Rules assert that national governments are responsible for the introduction of various measures to secure full participation and equality for 'persons with disabilities'. There are 22 specific recommendations covering all aspects of social life. They also identify the need for legislation to support disabled people's rights and the inclusion of organisations of disabled people in drafting and evaluating disability policy (UN 1993).

These are the latest in a long line of international measures to promote equal rights for disabled people that date back to the early 1980s. Yet progress has been slow both in the wealthy nations of the West and especially in the poorer nations of the majority world (Coleridge 1993; Charlton 1998; Stone 1999). This raises the question why are such seemingly well-intentioned policy directives only marginally effective?

Citizenship and the law

Rights are little more than a series of entitlements which are inextricably bound up with the notion of citizenship. For T. H. Marshall (1950), civil, political and social rights constitute the basis of modern citizenship. In western culture the civic element is associated with the revolutionary struggles of the 18th century and is composed of the rights necessary for 'individual freedom'. Political rights are those that are linked to campaigns for universal suffrage in the 19th and early part of the 20th century. Social rights include a range of economic and welfare entitlements deemed essential for an individual 'to live the life of a civilized being according to the standards prevailing in the society' (Marshall 1950: 15). However, it is increasingly evident that:

> civil and political rights are not worth an awful lot unless they are backed up by a certain basic social security which enables people to make use of the rights, and makes it impossible for others to push them around in such a way that the rights become an empty constitutional promise without any substance. (Dahrendorf cited in Commission on Citizenship 1990: 7)

Hence, as most societies are characterised by vast inequalities of wealth and power, legislation is considered necessary to secure the rights of economically and socially disadvantaged people. But, hitherto, civil rights legislation has been only marginally effective. This is evident for all marginalised groups, but particularly so for disabled people (Oliver and Barnes 1998).

One reason for this unfortunate but not unexpected situation is that unlike sex, for example, what is and what is not considered an impairment or 'disability' is a highly contentious issue. Accredited impairments come in a variety of forms; they may be physical, sensory or cognitive, obvious or invisible, permanent or intermittent. Disabled people, unlike women and people from minority ethnic groups must prove that they are in fact 'disabled' under the terms of the Act before litigation can begin. For example, under the ADA working is seen as a major life activity and the courts expect individuals to be 'substantially disabled' across a whole range of jobs is order to show that they qualify under the Act. Also, people using corrective devices such as spectacles or medication to minimise the negative effects of impairment may not be considered disabled (Perkins *et al.* 1999). Further, while there have been a number of well-publicised victories under the ADA, there is a growing awareness that it has had most impact on those whose impairment does not 'effect their performance'. Hence, those who are most likely to benefit are generally white, middle-class, well-educated people with physical or sensory conditions (Sayce 2000).

Additionally, employers with less than 15 workers are not covered by the Act and bigger firms are debarred from discriminating against 'qualified' disabled people only. Under the ADA it is also up to the disabled employee to seek 'reasonable accommodation'. But their views may be overruled by those of the employer. The primary aim is to reach an 'amicable agreement'. Therefore the majority of disputes are settled out of court and 95 per cent of those that enter the courtroom are ruled in favour of the employer (Miller 2000). Furthermore, a report by the independent National Council on Disability entitled 'Promises to keep: a decade of federal enforcement of the Americans with Disabilities Act' examined the enforcement activities of four key federal agencies: the Department of Justice, the Equal Opportunities Commission, the Department of Transportation and the Federal Communications Commission. It found that:

while the Administration has consistently asserted its strong support for the civil rights of people with disabilities, the federal agencies charged with the enforcement and policy development under ADA have, to varying degrees, been underfunded, overly cautious, reactive and lacking any coherent and unifying national strategy. In addition, enforcement agencies have not consistently taken leadership roles in clarifying 'frontier' or emergent issues. (Bristo 2000: 1)

Britain's DDA is similarly flawed. It is based on the orthodox individualistic medical view of disability: impairment is the cause of disability rather than the way society is organised. Hence it retains the notion that disabled peoples' requests for meaningful change are unrealistic and unnecessary. It provides only limited protection from direct discrimination in employment, the provision of goods and services, and in the selling or letting of land. As in the ADA, people must prove that they have impairment before a case can be brought. To date, 74 per cent of the cases are withdrawn or settled before a full tribunal hearing, while a further 10 per cent are dismissed (Meager *et al.* 1999). The overwhelming majority of employers, over 90 per cent, are not even covered by the Act and those that are can easily claim exemption if they can demonstrate that compliance would damage their business (Gooding 1996).

Furthermore, when the DDA came into force in 1996 there was no enforcement agency with which to monitor and police the Act until April 2000. This is in stark contrast to the situation in America and, most importantly, to other British anti-discrimination laws such as the 1975 Sex Discrimination Act (SDA) with its Equal Opportunities Commission (EOC) and the 1976 Race Relations Act (RRA) and the Commission for Racial Equality (CRE). But even these bodies have been only marginally effective: sexism, heterosexism and racism are as evident today as they were in the 1970s. A key factor in explaining the relative failure of the SDA and the RRA is their semi-autonomous status. Although formally 'independent', funding and appointments are controlled by politicians and policy makers. Hence, successive governments have been able to coerce both organisations into concentrating the bulk of their activities on 'education and research' rather than enforcement (Gregory 1987).

But after intense lobbying from a variety of sources, Tony Blair's government established the Disability Rights Commission (DRC) in April 2000 to 'work towards the elimination of discrimination against disabled people'. The DRC has 15 commissioners including representatives of employer's organisations. It is chaired by Bert Massie; previously the Director of the government-sponsored RADAR, Britain's largest disability organisation controlled and run by non-disabled people. The Commission has the power to take up cases on behalf of both individuals and organisations. But early indications suggest that like the EOC and the RRA, its main tasks will include the production of new codes of practice, the updating of existing ones, the provision of information and advice, conciliation, and 'research' (Wilkinson 1999: 12). Given the nature and extent of the discrimination encountered by disabled people there is little here to suggest that the DRC will be any more successful than its contemporaries for sex and 'race'.

The arrival of the DDA brought an end to the uneasy coalition between organisations *of* and *for* disabled people. The majority of BCODP's member organisations claimed the Act was weak and unworkable. But six of the main charities *for* disabled people – RADAR, the Royal National Institute for the Blind, the Royal National Institute for the Deaf, MENCAP, MIND and

SCOPE – agreed to work with the government to implement the new law. Equally important, key figures within Britain's disabled people's movement have been coopted into the official echelons of power. For example, Jane Campbell, a leading disability activist and ex-Chairperson of the BCODP is now a member of the DRC. This parallels the tendency for American disability rights leaders to be incorporated into formal and informal associations of civil rights lobbyists (Charlton 1998). It also mirrors divisions in other political movements between those with a more 'reformist' tendency who believe that the system can be changed from within, and those who maintain that members' interests are diluted as organisations and activists are coopted into the structures of power.

It is likely that as in America the DDA will benefit a minority of disabled individuals and is unlikely to have a significant impact on the lives of the disabled population as a whole. Indeed, the DDA may give a false impression that disabling barriers are being dismantled. Recent discussions of the question of rights have stressed the notion of 'mutuality' as a philosophy of reciprocal rights and responsibilities. This has been accompanied by the need for an:

> overhaul of the welfare system on the basis of a new entitlement to benefit and reciprocal responsibilities to make self provision against risk. (Christie 1999: 56)

The danger is that this 'overhaul' of the system signals yet another lurch to the right and further erosion of the welfare safety net upon which so many disabled people have little choice but to depend. The situation is even more problematic in the nations of the 'developing' world where western notions of individual rights are directly at odds with more collective ideologies and where resources are extremely scarce (Stone 1999). For a disabled individual to contest a denial of rights through the courts requires considerable resources, both economic and social. Yet the overwhelming majority of disabled people simply do not have access to those resources.

Something old, something new?

The transition from conventional politics to more overt forms of political action by disabled people and their organisations marks a new direction in disability politics. It has been likened to a 'new social movement' by disability theorists such as Mike Oliver (1996a) and an old-style, long-term 'liberation struggle' akin to feminism by Tom Shakespeare (1993). However, determining whether the disabled people's movement belongs to the 'new' or 'old' category, or something in-between, is far from straightforward.

New social movement theory centres on the distinctive features of recent political movements in societies across North America and Western Europe; in particular, those concerned with global ecology, human rights, animal rights and world peace. During the 1980s several commentators identified a 'new' core conflict in western society linked to such factors as the collapse of conventional work patterns, changing welfare systems, and the harsh economic and social conditions of the period. Whereas 'old' political movements, such as the trade union movement, were concerned mainly with economic issues, new social movements are said to focus on wider cultural change and the physical and social environment. They draw disproportionate support from the middle and upper middle classes, are international in structure, and have essentially non-economic agendas (Macionis and Plummer 1998).

Shakespeare (1993) maintains that the claims surrounding new social movements overstate the contrast with earlier forms of political action. He draws attention to the links between the women's movement of the 1920s and feminism of the 21st century. While acknowledging that there are significant differences between the traditional, paternalistic organisations *for* disabled people of the pre-1970s and the newer more representative organisations of today, he notes that self-organisation among disabled people can be traced back to the 1890s with the formation of the National League of the Blind and Disabled (NLBD) and the British Deaf Association.

Nonetheless, it may be argued that the disabled people's movement can be defined as a new social movement on the basis of four key characteristics. First, it is marginal to conventional politics. Second, it offers a critical evaluation of society. Third, it embraces (qualified) post-materialist/acquisitive values; and fourth it is international in character. These are in addition to the criteria used to evaluate all social movements: namely, their impact on general political or economic changes, specific policies, effecting a shift in public opinion, or the sponsoring of new organisations (Campbell and Oliver 1996).

With regard to the first criterion, until very recently organisations controlled and run by disabled people were undoubtedly peripheral to conventional political structures. Historically, organisations *for* disabled people, some of which date back to the 18th century (Gleeson 1999), dominated disability politics. Many are concerned solely with impairment-specific issues. They are increasingly involved in service provision as governments across the world seek to reduce the cost of state welfare. But disabled people's growing disillusionment with these organisations and their activities prompted an unprecedented growth in campaigning, self-help and activist groups in the closing decades of the 20th century. The emphasis was on indigenous organisation and self-reliance and a political rather than a therapeutic orientation. The central aim is not to modify their own behaviour in deference to traditional expectations of disabled people, but rather to influence the behaviour of groups, organisations and institutions (Anspach 1979; Campbell and Oliver 1996).

In Britain, self-organisation began in earnest in 1965 with the formation of the Disablement Incomes Group (DIG) by two disabled women Berit Moore and Megan de Boisson. In the late 1960s DIG became a focus for political activity attracting the attention of both activists and academics alike. However, following its colonisation by 'non-disabled experts' and a largely unsuccessful campaign for comprehensive disability income new groups emerged. One notable example was the influential Union of the Physically Impaired Against Segregation (UPIAS). Such organisations represented a 'powerful source of mutual support, education and action' for disabled people (Crewe and Zola 1983). Their stated aim was to present members' collective needs, both to statutory agencies and political parties, at both local and national levels. A further significant development was the emergence of the BCODP. Initiated by members of the UPIAS, it had representatives from only seven national groups at its first meeting in 1981. By July 2000, it had a membership of 130 organisations of disabled people representing over 400,000 individuals (BCODP 2001).

A further defining feature of the disabled people's movement is its critical evaluation of society and its systematic oppression of disabled people. The barriers are embedded in policies and practices based on the individualistic, medical approach to disability. Consequently, the removal of such obstacles involves far more than gaining control over material resources and the range and quality of services. It requires a fundamental reappraisal of the meaning and hence medicalisation of disability and a recognition that the multiple deprivations experienced by people with accredited impairments are the outcome of hostile physical and social environments or the way society is organised (Barton 1993a).

The choice of 'unconventional' political tactics, much in evidence in the United States in the late 1960s and 1970s and Britain in the 1990s, provides another example of a sustained critique of conventional society. Indeed, some groups such as Britain's NLBD have been engaged in this type of protest since the 1920s. But the shift from 'old' to 'new' politics has intensified over recent years. More recent British initiatives include the Campaign for Accessible Transport (CAT), the Campaign Against Patronage, and the 'Rights not Charity' march of July 1988. Since then there has been a growing number of demonstrations against a range of issues which have presented a 'new image of disability' in the media. A major demonstration against Independent Television's charity show Telethon was held in 1992 which drew over 2,000 disabled activists. It was the last such event. This and other successes led to the formation of DAN. With a voluntary self-funding membership of over 1,000 disabled individuals DAN has organised more than 200 local and national demonstrations (Pointon 1999). All of which poses a direct challenge to orthodox notions of disability and a passive disabled identity.

The commitment by new social movements to 'post-materialist' or 'post-acquisitive' values, over and above those that have to do with economics and material needs, is based on an opposition to conventional political demands for more resources. Yet such claims may be somewhat overstated. While there is no doubt that other movements such as environmentalists and the peace movement champion selected post-acquisitive values, the same cannot be said of those representing women, minority ethnic groups and disabled people. Within feminism, for instance, there is a central concern with equal pay, gender inequality at work and discriminatory benefit systems. Indeed, the whole thrust of the international disabled people's movement has been to channel more resources to disabled people and to the services upon which they have to depend. Yet the emergence of 'disability culture' and the affirmation and celebration of a positive disabled identity pose a direct challenge to conventional assumptions about impairment and disability and the stigmatisation of difference. Hence, the disabled people's movement is about far more than resource allocation and redistribution. As with feminism and lesbian and gay movements, it presents a radical countercultural politics, which strikes at the very heart of western values and culture (Fagan and Lee 1997).

This raises questions about its representativeness. Early criticisms centred on the American movement and its notion of 'independent living' – a philosophy of self-reliance, individual rights, and 'radical consumerism' (DeJong 1983). The stress on self-reliance and consumer sovereignty is misplaced within the context of the stark inequalities of modern capitalism as it inevitably favours some more than others. In Britain, the emphasis on citizenship is important and developing, but the movement's main efforts have been invested in building a collective organisation for the benefit of all disabled people (Campbell and Oliver 1996).

A related issue concerns how many individuals with impairments 'self-identify' as disabled people. For advocates, the traditional focus on individual functional limitations has been replaced by the notion of 'disabling barriers and attitudes'. Exactly what constitutes a 'disabled person' is not fixed but contingent on changing social circumstances and contexts. It is unequivocal that large numbers of those labelled 'disabled' by official statistics do not identify with the disabled people's movement or get involved in political activity of any kind. Similar conclusions can be applied to other social movements such as feminism or anti-poverty movements.

Nonetheless, it is widely recognised that older disabled people, disabled individuals from minority ethnic groups, people with learning difficulties and mental health system users and survivors are underrepresented in the disabled people's movement. Therefore, for it to continue to be an effective force for change, it must encourage more people with a range of impairments to consciously adopt a positive 'disabled identity'. This form of identity politics necessitates the subordination of individual circumstances to a collective consciousness, which is in direct opposition to an overtly individualistic and disabling society. The difficulty is that for many people, both with and without impairments, in rich and poor countries alike, an orthodox 'disabled' or dependent identity represents a degree of stability and security in an increasingly unstable and insecure world.

This relates to further criticisms. A key factor in the politicisation of disability has been the globalisation of the disabled people's movement. Disabled People's International (DPI) was formed by disabled activists in 1981. Its first world congress was held in Singapore and attracted 400 disabled delegates with all types of impairment and cultural backgrounds from across the world. They united around a common purpose: the empowerment of disabled people through collective political action. For DPI the prerequisite for change lies in the promotion and nurture of grassroots organisations and the development of high levels of public awareness of disability issues among the population as a whole (Driedger 1989).

The DPI has acted as a major stimulus for discussions on the creation and spread of impairment and disability through poverty, industrial development, pollution and war. By coming together at the international level, disabled people have created new forms of self-organisation. The British disabled people's movement, for example, drew heavily on the American experience; in particular, the promotion of 'independent living' options. Indeed, besides America and Britain, there are now CILs or similar organisations in most 'developed' countries such as Australia, Canada, Japan and Europe and in 'developing' nations of the majority world such as Brazil, Nicaragua and Zimbabwe (Charlton 1998). A further example of the impact of the disabled people's movement at the international level is found in the primacy given to disability issues within transnational organisations such as the United Nations, the International Labour Organization, and the World Health Organization (Hurst 2000).

While organisation at the international level has encouraged national movements to learn from the experience of those in other countries, there remains considerable variation. Some national bodies such as those in Sweden, Norway and Finland, where traditional welfare systems remain relatively intact, are composed mainly of confederations of impairment-specific, self-help groups and tend to favour a broadly conventional individualistic perspective. In other 'Western' countries such as the United States and Britain and in several poorer nations of the majority world such as South Africa and Uganda, services have developed in very different ways accompanied by a more radical barriers approach (Hurst 2000).

Conclusion

The experience of other social movements illustrates the potential for assimilation into the political system in ways which effectively neutralise their political goals. These dilemmas will no doubt intensify as the influence of the disabled people's movement extends. The DPI now has consultative status on disability issues within the UN and disabled politicians have achieved national prominence around the world. Many disabled activists in both the USA and Britain are now government appointees. The risk that key figures are drawn ever further into the political system and lose touch with the grass roots has been a particular issue in America (Scotch 1989). This is because such appointments often appear symbolic rather than practical and thus generate serious divisions among activists and supporters.

In Britain, concern has also been expressed over the BCODP's continued involvement in conventional parliamentary lobbying groups such as Rights Now, as it appeared to be distancing itself from grassroots organisations and groups (GMCDP 2000). Equally worrying is the fact that as local organisations become ever more involved in service delivery their priorities change. In America, for example, in the 1970s CILs were in the vanguard of disability politics, but in the 1990s:

> Most CILs do not hire politically active people, do not have organizers, and have no strategic view of how to effect social change. Many executive directors of CILs and disability rights groups are apolitical, outside narrowly defined disability related issues. Most disability rights groups avoid demonstrations because they are considered outdated, or because they would alienate funding sources. (Charlton 1998: 122)

By way of contrast, it is important to remember that the emergence of the disabled people's movement has offered people labelled disabled a real political voice. It has also had a significant influence on politicians, policy makers and the population at large. At the structural level, the most important effect of disabled people's self-organisation is legislative victories such as the enactment of anti-discrimination laws around the world. Although each of these measures falls far short of what disabled people's organisations campaigned for, they do represent significant advances in disability policy. Equal rights for disabled people is now firmly on the political agenda at both national and international levels. Similarly, user involvement in the planning and delivery of services is increasingly prevalent throughout the world.

Whether such developments signify the assimilation and effective neutralisation of disability politics into the established structures of power, or another stage in a long and arduous struggle for a fairer and more just society has yet to be determined.

Questions

- How and in what ways has the emergence of the disabled people's movement made a significant contribution to the development of a positive disabled identity?
- Should the disabled people's movement view the inclusion of some of its leaders into conventional political institutions in a positive or a negative light?

CHAPTER 3

Disability and the constitution of dependency

Bill Hughes

Introduction

For the organic intellectuals who have helped to make disability studies a theoretical expression of the disability movement the meaning of dependence and independence has been a crucial point of debate (Barnes 1990, 1995; Barton 1989; BCODP 1986; Finkelstein 1981; Lakey 1994). Indeed one can trace the current form of disability politics to the Independent Living Movement (ILM) that flourished originally in the USA in the later part of the 1960s. Since the heady days of counterculture politics, the everyday praxis of disabled people has changed markedly. The resignation associated with dependency and oppression is now infused with a language of opportunity, emancipation and pride (Paterson and Hughes 2000). Though much remains to be done in the struggle to transform the material and cultural conditions of disabled people's lives, the social movement of disabled people has begun to undermine the pejorative mythology that disability is necessarily a form of dependency.

In the medical model of disability the constitution of dependency is explained as the outcome of a biophysical or mental deficit. This deficit brings about restriction or curtailment of activity, mobility or function such that one becomes dependent, not able to look after oneself and, therefore, lacking in autonomy. The burden of this deficit must be picked up by others, either in person or by virtue of the benevolence of the state or some voluntary charitable organisation (Barnes *et al.* 1999: 20–27). The logic of the argument that leads from impairment, to disability, to economic, social and emotional cost to the community, is commended to us as unassailable. Dependency is the social outcome of an inherent or acquired biological abnormality. The 'invalid' is a fiscal burden but one who deserves the support and succour of the community. At the heart of this perspective is a moral mythology that constitutes disability as a tragedy (Oliver 1990). Fate is without pity but those whom it has made tragic and dependent must expect it – one assumes with grace and thanks – as the basic social response to their 'spoilt' lives.

Yet behind this logic – so-called – there lies a powerful process of social and historical constitution. Dependency is not a label that can be objectively applied to a given person or group and it is easy to make the argument that we are all, to some extent, dependent on others. Such a view is intrinsic to all organic models of society and can be found in the writings of thinkers as diverse as Plato, Aristotle, Hegel and Marx. Whosoever argues that we are all products of our social worlds and can only realise ourselves within them claims that life implies interdependence and – regardless of 'ability' – some measure of dependency. One is reminded of the remark of the poet John Donne that 'no man is an island'. In addition to this caveat about the ambivalent and problematic nature of independence, it should be stressed that the meaning of dependency is contingent and, indeed, highly dependent on its cultural, social, economic and historical context. It is (the constitution of) dependency in the context of modern western society which will provide the analytical focus of this chapter. I will argue that modernity and western individualism valorises the autonomous subject and simultaneously constitutes disabled people as its alterity. This politico-cultural process of 'invalidation' is then materialised in socio-spatial arrangements that regulate disabled persons on the grounds that they can be defined as flawed bodies incapable of adequate social participation. Built into this constituting process is an (informal) denial of citizenship that is predicated on a medico-onto-logical argument that to be impaired necessarily means a life that is dependent on others.

Modernity and the autonomous subject

In modernity, the high value placed on independence and autonomy produces dependency as a wholly negative social attribute and as a form of alterity which, in turn, legitimates processes of exclusion and oppression. The argument is perhaps even more obvious in relation to the concept of 'normality'. Disabled people will easily recognise the validity of the claim at the heart of this quotation:

> If we consider what social scientists often say about 'normality' … and similar concepts in fields ranging from the policy sciences to medicine to psychology, we find very narrow assumptions that lead to practices that have untoward consequences for many people. (Hollinger 1994)

Indeed, the medical deficit associated with the application of the label of 'abnormality' invari-ably assumes a person who is in need of care and is, therefore, dependent upon others.

The othering or 'invalidation' (Hughes 1999, 2000) of disabled people in modernity has been partly achieved by their representation as a dependent population. One can argue that the category and indeed identity of disability is constituted out of a modern western value system in which notions of individuality, agency and personal autonomy are privileged. The anthro-pologist Clifford Geertz (1993) writes:

> The Western conception of the person as a bounded, unique, more or less integrated moti-vational and cognitive universe, a dynamic centre of awareness, emotion, judgement and action organized into a distinctive whole and set contrastively both against other such wholes and against its social and natural background, is, however incorrigible it may seem to us, a rather peculiar idea within the context of the world's cultures. (p. 59)

If one is not recognised as, quite literally, the embodiment of these (peculiar) values then one is not likely to be admitted to the party. It is at this categorical or discursive level that the inval-idation of disabled people is consecrated and reiterated but one must not forget that rapid economic change in the 19th century redefined the meaning of disability to the detriment of disabled people (Finkelstein 1980). If wage slavery is a dubious privilege, it at least suggests an element of economic autonomy that has been denied to disabled people since the industrial revolution. Exclusion from industrial production on the grounds of impaired labour power constituted disabled people as just another waste product of the new economic system (Oliver 1990). The capitalist mode of production made instant judgements about people's social and economic worth and the clear message for disabled people was that the labour market was closed to them. Productivist culture had no place for impaired labour power. It was surplus to value. In the 19th century, the judgement that people with impairments must be excluded from the creation of wealth because it depended on the mastery of repetitive corporeal activities became for disabled people the gateway to segregation, exclusion and oppression. Many disabled people became dependent upon the 'therapeutic state' (O'Neil 1986) or on the philanthropy of charitable organisations. They were offered no opportunity to express or establish their worth and value and as worth and identity became – as modernity matured – increasingly associated with employment and the autonomy that it afforded, then disabled people were condemned to abject poverty or relocated to and incarcerated in specialist medical spaces in which they became experimental matter.

The argument that disability is primarily economically constituted is invariably supplemented by reference to the ways in which the core bourgeois ideology of individualism disguises the systematic structures that make disability a product of social organisation and, therefore, a collective rather than personal problem (Oliver 1990). This argument leaves an important lacuna. Not only does bourgeois individualism mystify the social relations which produce disablement, it also creates a normalising framework in which a certain form of individuality is idealised. For disabled people, this normalising framework is invalidating because the form of individuality most prized in modernity is the autonomous, unitary subject. MacPherson (1962: 263–4), in his highly praised and much quoted study of the doctrine of individualism, wrote that in the ideal western model 'the individual is essentially the proprietor of his own person and capacities' and as such 'is human only in so far as free, and free only in so far as a proprietor of himself'. Freedom and dependency are not commensurate. More sinister for disabled people is the implication that those who are not individuals in the manner defined by the doctrine of possessive individualism are somehow less than human.

The western doctrine of individualism, therefore, projects an idealised historically and culturally constituted 'figure' that is essentially a model of self-contained physical and mental integrity. This 'figure', in the romanticist version of ideal personhood is 'heroic' and 'stands alone'. In its rationalist Kantian version – in so far as individual consciousness is the basis of practical reason – 'he' is mature, 'balanced', a unitary ego (Lukes 1973). Even the metaphors are discriminatory. The carnal ideal is 'upright' and the cognitive ideal is focused around self-reliance and self-determination as *the* objective of personal development. Mental and physical impairment are the shadow side of the enlightenment dream of flawless reason and the romantic myth of a harmonious and heroic combination of spirit and flesh embodied in personal nobility. These figures are more or less mini-portraits of the ideal citizen. Yet despite their differences, they both commend the independence of the 'skin encapsulated ego' and deride 'the collective sense of self, enclosed within a symbolic boundary far beyond the human body' that is common in many non-western and pre-modern social contexts, for example, 'in

Japan, where the group is considered to be more central than the individual' (Helman 1994: 17).

Indeed the category of the 'person' as an autonomous unitary self is – as the anthropological literature suggest – a modern western construction (Gergen and Davis 1985; Carrithers *et al.* 1985; Mauss 1938; Rose 1989). Rose (1989) writes:

> Social theorists from many different standpoints have questioned the universality of the contemporary western concept of the person: a bounded sphere of thought, will and emotion; the site of consciousness and judgement; the author of its acts and the bearer of a personal responsibility; an individual with a unique biography assembled over the course of a life. From the mid-19th century onwards, analysis proliferated of the rise of 'individualism' over the previous 200 years, linking it, among other things with Protestantism, with Romanticism, with the growth of the market society based on exclusive possession and with theories of natural law. (p. 217)

The discursive construction of the modern western person in this form has been a long and intricate cultural and political process which both creates a normative model for personhood and citizenship and at the same time constitutes certain social groups as 'in deficit' in relation to it. For example, a person with intellectual impairment becomes a political problem – in a formal legal sense – because they are constituted in deficit with respect to personhood on the ground that the site of consciousness and judgement is certified as sub-standard. How can a physically impaired person be a bearer of personal responsibility if the material possibilities for an autonomous life are denied them by the omnipresence of physical and social barriers to their participation in society? And how can these barriers be designated a constraint upon agency if politics is reduced to individual choice and individuality itself reduced to 'a bounded sphere of thought, will and emotion'? For disabled people the journey through modernity is not a comfortable one. How can it be so if we accept Bakhtin's view (1984: 321) that bodies in modernity have become 'narrow and specific, torn off from the direct relation to the life of society and to the cosmic whole'.

Elias (1978, 1982) presents this journey of modernity as a 'civilizing process'. He is intrigued by the link between sociogenesis and psychogenesis or the ways in which the development of culture and personality parallel one another. He traces the process of modern state formation from medieval times to the present and links it to the growth of emotional and carnal control. The process of rationalisation associated with the formation of the modern state and its bureaucracies mirrors the process by which modern men and women acquire an intense sense of shame about bodily functions, processes and desires. As the rationality of the social world ossifies, its participants lose spontaneity, become less emotionally expressive and develop intricate social skills of self-regulation and self-control. The 'individual', writes Elias (1982: 232) 'is compelled to regulate his conduct in an increasingly differentiated, more even and more stable manner'.

'Civilization' for Elias is the process of change that simultaneously transforms the social and the emotional. Modernity is the process of the social regulation of impulse and instinct. It implies the fabrication of a new mode of being in which the corporeal and the emotional – all that is spontaneous and uninhibited – is brought under the jurisdiction of social norms and all that is not is marginalised and excluded. One is reminded of Neitzsche's view that 'the moral and institutional climate of modernity is not conducive to the eloquent expression of the affects'. It is inimical to that which fosters growth, life and liberation' (Hughes 1996: 41). Elias characterises the civilising process as a shift from external control to self-control, that is – in the original German – from *fremdzwang* to *selszwang*. The modern self is constituted as a result of its role in the process of internalising social norms of control in the form of manners, rules of hygiene and other behavioural codes and mores to do with the conduct of everyday life and practices of the body. In modernity, the unregulated physical self becomes a shameful thing, a source of embarrassment that requires constant vigilance.

What Elias does not point out, however, is that this journey of modernity marks off certain bodies as unregulated, as sources of embarrassment and shame. Impaired people come to represent the alterity of rational embodiment and a reminder of a 'grotesque' pre-modern world in which the boundaries of body and self were uninhibited by the constraints of propriety and the behavioural and emotional rules of containment and self-restraint. Such persons become socially undependable, 'disfigured' by a culturally dominant perception of personhood. Their fate is exile and invalidation. They are not permitted to make the transition from *fremdzwang* to *selszwang* but remain subject to external controls and constraints which limit opportunities for autonomous action.

Dependency and space

Dependency is never simply an ontological status. It arises out of processes of social constitution. With respect to disabled people these processes are inextricably linked to a politics of space, to a strategy of regulation and physical containment which developed in the 19th century. Foucault (1967) refers to these developments as the period of the 'great confinement' during which certain social groups, including disabled and mentally ill people, were excluded from participation in mainstream culture and denied access to the sites of privilege and power. The (mis)management of impaired bodies in modernity has developed through 'special' spatial arrangements which have served to reinforce the culturally dominant notion of personhood in which agency and autonomy are defining factors.

As myself and a colleague have argued elsewhere, the policy response to impairment in modernity, prior to the prioritisation of Community Care provision in the west in the latter half of the 20th century, was essentially anthropoemic (Hughes and Paterson 1997) – a form of the 'disposal' of human beings in which those identified as some form of threat to the community are segregated or eliminated. Aristotle's claim that for the sake of the integrity of the polity, infanticide was the 'solution' to deformed children, is a classical anthropoemic conception of social order which was later implemented clinically by the Nazis during the second world war. In western liberal democracies during the 19th century, for disabled people exile was the preferred response. This took the form of a segregationist policy that involved two forms of the management or government of bodies in social space; namely, segregation and medicalisation.

1) Segregation: The first arises out of the establishment of disabled people as a distinctive population which, as we have seen, is an historically contingent product of power raised to a 'truth' by the application of normalising judgement. As disabled people became invalidated by

the material and cultural processes described in the previous section, policy makers felt compelled to address *the management and regulation of the spaces between non-disabled and disabled bodies*. The 'total institutions' (Goffman 1968) of the Victorian era fulfilled this particular requirement of social order by distinguishing between autonomous and dependent populations. 'Deviant' or dependent populations were incarcerated in 'austere and rational bureaucratic organizations' which were 'created for the classification and segregation of the poor, the mad, the sick, the young' (Johnson 1993: 143). One could and should add disabled people to the list but as usual, they are either subsumed under the category of 'the sick' or omitted altogether. The political act of confining disabled people transformed the moral line between acceptable and unacceptable persons into a practical system of disposal which placed the latter in the shadowy margins of social life. Geographical separation, as a tactic of social distancing, was regarded as the best cure for the fear of the stranger and the possibilities of contamination that such a person was assumed to epitomise (Bauman 1995). By this means, disabled and non-disabled bodies were separated and kept apart. This process created a spatialised apparatus of security which kept the threat of impairment in (not so) splendid isolation, be it 'special' schools or other segregated spaces dominated, primarily, by medical supervision. 'Such segregated spaces', Rob Imrie (2000: 7) argues, are 'infused with values which identify disabled people as different and usually inferior to the rest of society'.

By implementing a strategy of exclusion, an alliance of the 'therapeutic state' and philanthropic organisations and individuals exercised a complex form of power which put disabled people in their (isolated) place. This place was one which was 'out of sight' (Humphries and Gordon 1992). The consequences of such a strategy were the exacerbation of dependency and the virtual closure of opportunities for disabled people to participate in the public sphere or in civil society in any meaningful way.

2) Medicalisation: The daily government of impaired bodies in these segregated spaces became dominated by expert cadres. They became constituted in order to supervise and regulate the social disorder promised by 'special' populations that had been discursively constructed as bio-politically problematic (Foucault 1979). Disabled people confined to medical spaces came under the jurisdiction of the medical profession and its allied para-professions. Impaired bodies, therefore, became redefined as 'sick bodies' in need of confinement and rehabilitation and as a consequence disabled peoples lives were depoliticised. These 'therapeutic' spaces provided an enabling environment for the virulent expansion of medical power but had a profoundly disabling and debilitating effect on the disabled people who were forced to spend their lives in them (Illich 1975; Illich *et al.* 1977). Incarcerated populations became institutionalised (Goffman 1968) apathetic and demotivated. Such places not only discouraged autonomy and agency but were organised to produce docile and dependent residents.

Even disabled people who remained outside these 'special' spaces of confinement were both denied opportunities for social participation by the disabling structural barriers that hindered their every move and by the medical profession whose control over disabled people extended into the community. 'The sum of these disabling characteristics is an ideology that converts citizens to clients' and 'communities to deficient individuals' (McKnight 1977). The spatialisation of disability in modernity was profoundly claustrophobic: disabled people had their needs and interests defined for them by a class of supervising experts and were further confined by a world that was both emotionally and structurally hostile. This hostility was omnipresent because the carnal information and norms that underpin the construction of the physical and social environment are inimical to the needs of disabled people. 'Any body that is excluded from making a contribution to the construction of the social world cannot find a home in it' (Paterson and Hughes 1999: 604). Access to the spaces that non-disabled people take for granted was simply not available to disabled people. Therefore, if institutionalisation was not a disabled persons destination and destiny then a highly privatised, restricted life of limited mobility was the appealing alternative. In either context, disabled people were likely to become highly domesticated 'objects of care', 'emplaced' (Casey 1997) in a context which constrained self-determination and social participation. Such demarcation of spatial opportunities, profoundly constrained by a disablist public transport system, helps to transform dependency into a master status and thus produce for disabled people a highly supervised world in which they are continuously subject to the oppressive gaze of power (Hughes 1999). Even where this gaze is informed by informal loving forms of care, the emasculation of autonomy is always possible. 'The impulse to care for the other, when taken to its extreme, leads to the annihilation of the autonomy of the Other, to domination and oppression' (Bauman 1993: 11).

Citizenship suspended

Citizenship assumes autonomy. It is not commensurate with domination and oppression. Lives marked by confinement and supervision know freedom, equality and choice as mere words. The history of disability in modernity has been one of citizenship suspended. If the rallying cries of the radical bourgeoisie were not necessarily music to the ears of the proletariat, they were meaningless to those who were excluded from the slavery of wages and who were expected to live out their lives under the protective wing of the almoner, the physician or some other benefactor. Life under the aegis of philanthropy and welfare expertise is a life in which autonomy and agency are abrogated. Emancipation for disabled people embodies a simple goal: the abolition of the ties that bind them to dependency, the freedom to explore the world, themselves and their fellows in a manner unimpeded by the ubiquitous social and cultural constraints out of which their lives have been fabricated. Disabled people demand the right to live independent lives. Social intervention in the lives of disabled people in modernity has been a series of costly errors (Hales 1996). It has produced services which demean, spaces which confine, norms and values that bifurcate humanity into valid and invalid bodies. Where the non-disabled majority regard intervention in the lives of disabled people as the march of progress, as a humanitarian response to the tragedy of impairment, as a triumph of welfare wisdom, those who are the recipients of this great and good adventure are not only not convinced but are also making the argument that all the help and paternalistic good intentions amount to a failure on a grand scale which can be summarised politically as a denial of citizenship. The agency and autonomy that has been denied to disabled people has erupted into a social movement, a struggle in which the organised voice of disabled people is beginning to be heard.

The disability movement has been *the* central player in the struggle for anti-discrimination legislation (ADL) in many western countries. The barriers model of disablement suggests a political process which focuses metaphorically and literally on clearing away the many and varied structural hurdles that stand in the way of disabled people's full participation in the life of the community. This suggests a social participation model of citizenship in which dependency is the generic barrier which legislative action should aim to remove. Davis (1996) writing as a disability activist argues that disabled people need equal rights:

> We have said that we do not want legislation which treats us as people with special needs but which instead outlaws and requires removal of the environmental and social barriers which prevent us from participating on equal terms in the ordinary activities of daily life. We have pointed out that we need legislation which enables us to take control of our lives, live independently and make a contribution to society. (p. 124)

The disability movement defines emancipation and the route to it through equal rights in the relatively concrete terms of independent living. This embodies a political clarity with respect to citizenship which is generally absent on the political left. Traditionally, the political left has been suspicious of the bourgeois doctrine of civil rights on the grounds that legislative action which might enhance formal rights obscures the struggle for economic emancipation. However, since the revolutions of 1989 demonstrated the importance of civil society as locus for the attainment of liberty, there has been a revival in the fortunes of the idea of citizenship: 'For the left, citizenship has been the focus for a new concern with rights' (Andrews 1991: 12). This has provided new social movements – like the disability movement[1] – with the opportunity to develop a debate about citizenship which articulates, at least to some extent, with the 'new' language of the 'traditional' left. As if to mark this articulation, Driedger, in 1989, described the Disabled Peoples International (DPI) as 'The last Civil Rights Movement'.

The politics of disablement is about reversing the processes which have constituted disabled people as dependent 'subjects' and while this 'strategy' involves the practices of claiming and asserting civil and social rights, it cannot be the 'be all and end all' of disability politics. If disability politics is to eliminate the ways in which dependency is constructed and reconstructed, it must challenge the multifaceted way in which disabled people have had citizenship denied and suspended. These include problems of physical and social access, the disablist nature of social, welfare and medical services locally, nationally and internationally as well as the myriad ways in which disabled people have been denied the right and opportunity to define their own needs and supervise their own lives. Such a conception of politics is well placed to tackle the material constraints which constitute disability as dependency but perhaps less efficacious when it comes to challenging disablism in the cultural (inter)personal and embodied domains.

For example, contemporary debates about citizenship are still saturated with the values of liberal individualism and in modernity the juridical model of citizenship as legal personhood (Marshal 1964) although universalistic and potentially inclusive, does not attend to the particularistic and 'real' sociological problems of othering and invalidation which have helped to constitute disabled people as a dependent population. Indeed, such a model has been, as I have suggested above, disabling and disablist. Furthermore, it is difficult for any collectivist political tradition to be completely content with a debate about citizenship which owes so much to liberalism even if it is of a cosmopolitan and inclusivist hue. Indeed, 'when dominant, the juridical model seems to be depoliticizing and desolidarizing' (Cohen 1999: 249). These are debilitating processes which the disability movement must avoid not simply for purely political reasons but because they will emasculate the development of a pro-active culture of disability which has begun to embed disability politics in common bonds of embodiment. Given that we live in a 'somatic society' (Turner 1996) in which the modernist separation of the body and politics is no longer tenable, it makes sense for disability politics to embrace not only legislative change but also the cultural politics of identity and difference. The oppression of disabled people (and the forms of dependency in which it manifests itself) is not only material and structural but also has aesthetic (Hughes 1999, 2000) and carnal (Paterson and Hughes 1999) dimensions which a 'traditional' politics of equal rights is not fully equipped to deal with. I will attempt to illustrate the importance of cultural politics and its value with respect to the constitution of disability as dependency by giving one example.

The disability movement must be careful about placing too much emphasis on the legislative route to citizenship because in our contemporary 'enterprise culture' the political right have developed a model of civic participation in which 'active citizens' are 'successful, self-reliant, enterprising, consuming and property owning' (Lister 1990: 16). In this model, wealth and independence – qualities inimical to the experience of disability in modernity – are the essential qualifications for any claim to citizenship. This idea merely reiterates – in contemporary form – the good old-fashioned Victorian values about individual worth and proper personhood which were so central to the cultural constitution of disability as dependency during the period of the 'great confinement'. Of course 'the right' does not have exclusive access to the debate over citizenship but with enterprise culture in such a commanding position globally, its influence over the meaning of citizenship cannot be underestimated. The disability movement must make advances by way of ADL but it must also contest this discourse on citizenship.

Conclusions

In modernity, impaired people have become, quite literally, the embodiment of dependency. Opportunities have been closed by an individualistic culture that fetishizes autonomy and agency by assuming that these are qualities which are, ontologically, either present or absent. Where the exercise of power identifies their absence in individuals or populations, then systematic processes of exclusion become vindicated. The 'civilizing process' (Elias 1978, 1982) exacerbates the problem by narrowing the possibilities for bodily and emotional expression and performance (Barnes *et al.* 1999: 64). The generic lesson to be learned is that where cultures identify 'deformity' in some of their members, what in fact we may be witness to is a deformity of culture, a process by which dominant values invalidate certain kinds of being often in the name of a sham sense of homogeneity or a narrow notion of human virtue. Modernist bourgeois individualism demands that each one of us take a proprietorial grip upon our own person and capacities, yet at the same time, it sets in motion the closure of opportunities for disabled people to do just that. The exclusion and oppression of disabled people works itself out against a background where moral personhood cannot be divorced from the abstract humanist notion of the unitary subject, the self-contained, skin-encapsulated ego that epitomises physical and mental integrity. The naturalisation of this value system is productive of social exclusion, inimical to the celebration of diversity and constitutive of second-class citizens. Modernity has institutionalised this value system by creating closed and demeaning spaces in which disabled people are expected to live out their lives in a manner that is supervised and controlled by professional experts whose dominance of disabled people's lives has been an important factor in the fabrication of dependency.

However, this process of constitution and fabrication is being reversed. Despite the reactionary aesthetic (Hughes 1999, 2000) and material forms (Barnes 1991; Oliver 1990) of disability discrimination that continue to haunt contemporary culture, there is a powerful trend – sponsored by fragmented but nonetheless forceful (new) social movements – that stands for the value of diversity and the celebration of multiple and heterogeneous identities (Humphrey 1999). This is potentially a more positive cultural context for disabled people. They can and have begun to exercise the power and autonomy which they have been denied by centuries of discrimination. The changing nature of work in a post-fordist society as well as new technologies (Finkelstein 1980) have helped to usher in a period of cautious optimism in which, theoretically at least, there are more opportunities for disabled people to live independent lives. Disabled people are demanding personal assistance rather than 'care'. As a rejoinder to the paternalism, infantilisation and professional interference that has been the lot of impaired people since the onset of industrialisation, disability activists are making sustained demands on the legislature to tackle structural forms of discrimination. Impaired people are expressing pride in themselves and questioning the discourse which represents disability as a personal tragedy (Morris 1991). As Drake (1996: 162) argues, 'the notion of charitable benefaction is anathema to disabled people and they are rejecting those agencies who espouse it'. Disabled people have broken out of the medical spaces in which they were imprisoned during the period of the 'great confinement' and they are rejecting both the medicalisation of their lives and the medical model which has traditionally dominated how those lives have been understood. These are just some developments which suggest that – largely as a result of collective agency – the threads of economic, cultural and social life which have constituted disabled people as dependent are beginning to unravel.

Questions

- Consider the ways in which the western, idealised notion of the autonomous individual contributes to the oppression of disabled people.
- Disability politics today is primarily about gaining access to the social and physical spaces from which people with impairments were excluded during the march of modernity. Discuss this contention.

Note

1. It should be noted that there has been some debate within the disability movement as to whether the category of 'new social movement' is an adequate tool for analysing the disability movement. For an overview of this debate see Barnes *et al.* (1999: 153–81). For more in-depth coverage see Oliver (1990, 1996a) and Shakespeare (1993).

CHAPTER 4

Bending towards justice

Marcia H. Rioux

Introduction

Political struggles for the rights of disabled people have an auspicious history in Canada as they do elsewhere. These struggles form part of the earliest political history of the country and set the stage for the social and legal construction of inequality that still acts as a barrier to full citizenship. Fortunately the nature of those political struggles is very distinct from the political struggles framed by the disability rights movement that has developed in the past 25 years.

In this chapter, I use early Canadian history as an introduction for looking at the nature of the current political struggle for change in which the disability rights movement is involved. I place that in the context of the evolving international norms and standards that frame disability as an issue of human rights and social justice, rather than social development and charitable aid. Recognising empowerment and control as central to the struggle for change, I argue that freedom is a fundamental right that has to be won to address the political disenfranchisement, economic disempowerment and social inequality that are the reality of disabled people universally. Being active participants in their own lives and in the transformation of their societies (that is, being free) is central to people overcoming the entrenched repression imposed by a model of caring for people. This challenges the current social and political lethargy that accepts the current position of disabled people as a natural state of affairs and the framing of the issues of disability as issues of services, income and care. Evidence of the changing nature of the struggle is found in Canadian law and jurisprudence in which the political struggle has clearly coalesced around freedom and agency.

Historical struggles

As a political issue disability was evident as early as the mid-1700s in Canada. Britain, in its zeal to be rid of those deemed 'undesirable', shipped them to the colonies. To Australia, they shipped the prisoners to populate that country and to get rid of them. In the case of Canada, they shipped, what were termed 'the poor, the indigent and the mentally and morally defective'.

This led to some dissension in the early days in Canada. In 1766, a group of prominent citizens of Halifax, Nova Scotia (one of eastern Maritime provinces) lodged a complaint with the English Lords of Trade and Plantations against an unimpeded influx to Nova Scotia of the 'scum of all the colonies'. He included:

not only useless but very Bothersome to the Community, being not only those of the most dissolute manners, and void of all Sentiments of honest Industry, but also Infirm, Decrepit, and insane, as well as extremely indigent persons, who are unable to contribute anything towards their own maintenance. (Green 1986)

Two years later the citizenry voiced its concern that the so-called 'scum' continued to place a heavy burden on a relatively weak economy, with a small population and a limited tax base (Franklin 1986). Accordingly, it sought legislation to prevent the immigration of disabled, infirm and other 'useless' people into Canada.

In 1896, Dr Bodington, the Medical Superintendent of the Province of British Columbia, on Canada's west coast, joined a growing number of those in the west who complained about the United Kingdom:

> … shipping off to the Colonies weak minded young people who are unmanageable at home and unable to make a career for themselves, or earn a living.

On his own initiative Dr Boddington shipped five such individuals back to England and urged the government to deport to the mother country 'other chronic lunatics' (British Columbia 1897; British Columbia Assembly 1898).

The British government disallowed exclusory legislative bills in Nova Scotia and elsewhere because its own interest lay in the immigration of 'such' people to its colonies. Indeed, Britain had given justices of the peace the power to sentence vagrants – including individuals with disabilities – to houses of correction until 'the justices could place them out in some lawful calling … either within this realm or his majesty's colonies in America', (*England, An Act to Amend and Make Effectual the Laws Relating to Rogues, Vagabonds, and Other Idle and Disorderly Persons, and to Houses of Correction*)

In 1895, Dr Bruce Smith, the Ontario Inspector of Hospital and Charities, complained that the ever-increasing number of what he called 'feeble-minded' in the province needed to be checked and prevented, and further:

> There is another point that must not be lost sight of and that is the fact that we are alto-gether too lax in regard to allowing undesirable immigrants to find shelter in this province. Too often … mental and physical degenerates have been landed on our shores and have finally drifted, wither through mental, physical or moral deficiencies into one or other of our great public Charities. The majority of the feeble-minded girls, who having fallen prey to some designing villain [by way of sexual intercourse] are sent to our Rescue homes, have only been a short time in this country…. (Green 1986)

These are not very illustrious early days in relation to disability in Canada. Some of the harsh words of the early settlers of our country can still be found today in the attitudes, laws, policies and programs that find their roots in the early rejection of disabled people – immigration proce-dures, sterilisation practices, pre-natal screening and selective abortion, institutionalisation, competency laws, education acts, medical care and triaging and others. But there have also been some significant victories. At the very least people are not still trying to ship disabled people out of the country. And relative to the goals of the disability rights movement, there are several legal cases and some social policies that suggest that the struggle for change is having an impact.

The nature of the struggle for change is not entirely clear. Alternative perspectives on the nature of disability, the political mechanisms to address disability, ethical imperatives invoked to justify actions directed towards disabled people, interpretations of the concept of disability, and disciplinary approaches to disability all impact on the way the struggle for change is manifested. There is not agreement on a singular, monolithic goal. To understand the move towards disability rights, as a political struggle, this article will first look at the emerging understanding of disability rights and then using some recent legislative action and legal decisions examine the way in which these reflect the way the struggle for change has evolved in Canada.

Shifting paradigms

Over the past 20 years, the paradigm of disability has shifted from a medical welfare model to a human rights model. The rights paradigm recognises non-discrimination and equality rather than goodwill as the goals of the liberation and inclusion struggle. Inspired by other rights movements (race, religion, gender) of the 1960s and 1970s, disabled activists now see their disability in the same political context as black people view their race and feminists their gender. In particular segregation and institutionalisation, which have been the hallmark of disability policy, are seen in the context of racial segregation and apartheid. 'Disability was reconceptualized by the activists as a different state of being rather than a tragic deviation from "normalcy", and a social status vulnerable to discrimination by non-disabled persons' (Degener 1995). Empowerment and self-direction are accepted as key to achieving equality of opportunity and citizenship in society (Cooper 1999; Oliver 1990; Barnes 1994)

This reconceptualisation of disability, by the rights movement generally, by disability rights advocates and reflected in some government policies and programmes recognises disabled people's criticism of the medical and individualistic approach to defining disability. As an individual pathology, disability is seen as a physical, psychological or intellectual condition that results in a functional limitation. This means that it gets framed as an individual, rather than a society problem, and one that can be prevented or ameliorated through medical, biological or genetic intervention or through therapy, rehabilitation services and technical supports. But there is no leverage or argument that either the society or the environment needs to be changed if the problem rests in the individual as this paradigm suggests.

The model adopted by the disability rights movement is grounded in a framework of social pathology (Rioux 1997), and recognises and gives attention to the effect of the environment and the social structure on the consequent disability of an individual (ICIDH 1981). It recognises that disability is not only the result of the individual impairment, but is the result of interaction between individuals and the environment that is not intended or designed to enable participation (Roth 1983). It also recognises that the social causes of disability extend to the way in which social, economic and political structures contribute to disablement (Oliver 1990). The solution to the issues arising from disability is political. It recognises that beyond equal treatment or equal opportunity, notions of discrimination have to encompass the concept of 'equal environmental opportunity' to enable disabled people, to have opportunities equivalent to their non-disabled counterparts (Hahn 1993a, 1997a).

International norms and standards as guidelines for the struggle for change

Internationally, in civil society, in state governments (Jones and Marks 1999) and within the United Nations system, there has been a reflection of this shift in paradigm. The emergence of international norms and standards relating to disability has carried with it the potential to transform an almost universal pejorative cultural resistance to the equalisation of opportunities for disabled people.

Following the designation of 1981 as the International Year of Disabled Person, the United Nations General Assembly adopted the *World Programme of Action concerning Disabled Persons* (1982). The *World Programme* identified as its goal the 'full participation of persons with disabilities' in social life and development on the basis of equality. In 1993, the General Assembly adopted the Standard Rules on the Equalization of Opportunities for Persons with Disabilities (UN G.A. Res.48/96). The Standard Rules were important in so far as they supplement and provide greater specificity on the rights of disabled persons in light of conventional established rights. In 1998, the United Nations Commission on Human Rights adopted Resolution 98/31, Human Rights of Persons with Disabilities, reaffirming their commitment to the full participation of persons with disabilities in all aspects of life and to its promotion and application in international and domestic contexts.

Other international instruments articulating guidelines and standards on a range of disability-related issues include the 1975 Declaration of the Rights of Disabled Persons, the 1991 Principles for the Protection of Persons with Mental Illness and the Improvement of Mental Health Care, the 1993 Proclamation of the Economic and Social Commission for Asia and the Pacific on the Full Participation and Equality of People with Disabilities in the Asian and Pacific Region, the Tallin Guidelines for Action on Human Resources Development in the Field of Disability and the recent adoption of the Inter-American Convention on the Elimination of All Forms of Discrimination against Persons with Disabilities. These and other instruments are significant both in terms of their support for persons with disabilities, their value as authoritative interpretations of broad treaty obligations for disabled persons and for their potential contribution to the corpus of customary international law in the field of disability rights. The Standard Rules emphasise the goal of equalisation of opportunities as a fundamental concept in disability policy.

The principle of equal rights implies that the needs of each and every individual are of equal importance, that those needs must be made the basis for the planning of societies and that all resources must be employed in such a way as to ensure that every individual has equal opportunity for participation. Persons with disabilities are members of society and have the right to remain within their local communities. They are entitled to receive the support they need within the ordinary structures of education, health, employment and social services.

In addition, disabled persons are described as citizens with equal rights and equal obligations, who should receive assistance in assuming 'their full responsibility as members of society'.[1]

The most recent recognition of the status of disabled people is the adoption by the UN Human Rights Commission of Resolution 2000/51, which recognised disability as an issue of human rights. The resolution recognises that:

… any violation of the fundamental principle of equality or any discrimination or other negative differential treatment of persons with disabilities inconsistent with the United Nations Rules on the Equalization of Opportunities for Persons with Disabilities is an infringement of the human rights of persons with disability' (para. 1).

The Commission in the Resolution invites all human rights treaty monitoring bodies to monitor the compliance of states with their commitments under the relevant human rights instruments and to include those with disabilities in complying with their reporting obligations to the UN (para. 11). The High Commissioner on Human Rights is called upon to work with the Special Rapporteur on disability of the Commission for Social Development, to examine measures to strengthen the protection and monitoring of human rights of persons with disabilities (para. 30).

This is the international context for social change in Canada. These are indicators that disability has been recognised as a legitimate issue of public concern. It also suggests that the political activism of the disability rights movement has had an impact. Further, there is recognition that the non-government sector speaking for disability includes disabled people themselves and not just their families or service providers or medical charities.

Control and empowerment as ends in the struggle for social change

The struggle for social change is therefore a human rights struggle (Minow 1990).[2] It is about entrenching fairness, dignity, diversity and equality in societies. The development and administering of tests, classifications and medical evaluations are not central to that struggle. Providing services, while important, is not the essence of the political struggle but a means towards empowerment. However, it would appear that how to classify people's condition has received much more attention than the monitoring of human rights and the abuse of people's rights in their societies. Empowerment and control are central to the struggle and benchmarks against which to test policy choices, legal decisions and service models (Hahn 1997a).

The litmus test about the struggle for change is, therefore, how much progress there has been to end the political disenfranchisement, economic disempowerment and social inequality that are the reality for disabled people. Providing services and care do not lead to empowerment. It is the right to choose – the right to self-determination that will lead to the societal transformation in which 'difference [will no longer be considered] disruptive (if not threatening) and community involvement a luxury at best and an intrusion at worst' (Funderburg 1998).

Freedom as a fundamental right

The political question and the basis for the political struggle is related to the nature of empowerment. What prevents the exercise of rights? What constitutes the exercise of real freedoms? Amartya Sen, the winner of the 1998 Nobel Prize in Economics, argues in his recent book, *Development as Freedom* (Sen 1999), that:

development[3] requires the removal of major sources of non-freedom: poverty as well as tyranny, poor economic opportunities as well as systematic social deprivation, neglect of public facilities as well as intolerance or overactivity of repressive states.

He explains that even with the unprecedented increase in wealth and material goods, millions of people living in rich and poor countries are still unfree. That is, they are unable to live as they would like. What people can positively achieve, he holds, is influenced by: economic opportunities, political liberties, social powers, the enabling conditions of good health, basic education and the encouragement and cultivation of initiatives, and the liberty to participate in social choices.

With adequate development opportunities, individuals can effectively shape their own destiny and help each other. They need not be seen primarily as passive recipients of welfare or charitable help. People can be active participants in the transformations that will change their lives and the societies in which they live.

Applied to disabled people, it is easy to see the non-freedoms that characterise their lives. They have none of the characteristics that Dr Sen argues are essential to positive achievement. This is not, however, simply a case that they are poorer, are un- or underemployed, are more likely to be subject to abuse, are denied access to education in their community schools, are not given control over their own welfare assistance and so on. While these inequities in and reduction of health and well-being of disabled people need to continue to be addressed, there are other non-freedoms that require urgent attention.

It is the very essence of lives as 'cared for' people and the contingent dependency that are the most important non-freedoms faced by disabled people. To be a passive recipient of services, income and care disempowers and depoliticises an individual. This includes the profoundly personal decisions of everyday life

In some cases, not having the agency and autonomy to make decisions will not affect the immediate health of an individual. He or she may still have enough nourishing food and a good bed to sleep in, to be confident that no physical risk is encountered. But if the individual does not have agency, they are disempowered. And the consequence is a general acceptance that the disempowered disabled individual is a natural state of affairs. It is considered acceptable not to worry about the process if the end is achieved.[4] The end is argued to justify the means. But in fact, there is a demonstrated effect of having control of one's environment on the status of health and well-being. This provides a powerful argument for re-thinking some conventional assumptions. For example, there is a tendency to assume that if an individual needs support, then that need transforms him or her into a passive recipient of care thereby justifying the curtailment of freedom and choice. However, if as Dr Sen would argue the end is empowerment, the end is freedom, then not empowering people is a contradiction of justice.

Freedom and empowerment also involve responsibilities that the individual has to be able to exercise. However, the substantive freedoms that people have to exercise their responsibilities are contingent on the personal, social and environmental circumstances. For example, a child who is denied the opportunity of inclusive elementary schooling in their neighbourhood school is not only deprived as a youngster, but is also disabled throughout life by not being able to do the things that rely on reading, writing, social skills and the curiosity that is learned in school. The adult who is not allowed to express their sexuality is not only denied the ability to have children but also the freedom to have the responsibility of a physically expressed emotional relationship. An individual who is placed in an institution or protective group home is not only deprived in terms of well-being but also in terms of the ability to lead a responsible life, which is dependent on having certain freedoms. 'Responsibility requires freedom' (Sen 1999: 284).

Without the substantive freedom and capability to do something, a person cannot be responsible for doing it. So the struggle for change for disability rights advocates is for the opportunity for choice and for individuals to be entitled to make their own substantive decisions. This social commitment to individual freedom operates not only at the state level but also in other places, in community-based settings, in political and social organisations, in NGOs and in the workplace.

Being protected from the freedom and empowerment needed to make choices and act responsibly is a common experience for disabled people. There is a great deal of information and knowledge about how to provide the maximum freedom for decision making. However there is a reluctance to use that information to enhance the freedom and rights that people have. There are a number of probable reasons. First, governments in many countries do not trust their own ability to set up appropriate accounting systems so that individuals with disabilities, rather than service agencies or charities, can be held accountable for determining needs and for managing the costs. Second, social values about disability are still very negative, and conventionally people who are devalued are subject to controls on their freedom. Third, myths are still prevalent that suggest that freedom and responsibility of disabled people have to be curtailed for their own safety or for their best interests. It is a form of conventional paternalism based on the presumption of the diminished capacity of the disabled person to understand his or her own circumstances. Fourth, there is a generalised fear about difference in many societies that leads to a perception that freedom to choose might be dangerous to society generally. Fifth, disability is viewed as a negative, abnormal state rather than simply diversity. In that context limitations on freedom and choice are interpreted as appropriate.

One of the important freedoms that people must have is the freedom to act as citizens who matter and whose voices count rather than living as recipients of state or charitable largesse. The struggle for change is to undermine, to attack the commonly held view that disabled people are simply patients or clients to whom benefits will be dispensed. It is to reinstate adults being in charge of their own well-being – to enable each individual to decide how to use their capabilities, no matter how those capabilities might appear to others. But the capabilities that a person does actually have depend on the nature of social arrangements, which is crucial for individual freedom. And that is where the state and society must take an active part in ensuring that the conditions for freedom, for choice, for empowerment are in place, as it is the state that has established the conditions that result in non-freedom.

There are both social responsibilities and individual responsibilities in achieving freedom and empowerment. Social responsibilities include such mandates as: ensuring welfare is unhindered by regulations that restrict the well-being of people through where and how they live and who they live with; directly addressing blatant forms of discrimination, both direct and systemic; ensuring public accessibility to transportation, public services and places normally open to the public; gearing teaching to accommodate the diversity of students and maximise learning; providing people with the support they need to make decisions (for example, replacing incompetence proceedings with legislated supported decision making); and putting in place economic policies that provide opportunities for disabled people to work.

Individuals have a parallel responsibility to make choices about how they want to live their lives – about what job they want to take; about what educational facilities they enrol in and how they use the education they attain; about what use to make of the opportunities they have available to them. Freedom is then the empowered individual's right to make choices not within the narrow confines of externally defined limitations but within the full range of possibilities and within their own understanding of what well-being means to them. It includes both the right to make decisions and the opportunities to achieve those outcomes that are individually valued. Sen draws the distinction between the derivative importance of freedom (dependent on its actual use) and the intrinsic importance of freedom (in making an individual free to choose something he or she may or may not actually choose) – that is the process aspect of freedom and the opportunity aspect (Sen 1999: 292).

The Canadian framework for disability equality rights

Some recent legal cases in Canada provide insight into the nature of the political struggle of disabled people to have that freedom entrenched in law (Lepofsky 1997)[5] and policy; to establish human rights practices for disabled people; and to clarify what equality means. In each of these cases, the disability rights movement played a key role in decisions that recognised that the social change that was being pursued in the cases was about the freedom and agency of disabled people. The effectiveness of the struggle for substantive social change is reflected in these cases. These cases indicate that the courts are beginning to recognise the importance of the voices of disabled people and the manner in which they structure the injustice that they face.

Within the Canadian context, human rights protections for disabled people include both constitutional entitlements and federal and provincial statutory provisions.

Since the coming into force of the Canadian Charter of Rights and Freedoms in April, 1985, Canada has had the distinction of a constitutional guarantee of equality rights for persons with 'mental and physical disabilities'. Section 15 provides:

1. Every individual is equal before and under the law and has the right to equal protection and equal benefit of the law without discrimination and in particular, without discrimination based on race, national or ethnic origin, colour, religion, sex, age, mental or physical disability.
2. Subsection (1) does not preclude any law, program or activity that has as its object the amelioration of conditions of disadvantaged individuals or groups including those that are disadvantaged because of race, national or ethnic origin, colour, religion, sex, age, mental or physical disability.

As a constitutional provision, this guarantee of equality rights applies to all levels of legislative authority in Canada. That includes law at the municipal, provincial and federal level, including taxation, immigration, education, health care and even human rights protections. For the past 15 years, section 15 has provided an important process for defining and clarifying the rights of citizens. It has provided a context in which the discourses as well as the legal and policy considerations of disability have gradually taken on an equality rights perspective. Since it covers both substantive and procedural rights under 15(1) and permits affirmative action under 15(2), it provides an authoritative instrument for challenging conventional thinking about disability as an individual deficit and advancing the alternative notion of disability as a social status. It also has provided the court the ability to determine the meaning of equality and to recognise notions of freedom and autonomy as elements of equality of outcome. In the first equality case to come before the courts (*Andrews v Law Society*, 1989), the Court adopted a contextual, effects-based approach that recognised disadvantage as central to the analysis of discrimination. For disabled people, this is important because that approach makes transparent the disadvantage produced by public policies or social practices that treat people exactly the same as their non-disabled counterparts result in the exclusion of disabled people.

The pressure from those in the disability rights movement and their allies in the equality rights movement that spurred the last-minute decision of the federal government to add *disability* to Charter section 15 is important to the history of the struggle for change that has taken place in Canada. It was evident even in the early 1980s that to redress the discrimination and inequality faced by disabled people required more than the existing human rights legislation. The federal government did not include a specific equality rights guarantee for disabled people in the original proposed patriation package in October 1980, although all the other listed groups were there as they are now. During the debate on the Charter of Rights and Freedoms between 1980 and 1982, when it was passed, the only new right to be added to section 15(a) was disability equality and that was done only after a significant debate on the merits of including it specifically, rather than as part of reading section 15(a) as an open-ended section:

> The federal government initially advanced the following arguments in opposition to the disability amendment. First, there was no need for a constitutional guarantee because statutory Human Rights Codes provided a better method for protecting disability equality. Second, terms like physical and mental disability were too vague and would pose problems for judicial interpretation. Third, the cost of providing equality to persons with disabilities was too high. Finally, disability rights might not have matured sufficiently in the mind of the public to justify their inclusion. (Lepofsky 1997; Lepofsky and Bickenbach 1985)

Those advocating for the disability amendment made the following arguments. 'Disabled people constitute a significantly disadvantaged minority in Canadian society who are subjected to widespread discrimination in the public and private spheres, and who need constitutional protection' (Lepofsky 1997). Civil rights or anti-discrimination legislation, based on individual complaints, it was argued, did not provide adequate protection for the extent and type of legislative redress and change needed. Disability rights advocates argued, with respect to definition, that disability was no more difficult to define than other constitutional terms and there were definitions in the literature at the time that could be used. In other words, definition was not nearly so uncharted as some tried to make it out to be. The government was reminded of Canada's international obligations, particularly in the United Nations Year of the Disabled Person (UNDP). Disability rights advocates opposed any arguments about costs, reasoning that arguments about the cost of equality was inherently unjust and discriminatory in itself as it was not applied to any other groups being protected by the Charter provisions. They also argued that the cost of exclusion would more than compensate for the cost of inclusion. In the end, mental and physical disability were added as listed grounds for equality rights.

In subsequent cases under the Charter of Rights and Freedoms the Supreme Court has adopted a contextual, effects-based approach that recognises disadvantage as central to the analysis of discrimination (*Andrews v Law Society*, 1989; *Turpin v R.*, 1989). The Court has enunciated constitutional equality principles that are of benefit to disability claims in a number of ways. First, the decisions have recognised that section 15 of the Charter is the culmination of Canada's legislative human rights tradition to secure full equality and full participation for disadvantaged groups who have traditionally faced discrimination. Second, section 15's prohibition against discrimination has been interpreted in the *Andrews* and *Turpin* decisions to encompass both direct discrimination and adverse effects discrimination. There is no requirement for plaintiffs to show that the discrimination was intentional. Third, the court in these cases, rejected the equal treatment model of discrimination (Rioux 1994) in favour of an interpretation of equality that recognised that equality may require differentiation in treatment. Fourth, the Court acknowledges that section 15 '…was intended to make real substantive changes to society' (Lepofsky 1997) and that the Court can grant comprehensive remedies to advance equality 'including requiring the spending of public money and the extension of benefits to previously excluded disadvantaged groups' (Lepofsky 1997: 291). Importantly the Court placed statutory Human Rights Code legal principles into section 15, which gave constitutional importance to the early decisions and interpretations under the federal and provincial Human Rights Codes. Fifth, legislative bans on discrimination require an affirmative duty to accommodate the needs of discriminated against groups.

This perspective on Charter equality rights as well as a number of decisions by the courts on cases specific to disability rights, both before and after the Charter came in effect, set clear guidelines for the struggle for change that is ongoing. The outcome of equality requires more than the removal of physical barriers and adaptation of the current structures. Equality for disabled people is about achieving a barrier-free society in which disabled people can fully participate. In that context, it is about the re-structuring of society and its institutions so that the participation of disabled people is not an exception but inherent to the political, social and economic life. It is not an issue of assimilation but of recognising the inherent differences as a basis for ensuring equality and redressing discrimination. It involves freedom and empowerment. Examining a few of the legal decisions provides some insight into the outcome for disabled people.

Outcomes in disability cases

Even before provisions of the Charter came into effect there were several cases that set the standard for equality, for autonomy and for freedom as the fundamental entitlements of disabled people.

In a case before the Divisional [Provincial] Court of Ontario in 1982, the court rendered a decision in *Clark v Clark* (1982). The case involved an application by the father of Justin Clark for a declaration that his disabled son was mentally incompetent. Justin who had lived for 18 of his 20 years in an institution had decided to leave the institution and move to a supported living arrangement in his community. His father, fearful that Justin could not cope outside the institution, had initiated legal proceedings to prevent Justin from moving. The case was significant for a number of reasons (Rioux and Frazee 1999). First, Justin was the first person in Canada to testify at a trial using a Blissymbol Board to give legal evidence. Second, the judge presiding in the case rejected expert evidence based upon medical and psychological tests, choosing to place greater emphasis on Justin's own testimony and that of witnesses who knew him well as a person. Third, the case was decided in favour of Justin's right to self-determination:

> I believe a courageous man such as Justin Clark is entitled to take a risk…. With incredible effort Justin Clark has managed to communicate his passion for freedom as well as his love of family during the course of this trial…. We have, all of us, recognized a gentle trusting, believing spirit and very much a thinking human being who has his unique part to play in our compassionate, interdependent society…. I find and I declare Matthew Justin Clark to be mentally competent. (*Clark v Clark* 1982: 383)

In 1982, this was a significant decision and reflected the emergence in Canada of a changing perspective on disability and a different standard by which to look at the place of disabled people in society. The disability rights movement was beginning to be heard.

In 1986, the Supreme Court of Canada recognised the rights of disabled people in a decision related to the non-consensual sterilisation of a woman with an intellectual disability (*Eve v Eve* 1986). In 1976, a mother of a 21-year-old woman attending a segregated school in the province of Prince Edward Island filed for a court injunction to enable her to provide the consent for her daughter to have a non-therapeutic sterilisation. Eve's mother argued that her daughter could not cope with being a mother, that Eve was at risk of becoming pregnant and that therefore it was in her best interests to sterilise her.

The Supreme Court ruled that no one can legally be sterilised without personally consenting, unless it is a matter of medical necessity. There is no legislation in Canada that permits a third party (including parents, next-of-kin, the Public Trustee or the administrator of a facility) to consent to a non-therapeutic sterilisation on behalf of an individual who is unable to consent on her or his own behalf. Mr Justice Laforest was unambiguous, when he held in the decision:

> … it is obviously fiction to suggest that a [substituted decision] is that of the mental incompetent (sic), however much the court may try to put itself in her place. What the incompetent would do if she or he could make the choice is simply a matter of speculation.

This case, the first Supreme Court case in which people labelled with intellectual disabilities were given leave to intervene, addressed the fundamental nature of rights and agency. In Canada, as in many Western nations, laws have been put in place to protect those not in a position to speak for themselves, people with intellectual disabilities, people who are ageing and children. But in the process of 'protecting', such laws often put disabled people in the position of having to prove that they are entitled to goods, services and opportunities that are considered rights for the non-disabled population. The result is that for many disabled people, rights become privileges to be earned. This legal model, which bestows rights as charitable privilege, emphasises benevolence and pity and puts in practice the exercise of control exercised through expert and professional decision making. The rationale for denying rights is paternalistic and usually argued from the perspective of the best interests of the individual concerned. This raises some fundamental questions about the basis of rights and claims by individuals to make their own decisions. It gives the authority in law to experts to decide who ought to be able to exercise their rights and to decide the criteria to exercise those rights. The court in the *Eve* case limited the *parens patriae* power, a beneficent, paternalistic area of responsibility, and argued that the right to procreate or the privilege to give birth is fundamental, thereby circumscribing the power of the state to an *a priori* restriction of rights-based on disability.

Importantly, the case was not argued on the individual capacity of *Eve* but rather on the efficacy and fairness of substituted decision making and the exercise of fundamental rights. The case is not about disability, but about state or others' power over individual agency and autonomy.

In another decision relating to sterilisation, in which Leilani Muir sued the Province of Alberta for wrongful sterilisation while she was a resident of an institution 30 years before, she received a significant financial award in a court decision in 1995 in recognition of the damages she suffered: (1) resulting from the sterilisation, allowed by the law of that Province, at that time; (2) associated with the humiliating categorisation of being labelled a 'moron'; and (3) connected with the improper confinement and detention in the institution and losses she suffered, including liberty, reputation, normal development experiences, enjoyment of life, civil rights, contact with family and friends and subjection to humiliation and disgrace, pain and suffering and institutional discipline.

The court in this case recognised that labelling in itself is a fundamental infringement of human dignity and the institution limited her liberty and other rights. It recognised that 'care' does not extend to treatment that imposes loss of liberty, loss of privacy, cruel punishment or unauthorised drug experimentation.

In October 1997, the Canadian Supreme Court delivered a decision, hailed by the disability rights movement, that many commentators have suggested will require provinces to take positive measures to remove barriers which limit access to public services for disabled people. *Eldridge v British Columbia* (1997) involved a claim by three deaf applicants that the legislation governing health care services and hospitals in the province was discriminatory because it neither included sign language interpreter services as an insured service, nor required hospitals to provide sign language interpreter services. The court ruled that the government had violated the equality provisions of the Charter of Rights and Freedoms in its implementation of the provincial Medical Services Plan. 'The court held that, in order for deaf persons to receive the benefit of medical services, they required communication with their doctors. Interpreters were not an ancillary service but an integral part of medical care. In providing a benefit scheme the state was obliged to provide the benefit in a non-discriminatory manner. Failure to provide interpreters meant that deaf people would receive an inferior quality of health care to hearing persons' (Mosoff and Grant 1999).

This decision is important for a number of reasons. First is court's holding that 'once the state provides a benefit, it is obliged to do so in an non-discriminatory manner'. This is important because it gives recognition to the entitlement of disabled people to government benefits, an entitlement that is not discretionary or charitable. It recognises the status of disabled people to receive what others receive, as a claim and not as government largesse.

The second point that has relevance is the interpretation of equality that the Charter protects. The denial of equality in *Eldridge* arose from the failure of the government to take action (rather than the imposition of a burden). The discrimination arose from the adverse effects of a public benefit scheme that failed to provide the same level of service (adverse impact discrimination). The court held that:

> To argue that governments should be entitled to provide benefits to the general population without ensuring that disadvantaged members of society have the resources to take full advantage of those benefits bespeaks a thin and impoverished vision of s 15(1). It is belied, more importantly, by the thrust of this Court's equality jurisprudence.

The important principle here is that there is a positive obligation on the government to remedy inequality notwithstanding that the benefit scheme appeared neutral and the remedy meant that the government had to spend money.

The third issue of relevance is the importance and centrality that the court placed on reasonable accommodation as a 'cornerstone' of ensuring equal benefit. The court included accommodation as a central element of section 15 and made clear in the ruling that it is the failure to provide reasonable accommodation that results in discrimination. It is not the disability.

The fourth issue of importance is the court's finding that '...governments should not be allowed to evade constitutional responsibilities by delegating the implementation of their policies and programmes to private entities'. In other words, it gave a broader scope to the applicability of the Charter. To the extent that an organisation or private entity is providing a specific government objective the Charter applies to those activities or programmes. Who performs the activity is secondary to the activity itself in determining if it is a government service that is being performed.

The fifth issue of importance is the court's holding that effective communication is an indispensable component of the delivery of a medical service. This is important to recognising the systemic nature of the discrimination against disabled people and recognising that the discrimination cannot be redressed without changes to the definition of the services government provides. The court began its analysis with the recognition of the historical exclusion and marginalisation of disabled people:

> It is an unfortunate truth that the history of disabled persons in Canada is largely one of exclusion and marginalization. Persons with disabilities have too often been excluded from the labour force, denied access to opportunities for social interaction and advancement, subjected to invidious stereotyping and related to institutions. This historical disadvantage has to a great extent been shaped and perpetuated by the notion that disability is an abnormality or flaw. As a result, disabled persons have not generally been afforded the 'equal concern, respect and consideration' that s. 15(1) of the Charter demands. Instead they have been subjected to paternalistic attitudes of pity and charity, and their entrance into the social mainstream has been conditional upon their emulation of able-bodied norms.

These cases reflect the direction in which the courts are headed in recognising discrimination, equality, empowerment, freedom, agency and full participation. It reflects the persuasive arguments that the disability rights community have made as *amicus curae* in each of these cases.

Conclusion

The struggle for change has, in itself, changed. It is no longer about better services in an unresponsive and ableist society. It is about equal outcome and entitlement, and about freedom and agency. Historically and legally it is possible to trace this evolution from exclusion to charity to service provision to freedom and rights. But it is not consistent. It is easy enough to find inconsistencies in legislation, in jurisprudence, in social attitude, and in practice. In many cases, there are different goals even within the same political jurisdiction and certainly cross-nationally. The continuing development of a strong disability rights movement and the legal entitlements that are being won in law courts do suggest however that the struggle for change is having an impact. Disability equality rights have found their way into recent international agreements and they are becoming a standard in jurisprudence in Canada. The voices of disabled people are being heard and given legitimacy. There is still a long way to go but some progress is being made. Martin Luther King, the leader of another great movement for social justice once said: 'The arc of history is long but it always bends towards justice'. The urgency felt by those who live outside the boundaries of justice is palpable. But as they push, we can see the direction the arc is bending.

Questions

- Recent United Nations resolutions of the High Commission for Human Rights have claimed that disability is an issue of human rights. Reframing disability as a rights issue rather than an issue of social development changes its context and makes it analogous to other human rights movements such as those based on ethnicity, religion, race and gender. Why has it taken so long for this to happen? What are the particular circumstances surrounding disability that have acted as barriers to this recognition?
- Why is it important that the goals of the struggle for social change are recognised as freedom and autonomy? Why is it not enough simply to provide more and better services for disabled people?

Notes

1. Standard Rules on the Equalization of Opportunities, Introduction para. 24-27. The *Standard Rules* in the preamble refer to other international instruments that are part of the legal framework for the human rights of disabled people notably *Universal Declaration on Human Rights;* the *International Covenant on Economic, Social and Cultural;* the *International Covenant on Civil and Political Rights;* the *Convention on the Rights of the Child;* the *International Convention for the Protection of the Rights of all Migrant Works and Members of Their Families;* the *Convention on the Elimination* of *All Forms of Discrimination Against Women;* the *Declaration on the Rights of Disabled Persons;* the *Declaration on the Rights of Mentally Retarded Persons;* the *Declaration on Social Progress and Development;* and the *Principles for the Protection of Persons with Mental Illness and for the Improvement of Mental Health Care.*
2. Martha Minow maintains that a rights-based strategy has to be a part of any strategy for political empowerment.
3. He contrasts this foundational view of development as freedom with narrower views of development in terms of GNP growth or industrialisation.
4. The simplest example is the assumption that as long as one has food that has the basic nutrients it is not relevant whether one chooses it or where it is served. The fallacy of such an assumption seems self-evident.
5. For an evaluation of legal entrenchment of Charter rights in Canada see David Lepfsky's paper.

CHAPTER 5

Feminism and disability: the theoretical and political significance of the personal and the experiential

Carol Thomas

Introduction

Those seeking to understand disability can learn a great deal from feminist research and theorising on the social position of women. This is not simply because the majority of disabled people *are* women, but because feminists have been engaged in the generation of new knowledge about the nature of the 'oppression' and social disadvantage of marginalised and excluded people for longer, and on a larger scale, than have disability theorists and writers. The history of the Women's Movement – that motor force behind second-wave feminist thinking – has already been written several times over, whereas that of the younger disabled people's movement has only recently begun to be documented (Campbell and Oliver 1996).

Lessons from feminism of relevance to disability do not, however, come in the form of theoretical and empirical work on disability or the social position of disabled women *per se*, but through the application in the field of disability studies of elements of feminist epistemology and other insights of a theoretical, empirical and political character. As Jenny Morris (1996) has pointed out, 20th-century feminism singularly failed to address the question of disability, and can actually be accused of contributing to disablist discourses and practices either by omitting to consider disability at all, or through its practice of uncritically reproducing disablist ideas, for example in the feminist debate on informal care (Morris 1991, 1993b, 1995, 1996). Nevertheless, despite disappointments, feminists have produced a rich body of ideas from which to draw in disability studies and politics. In the UK, there are recent signs of change in mainstream feminism in the form of an increased recognition that disability should be represented in discussions about dimensions of 'difference' among women (see, for example, Evans and Lee 2001), and in the appearance of a book on disability in a feminist series: Barbara Fawcett's *Feminist Perspectives on Disability* (2000).

Within disability studies, the work of applying feminist ideas to disability issues has, of course, already begun. There are a number of disabled women writing from an explicitly feminist perspective – Jenny Morris being the pioneer in Britain. Morris's work is representative of a small but growing literature of a scholarly character that analyses disability from a feminist perspective (Fine and Asch 1988; Begum 1992; Hillyer 1993; Wendell 1996; Marris 1996; Corker 1998; Corker and French 1999; Thomas 1997, 1999). In addition, there is a recent literature, much of it inspired by the feminist maxim that the personal is political, that aims to give voice to disabled women through the publication of their personal accounts, poems, stories and so on (Matthews 1983; Brown *et al.* 1985; Deegan and Brooks 1985; Finger 1990; Driedger and Gray 1992; Mason 1992; Atkinson *et al.* 2000; Traustadottir and Johnson 2000).

With reference to some of the analytical writings in this disability studies literature, and in the wider feminist literature, the aim of this chapter is to discuss the way in which feminist writers are critically engaging with the social model of disability. It reviews the debate between these writers and leading male social modellists, particularly Mike Oliver and Vik Finkelstein, with a particular focus on matters of the 'personal' and the 'experiential'. As we shall see, drawing attention to the personal and the experiential is viewed with suspicion and disdain by Oliver, Finkelstein and some other male writers (Oliver 1996a, 1996b; Finkelstein 1996a, 1996b; Barnes 1998). The main reason for this is their belief that a focus on such matters is diversionary: it saps the political energies of the disabled people's movement and bolsters oppressive models of disability (medical, individual, administrative). In their view, the social model of disability is a tool for identifying disablist social barriers 'out there' in the socio-structural environment, not for dwelling on the 'in-here' experiences of living with disability or impairment. Feminists, in contrast, reject forms of thought that posit a 'binary divide', that reproduce a dualism, between 'the personal' and 'the social'. They see the social and the political as just as present in the interstices and intimacies of day-to-day personal life, in the business of the 'private' dimensions of life, as it is in the 'public' domains of employment, education and other aspects of the wider social structure. For feminists, anti-oppressive politics have to develop from, and operate across, all of these fronts. However, it should be noted from the start that feminism is not a unitary perspective; there are a wide range of *feminisms* representing very different theoretical perspectives.

The chapter is structured as follows. First, recent debate among disability writers about the social model will be outlined in the form of a feminist critique and a social modellist counter-critique. In the second half, the personal and the experiential are explored in more detail, and some thoughts are offered on the ways in which disability theory and politics have gained from feminist ideas and debates.

Feminist critiques and social modellist counter-critiques of the social model of disability

As for others, the social model of disability is important to me for personal, intellectual and political reasons: it has helped me to self-identify as a disabled woman; it defines disability sociologically rather than bio-medically or individually; and it fits in with my (out-of-fashion) political inclinations that radical social structural change is necessary to advance the interests of disabled people, as it is for other socially excluded groups.

The central idea of the social model is that disability is socially created; it is *not* an inevitable consequence of being impaired. Impairment is causally unhooked from disability (Oliver 1996a; Barton and Oliver 1997; Thomas 1999) and disability becomes another form of social oppression. This conceptual severing of impairment from disability is the model's decisive liberatory move, and has enabled all types of social exclusions experienced by people with impairments to be correctly causally attributed to discriminatory social barriers and socio-cultural practices. 'Overcoming disability' can be politically reformulated to mean 'overcoming disabling barriers' – in employment, education, housing, transport systems, cultural arenas, and elsewhere. No one in disability studies would deny the profound political significance of this recasting of disability as *social*.

Feminist critiques

How, then, has the social model been critiqued by feminist writers such as Jenny Morris and others within the disabled people's movement? The following statements by Morris encapsulate some of the issues in question:

> ... they [male advocates of the social model of disability] have been making the personal political in the sense that they have insisted that what appears to be an individual experience of disability is in fact socially constructed. However, we also need to hang on to the other sense of making the personal political and that is owning, taking control of, and representation of the personal experience of disability – including negative parts of the experience.
>
> Unfortunately, in our attempts to challenge the medical and the 'personal tragedy' models of disability, we have sometimes tended to deny the personal experience of disability.... (Morris 1993b: 68)

> ... there is a tendency within the social model of disability to deny the experience of our own bodies, insisting that our physical differences and restrictions are entirely socially created. While environmental barriers and social attitudes are a crucial part of our experience of disability – and do indeed disable us – to suggest that this is all there is to deny the personal experience of physical or intellectual restrictions, of illness, of the fear of dying. A feminist perspective can redress this, and in doing so give a voice to the experience of both disabled men and disabled women. (Morris 1991: 10).
>
> ... there was a concern amongst some disabled women that the way our experience was being politicised didn't leave much room for acknowledging our experience of our bodies; that too often there wasn't room for talking about the experience of impairment, that a lot of us feel pressurised into just focusing on social barriers. (Morris 1996: 13)

These statements assert three things: i) the importance of taking account of the personal experience of disability; ii) the importance of acknowledging the personal experience of living with impairment; and iii) the necessity of recognising that some restrictions of activity *are* caused by the effects of impairment and cannot be causally attributed to 'social barriers'. This third point, that not all restrictions on activity are socially created, has also been made by Sally French (1993). She uses her personal experience of being visually impaired to show that some of the restrictions that she encounters (restrictions on activity and in social interactions) would remain even if all 'social barriers' were eliminated. That is, impairments, and not just social barriers, do 'cause' some restrictions on activity and disadvantages.

For similar reasons, Liz Crow has suggested that the social model should be renewed by including the experience of impairment:

What we need is to find a way to integrate impairment into our whole experience and sense of ourselves for the sake of our own physical and emotional well-being, and, subsequently, for our individual and collective capacity to work against disability. (Crow 1996: 59)

Thus, a fourth point is added: the capacity to engage in political struggle is weakened if people feel that aspects of their experience, and of their sense of self, are alienated or denied by the terms and conditions of that struggle.

Mairian Corker has also critiqued social modellist thought for its disinterest in the personal experience of living with disability and impairment, and for its setting up of a rigid discursive boundary between disability and impairment (1998). On the latter point, Corker and French state the following about the social model:

… though it is a ground-breaking concept, and one which has provided tremendous political impetus for disabled people, we feel that because the distinction between disability and impairment is presented as a dualism or dichotomy – one part of which (disability) is valorized and the other part (impairment) marginalized or silenced – the social model theory, itself, produces and embodies distinctions of value and power. (Corker and French 1999: 2) … the presupposition that the boundary between disability and impairment is solid does not allow us to explore adequately our experience of disability oppression because this experience is 'in-between' – discursively produced at the interface of society and the individual … (Corker and French 1999: 4)

Returning to Jenny Morris, she has explained the 'faults' in the social model approach with reference to the gendered character of the leadership of the disabled people's movement and its ideologues:

Like other political movements, the disability movement in Britain and throughout the world, has tended to be dominated by men both as theoreticians and holders of important organisational posts. Both the movement and the development of a theory of disability have been the poorer for this as there has been an accompanying tendency to avoid confronting the personal experience of disability. (Morris 1991: 9)

Corker's critique locates the faults in the modernist theoretical perspectives of this male leadership – their materialist or Marxist leanings. As a poststructuralist feminist within disability studies, Corker identifies the weaknesses, and exclusions, associated with the social model as bound up with its rootedness in problematic theoretical perspectives.

The social modellist counter-critique

Mike Oliver has done most to develop the social creation of disability thesis alongside the disabled people's movement, formulating it in terms of the social model (Oliver 1990, 1996b). In his reply to critiques by Morris, French and Crow, he has made a number of points (Oliver

1996a, 1996b). One is that the model does not amount to a theory of disability, and that a considerable amount of theoretical work is required (Oliver 1996a, 1996b). The social model is a 'pragmatic attempt to identify and address issues that can be changed through collective action rather than medical or other professional treatment' (1996b: 38). As a pragmatic definitional tool, the social model has had: '…unparalleled success in changing the discourses around disability, in promoting disability as a civil rights issue and in developing schemes to give disabled people autonomy and control in their own lives' (1996a: 39). This is a point with which few would disagree.

A second point is that '… the social model is not an attempt to deal with the personal restrictions of impairment …' (Oliver 1996b: 48). On the contrary, it is reasserted that there is no causal link between impairment and disability – 'disability is wholly and exclusively social … disablement is nothing to do with the body' (Oliver 1996b: 41–2). Oliver states that this is not the same as denying 'the reality of impairment' (Oliver 1996b: 42); it is not that 'the pain of impairment' is unacknowledged, but that this has not been focused upon because the key political task is to tackle the social barriers which cause disability: '…pain, medication and ill-health properly belong within either the individual model of disability or the *social model of impairment*' (Oliver 1996b: 49, my emphasis). In his view, attempts to integrate impairment into the social model of disability should be resisted because '…the collectivizing of experiences of impairment is a much more difficult task than collectivizing the experiences of disability' (Oliver 1996b: 51). Further:

> … engaging in public criticism may not broaden and refine the social model; it may instead breathe new life into the individual model with all that means in terms of increasing medical and therapeutic interventions into areas of our lives where they do not belong. (Oliver 1996b: 52)

Thus, for Oliver, the social model of disability still has the power to transform consciousness and to serve the struggle for disability rights, and should not be tampered with.

Vik Finkelstein's responses to the arguments advanced by Morris and Crow are made in a less tolerant tone. Finkelstein rejects the trend within the disabled people's movement, encouraged by some disability academics, towards a focus on 'experience':

> … over a period of time, the political and cultural vision inspired by the new focus on dismantling the real disabling barriers 'out there' has been progressively eroded and turned inward into contemplative and abstract concerns about subjective experiences of the disabling world. (Finkelstein 1996a: 34)

For him, the problem is that a focus on experiences – either of impairment or disability – dangerously diverts attention away from the causes of oppressive social barriers. In fact, focusing on experiences is a 'discredited and sterile approach to understanding and changing the world' (Finkelstein 1996a: 34) – leading to 'passive' pressure group politics limited to issues within the confines of personal experience. He calls for a return to a clear focus on the structural aspects of the social system, and the making of common cause with other sections of the community who are oppressed by the social system (p. 36). Another related thread in

Finkelstein's counter-critique is the tendency for academics to 'rectify' the social model, turning it into a politically neutered means of explanation:

> ... in the hands of a new and growing disabled elite teaching and presenting the [social] model at conferences, workshops and training sessions, the social model of disability progressively degenerated into a sterile prescription for 'explaining' our situation. There is an urgent need for the grassroots to regain its control over the social interpretation of disability because it is only here that the radical agenda can be returned to our struggle for emancipation. (Finkelstein 1996b: 1)

The personal and the experiential

At the heart of the feminist critique of the social model of disability, and of its defence, are two key questions: i) should attention be paid to the *personal experience of disability*?; ii) what are the consequences of acknowledging the personal experience of living with impairment and of recognising that some restrictions of activity *are* caused by the effects of impairment and cannot be causally attributed to disablist 'social barriers'? These questions will now be discussed in turn.

The personal experience of disability

For feminists, an engagement with their own, and others', personal experience is seen to be theoretically and politically essential. Understanding experience offers a route through to theorising the wider social position of women, and thus to laying the foundations for politically confronting their social oppression. In the 1970s and 1980s, many feminist writers invoked 'experience', both their own and other women's, as a way of challenging mainstream (malestream) social science which insisted on a version of itself as 'objective' and 'neutral', as theorising in a 'scientific' fashion at the level of the collective and the general (Stanley 1990). The purpose of giving authority to experience was, in part, to expose these mainstream approaches as in fact highly gendered – privileging a male viewpoint dressed up in the scientificity of 'objective knowledge'. It was argued that the malestream view of the world that dominated the social sciences was based on a male subjectivity (male subject = the 'norm'), and presented women, aspects of women's lives, and the feminine, as the 'other' (male = subject, women = object). The realm of the personal was coded as female and was therefore devalued and excluded (Stacey 1997). This was seen to be at the root of the exclusion of some areas of life as 'private' – and therefore not of central concern to sociologists and other social scientists.

> For many feminists the introduction of personal criticism is a strategic disruption of the smooth surface of abstract universalising theories that have constituted women in 'lack, invisibility, silence' (Miller 1991: 7). The embarrassment that personal modes may introduce into academic settings touches on the sense that 'emotion', 'experience' and 'autobiography' have no place in the discourse of knowledge and should be kept outside the doors of the academy. The authority of theory relies upon the exclusion of the personal to maintain its status. For some, it is precisely these conventions, based in the traditions of

objectivity and universal truth claims, that have been seen to protect the domain of theory in academy as a masculine preserve.... (Stacey 1997: 64).

It should be noted, however, that the concept 'experience' has not had a smooth ride within feminism (see the discussion in Thomas 1999). In recent years, feminist social and cultural theorists have disagreed about how to theorise experience, as feminism in general has fragmented into theoretical feminisms. Those adopting postmodernist perspectives have questioned traditional feminist assumptions that studying women's personal experiences gives unmediated access to experiential 'truths' (Bordo 1990; Stanley 1990; Haraway 1991; Skeggs 1995, 1997; Fuss 1989; Probyn 1993; Stacey 1997). Nevertheless, despite their theoretical differences, feminists retain their allegiance to the key importance of personal experience in their theoretical and political projects.

Given this background it is not surprising that feminists in disability studies view engaging with personal experience not as an optional extra, but as an essential part of developing an understanding of disability. Jenny Morris, Mairian Corker and other feminist writers bring personal experience into 'the social', and reject the social modellist insistence that it is separated off into the supposedly irrelevant realm of 'the private'. Feminists see a classic expression of (malestream) scientism in Finkelstein's assertion that a preoccupation with the private domain of experience is a 'discredited and sterile approach to understanding and changing the world' (1996a: 34). In their counter-critique to feminist criticisms of the social model, Oliver and Finkelstein continue to adhere to the view that some areas of life do not properly belong to the social, and should not occupy the minds of those attempting to challenge disability, that is, the operation of social barriers 'out there'. A good example of this private/public dualistic thinking is found in Oliver's (1996b: 48) discussion about why some of his 'personal experiences' as a wheelchair user do not qualify as disability concerns:

As a wheelchair user when I go to parties I am more restricted than some other people from interacting with everyone else and what's more, it is difficult to see a solution – houses are usually crowded with people during parties and that makes circulation difficult for a wheelchair user. But other people may find circulation difficult as well but for other reasons; they may simply be shy. The point I am making here is that the social model is not an attempt to deal with the personal restrictions of impairment but the social barriers of disability as defined earlier by DPI [Disabled People's International] and UPIAS [Union of the Physically Impaired Against Segregation].

From a feminist point of view, it is very problematic to view this party-going experience as defining 'the personal restrictions of impairment' rather than as an example of *disability* in action. To cite Oliver's preferred definition of disability:

[disability] is the disadvantage or restriction of activity caused by a contemporary social organisation which takes no or little account of people who have physical impairments and thus excludes them from the mainstream of social activities. (UPIAS 1996, cited in Oliver 1996b: 44).

Oliver is describing a social setting in which he is socially excluded (or disadvantaged) because the form of interaction between non-wheelchair users 'takes no or little account' of him, and takes place in physical spaces (houses) that are not designed for people like him. Furthermore, it *is* possible to see how these 'social barriers' could be removed – if the party was held in a fully accessible location/space and if non-disabled people behaved differently.

What Oliver's example really tells us is that party-going is believed to be part of 'private' or 'personal' life. For him, it follows that any restrictions of activity encountered in the private domain are 'personal restrictions of impairment'; they do not constitute disability. In his book, *Understanding Disability: From Theory to Practice* (1996a), Oliver makes this dichotomising of the personal (private) and the public (social, political) clear: 'There is a danger in emphasising the personal *at the expense of* the political because most of the world still thinks of disability as an individual, intensely personal problem' (1996b: 3, my emphasis). The consequence of this separation of the private and the public is that whole areas of disability experience, and thus of disablism, are eclipsed because they are located in the so-called private domain of life. It was this separation that enabled some male leaders of a number of left-wing political organisations in the 1970s to argue that issues of domestic violence, sexual relationships and women's roles as housewives and mothers, were not 'real' political issues because they were about 'private' life and belonged to the domestic domain (Rowbotham 1972; Coote and Campbell 1982). This was the origin of the feminist maxim that the personal *is* political.

The theoretical and political importance of the feminist insistence that the personal experience of disability must be taken account of now becomes clear. It allows the full extent of disablism to come into view. Alongside the possibility of identifying disablism in the shape of social barriers 'out there', it is possible to name as manifestations of disability those oppressive practices and restrictions that operate 'closer to home', in 'personal' life. Aspects of *social* life and social oppression so keenly felt by most disabled people bound up, for example, with family and sexual relationships, can be rightly seen as the terrain of disability, and thus of relevance to disability politics. Rather than de-railing the disabled people's movement, a focus on personal experiences can bring new dimensions of disability to light. In my book, *Female Forms: Experiencing and Understanding Disability* (Thomas 1999), I have used the term the 'psycho-emotional dimensions of disability' to try to capture some of the dimensions of disability that operate in the realm of the so-called 'private' domain of life, and readers may like to refer to the extended discussion there. I concluded that the UPIAS definition of disability needed to be reformulated to read as follows: disability is a form of social oppression involving the social imposition of restrictions of activity on people with impairments and the socially engendered undermining of their psycho-emotional well-being (Thomas 1999: 60).

The personal experience of impairment, and the consequences of recognising that some restrictions of activity are caused by the effects of impairment

As discussed, feminists in disability studies object to the social modellist denial of the experience of 'our own bodies', of the denial of living with features of impairment such as pain, fatigue and the threat of premature death. For many disabled feminists, the social model of disability, as it stands, is inadequate not only because important personal experiences of living with disability are left out of account, but so too are the personal experiences of living with impairment. Drawing on their own impairment experiences, feminists have also asserted that not all restrictions of activity they face can be attributed to social barriers; impairment does cause some of these restrictions. Oliver (1996a, 1996b) and Finkelstein (1996a, 1996b) defend the social model's complete independence from impairment concerns, and assert that any re-introduction of impairment issues risks revitalising oppressive medical, individualist or administrative models of disability. Oliver (1996a) concedes that there may be a case for a 'social model of impairment', but argues that the political priority is to work with the social model of disability. I would argue that feminists' reluctance, or refusal, to leave matters of impairment aside are, in fact, potentially of great assistance to disability studies and disability politics. This is for at least two reasons.

First, feminists' insistence on the relevance of impairment experiences has brought to light the important impairment-related *differences* that exist among disabled people (Corker 1998; Corker and French 1999). This has greatly enriched our understanding of the variety of life lived with very different types of impairment, a variety clouded by the generalising impairment categories: 'physical', 'sensory', 'learning difficulty', 'chronic illness', 'hidden impairments', and so forth. This enriched understanding, in turn, allows for the many different forms *of disablism* to be better identified, understood, and thus challenged. For example, the recent book edited by Traustadottir and Johnson (2000) on the personal experiences of women with learning difficulties adds greatly to our appreciation of the particular, as well as the shared, ways in which disablism manifests itself in the lives of people with specific kinds of impairment. This feminist sensitivity to difference in matters of impairment also supports the need to pay attention to other differences among disabled people, for example, those associated with gender, 'race', sexuality, class and age. This contributes towards ensuring that the disabled people's movement is inclusive and tolerant, rather than exclusive and bigoted.

Second, feminists' attention to impairment experiences has helped to encourage theoretical work on the nature of impairment. One dimension of this has been thinking on the *social*, in addition to the biological, character of impairment. The social modellist imperative to bracket impairment off as having nothing to do with disability (Oliver 1996b), and then to leave it aside as irrelevant in the struggle for disability rights, has the great danger of naturalising impairment, of relegating it to the domain of the 'purely biological' (Abberley 1987). Bill Hughes and Kevin Paterson (1997: 329) have expressed the point particularly clearly:

> ... there is a powerful convergence between biomedicine and the social model of disability with respect to the body. Both treat it as a pre-social, inert, physical object, as discrete, palpable and separate from the self. The definitional separation of impairment and disability which is now a semantic convention for the social model follows the traditional, Cartesian, western meta-narrative of human constitution.

Feminists such as Mairian Corker (1998) and myself (Thomas 1999) have, from different theoretical perspectives, argued for the *social*, or bio-social, theorising of impairment. This is important both because it has the effect of forcing us to clarify our theorisation of disability and because a sophisticated understanding of impairment is essential in this fast-moving age of genetic science and engineering (Shakespeare 1999). In this latter area, the political and personal stakes are very high indeed for disabled people.

Another dimension of theoretical work on impairment relates to the observations by Morris (1991, 1996), French (1993) and other feminists, based on their personal experiences, that some restrictions of activity are caused by impairment. This requires us to think through, rather than avoid, the intersection and interaction of disability (social oppression) and impairment (bio-social features of our bodies). My own solution has been to distinguish disability from what I have called 'impairment effects' (Thomas 1999). I would argue that the identification of the reality of impairment effects in no way weakens the potency of the social conceptualisation of disability. It offers no succour to the 'medical model' of disability. On the contrary, it has enabled me to clarify my ideas on the *social relational* character of disability (Thomas 1999). Thus, an engagement with impairment, and impairment effects, facilitates the development of disability theory.

Summary

This chapter has discussed some of the ways in which feminist ideas on the personal and the experiential can contribute to disability studies and disability politics. It has explored this through a focus on recent debate about the social model of disability between feminist writers and leading male figures within disability studies. It has shown that the feminist critique of the social model highlighted a number of issues: the importance of taking account of the personal experience both of disability and impairment; the necessity of recognising that some restrictions of activity *are* caused by the effects of impairment and cannot be causally attributed to 'social barriers'; and the importance of recognising that the capacity to engage in political struggle is weakened if people feel that aspects of their experience are alienated or denied by the terms and conditions of that struggle. Those defending the social model have stressed that it has had unparalleled success as a political tool in the struggle for disability rights, that impairment has no place in the social modellist schema, and that a focus on personal experience, either of disability or impairment, is inward looking, diversionary and dangerous, not least because paying attention to impairment lets the medical model in by the back door.

The two key questions raised in this debate have been further examined, with reference to the wider feminist literature on the significance of impairment. In answer to the first question – should attention be paid to the personal experience of disability? – I have argued in the affirmative. Pursuing a feminist engagement with the personal experience of disability has helped to expose the deep-rooted 'private/personal' versus 'public/social' dualism in social modellist thought, a dualism which mistakes 'the personal restrictions of impairment' (Oliver 1996b: 48) for what are, in fact, manifestations of disability. This exposure is important both theoretically and politically because it allows previously shrouded dimensions *of disability* associated with the more 'close to home' aspects of life to come into the full light of day.

In answer to the second question – what are the consequences of acknowledging the personal experience of living with impairment? – I have argued that the feminist insistence on taking account of impairment experiences assists rather than damages disability theory and politics. This is because it draws attention to *differences* among disabled people. I have suggested that this apparently divisive move is ultimately politically unifying because it facilitates inclusivity; differences in *disability experiences* associated with variable forms of impairment, as well as with gender, 'race', sexuality, age and class, can be better understood and addressed. Finally, paying attention to impairment has exposed the need to theorise impairment *socially*. This, in turn, requires us to sharpen up our theoretical understanding of disability and to examine the interaction of disability and impairment effects. Disability studies and disability politics can only gain by tackling this kind of theoretical work.

Questions

- Why is the feminist maxim that 'the personal is political' important for disability studies and disability politics?
- What previously hidden features of disablism can be exposed by paying close attention to the personal experiences of disability?

CHAPTER 6

Adjudication or empowerment: contrasting experiences with a social model of disability[1]

Harlan Hahn

In the initial phase of the 21st century, the disability movement in the UK and the United States faces a crucial juncture that could determine its future plans. Although disabled activists and researchers in both countries seem to have arrived at this crossroads by different routes, they confront similar choices that can be expected to have lasting implications. While British leaders may be able to glean some lessons from mistakes that have been made by Americans, disabled people in the US obviously could derive great benefits from the rich theoretical legacy that has guided and informed comparable endeavors in the UK. Fundamentally, the struggle of disabled people in both nations can be viewed as twin strands within the international disability movement. Although their activities are inspired by similar objectives, the evolution of events in both countries has been shaped by different cultural influences and conceptual perspectives. Whereas the diversity of the population and the background of the civil rights movement of the 1960s has produced more emphasis on legal principles in the United States, the British experience has embodied an increased appreciation of harsh economic realities and conflict between dominant and subordinate classes. Both orientations seem to face formidable obstacles. The American emphasis on legal rights has been substantially subverted by restrictive judicial interpretations of anti-discrimination laws; and the hegemonic nature of multinational capitalism has promoted despair among some theorists on the left in Britain about the prospects for sudden massive change in the social and economic system. While the paths that the disability movement might chose in either country cannot yet be predicted, these circumstances seem to provide a major opportunity to examine new alternatives to existing remedies.

This analysis begins with a brief description of the emergence of the 'social model' of disability in Britain and the United States. Both viewpoints stress the social construction of disability in contrast to the 'medical model' which concentrates on bodily impairments. Perhaps the principal differentiating feature of the definitions that launched the disability movement in both nations is the emphasis in the UK on the concept of 'oppression'. The second part of this presentation focuses primarily on the interpretation of anti-discrimination laws by American courts. Much of the judicial opposition to disability rights can be attributed to my failure, as an American theorist, to develop a 'minority group model' of disability that adequately encompasses the notion of oppression. This weakness, however, also provides a useful opportunity to revisit the sources of various conceptual traditions and to re-examine their implications accordingly. This approach is the major focus of the third section of this analysis. The harsh opposition expressed by a group of writers associated with the World Health Organization betrays both a serious misunderstanding of my work and an apparent inability to recognise the potential application of a broadened and expanded version of the 'minority group' perspective in other contexts. A significant portion of the fault may be traced to the structure of the judicial system as well as the behaviour of lawyers instead of conceptual inconsistencies. The theoretical development of research on this subject might profitably explore further applications of the basic ideas of political economy to the field of disability studies as well as innovative approaches to potential remedies. This aim is pursued by a brief examination of the concept of 'empowerment' in the fourth segment of this analysis. Although a full synthesis of the arguments does not seem feasible here, the concluding portion attempts to reweave some untangled strands of the presentation.

At the outset, I also want to acknowledge that much of what I intend to say here is a product, directly or indirectly, of more than 55 years of experience with a significant disability as a result of polio in 1945. I do not, of course, claim to speak for all disabled people; but I do regard disability as an experience rather than as a disease or a defect. In some instances, I can trace the impact of this experience on my own thinking, and I will attempt to note it accordingly. In other contexts, the influence may be so subtle that too much explanation would be required to uncover it. But I also consider disability, despite the everyday problems that stem from living in a disabling environment, a positive experience and a source of creative insights that may not be as readily available to non-disabled brethren. Furthermore, it is my hope that the candid admission of these facts could eventually aid in the discovery of what many of us call a 'disability culture'.

A short history of the social model of disability in the UK and US

In both the UK and America, theorists and policy makers have had more than 25 years to explore the ramifications of a social model of disability. An important impetus for this approach in Britain, of course, was the 1976 declaration of UPIAS, the Union of the Physically Impaired Against Segregation, which stated in part (as quoted in Oliver 1996a: 22):

> In our view, it is society which disables physically impaired people.... Thus, we define ... disability as the disadvantage or restriction of activity caused by a contemporary social organization which takes no or little account of people who have physical impairments and thus excludes them from participation in the mainstream of social activities. Physical disability is therefore a particular form of social oppression.

There are many concepts in this document that deserve additional analysis. At this stage, particular attention might be directed at the concept of 'oppression' as well as the observation that 'contemporary social organization' forms a source of the restrictions and exclusion encountered by disabled people on a daily basis. The latter notion opens up the possibility for comprehensive investigations of the linkage between the specific difficulties encountered by disabled persons and broader configurations such as the structure of the community and the nature of the economic system. For example, a wheelchair user, who realises that her isolation is caused primarily by architectural barriers such as stairs rather than by paralysis, may thus be permitted to move beyond this awareness to explore the manner in which ubiquitous aspects of the environment that exert a discriminatory impact on disabled people have been shaped by dominant economic and political forces. Similarly, the reference to 'oppression' serves not only as a reminder of the relentless struggle with a world designed exclusively for the benefit of non-disabled individuals but also as a standard for measuring the subjugation and exploitation that disabled women and men encounter constantly. The lack of an explicit admission of the reality of oppression has had an inhibiting effect on the strivings of disabled Americans. Most importantly, the social model in Britain was initiated and formulated by disabled people themselves rather than by professionals or politicians acting on their behalf.

By contrast, the origins of the modern disability rights movement in the US can be traced to the insertion of section 504 into the Rehabilitation Act of 1973, almost as an afterthought, by Congressional staff members (Scotch 1984). This provision stated:

> No otherwise qualified handicapped person shall, by reason of his handicap, be denied the benefits of, or participation in, any program receiving substantial Federal financial assistance.

The language in this new section of the Rehabilitation Act was adopted almost verbatim from an earlier civil rights law. As legislators and administrators gradually began to comprehend the meaning – and the potential expense – of this obligation, they postponed signing regulations to implement the new mandate until the Nixon and Ford administrations had left office. As a result, the birth of the modern disability rights movement in America was also delayed until 1977 when sit-ins and protests focused on securing the approval of these administrative rules (Shaw 1996; Johnson 1999) instead of passing new legislation. Hence, the definition of the problem as well as the remedy was drafted by officials lacking personal experience with disability in a manner that appeared to replicate common paternalistic relationship between non-disabled professionals and disabled people.

In addition, this formulation of section 504 contained other weaknesses that created serious gaps in protecting the civil rights of disabled Americans. The phrase 'otherwise qualified', for example, was probably intended to avoid foolhardy lawsuits such as so-called 'blind bus driver' controversies. Yet, in combination with legislative definitions that tend to equate disability with functional restrictions, an inability to work, or other deficiencies, the courts have forced disabled plaintiffs to pass through a narrow gauntlet that often results in the rejection of their claims. Put simply, many judges have concluded that, if a person is 'handicapped', they are not apt to meet the requirements for a particular job; but, if they are 'otherwise qualified', they may not have standing to bring a case to the courts as a 'handicapped' plaintiff. Furthermore, neither the language of the law nor its conceptual foundations provide a basis for investigating or prosecuting structural sources of discrimination against persons with disabilities. Although section 504 was limited to entities that received federal funds, this provision still included a vast range of organizations in the so-called private sector. The adoption of the Americans with Disabilities Act (ADA) in 1990, of course, extended the prohibition of discrimination against disabled citizens to private as well as public realms of society.

By contrast, of course, progress toward the enactment of comprehensive anti-discrimina-tion laws in the UK was much slower and hampered by increased obstacles. Although promi-nent British advocates in the disability movement including Oliver (1996a) thought that the passage of such measures was 'inevitable' (p. 49), powerful Members of Parliament in 1990 still expressed doubt 'whether blanket anti-discrimination legislation ... is the appropriate way to proceed' (quoted on: 156). Great Britain had adopted a 'quota system' in 1944 to promote the employment of disabled workers which went beyond the 'affirmative action' requirements in section 503 of the US Rehabilitation Act, but there has been little enforcement or compliance with these responsibilities in either country (Hahn 1984b; Percy 1989).

As a result, early indications of judicial reactions to the principle of disability rights have emerged almost exclusively from US courts. For many activists and researchers with disabilities, most opinions could hardly be described as encouraging. In general, appellate judges have relied on a narrow reading of statutory and constitutional provisions to reach decisions unfavourable to disabled Americans in the preponderance of cases. Many errors in these rulings probably have resulted from prevalent cultural misconceptions about disability. Intense adherence to the medical model, for example, compelled US researchers in the United States to devote much of their time to the arduous task of explaining an alternative conceptualisation. Moreover, by approaching issues of civil rights within the traditional context of a 'functional limitations' model rather than a 'minority group' paradigm of disability (Hahn 1982b, 1983, 1984a, 1985a, 1985b, 1985c, 1986a, 1986b, 1987a, 1987b, 1991, 1993a, 1995), non-disabled lawyers and judges abrogated their historic role of defending disadvantaged minorities and seeking to fulfil the promise of equality. The individualistic orientation of US law also has relied upon a particular theory of prejudice in the social sciences that was first advanced by Myrdahl (1940). According to this reasoning, the cognitive discomfort created by a perceived discrepancy between clear evidence of injustice and the public belief in cherished values such as freedom and equality may promote a process of social change that will eventually result in the reduction or eradication of bigotry and discrimination. But disabled people have not been popularly recognised as a minority group, and the judicial branch of government has often refused to implement statutes intended to grant them equal rights. Hence, disabled Americans appear to be confronted by a difficult choice between either (a) re-educating the judiciary and the public about the nature and meaning of disability or (b) pursuing alternative strategies of empowerment which are not as dependent on the legal process.

In contrast to the individualistic premises and structural-functional influences that perme-ated the socio-political definition of disability in the USA, scholars in Britain were able to draw upon a much more fertile intellectual legacy. Consequently, their contributions include a perspective based on historical materialism which regards 'disability and dependence ... [as] the "social creation" of a particular type of social formation; namely, industrial capitalism' (Barnes 1996: 44). This orientation, in the skilful writings of Michael Oliver, for example, yielded both an incisive criticism of the hegemonic perception of disability as a 'personal tragedy' (1990) and an enhanced understanding of disability (1996a). This approach was expanded in Australia by Gleeson (1999) to encompass the notion of 'embodied historical geographical materialism'. Although legal arguments based directly on Marxist principles may encounter resistance in American courts, they offer a more parsimonious vantage point for analysing the social model of disability. They seem to offer a solid foundation for educational innovations as well as increased public discussion and debate. Perhaps even more significantly, conceptual frameworks based on these ideas introduce a new potential to increase the voice of disabled citizens in public decision making through systemic or structural changes in the decision making instead of simple modifications of government policy or law.

Judicial interpretation of US anti-discrimination laws

One of the most problematic barriers encountered by the disability movement nearly everywhere is signified by the concept of paternalism (Hahn 1983). In Britain, this obstacle has been fostered by a strong tradition of dependence on private charities and by a pervasive belief that persons with disabilities can be numbered among the 'deserving poor'. Another form of paternalism can be traced to the behaviour of non-disabled professionals who sometimes indicate that they know more about the problems of disability than disabled people themselves. Thus, leaders of the disability movement in both countries occasionally have expressed a private wish that opponents would openly display their biased views of disabled people instead of attempting to cloak their feelings in language that inhibits frank disagreements, dialogue, and possible compromises.

More importantly, judges and lawyers have sometimes invoked sympathetic feelings toward disabled people in an attempt to discredit arguments for civil rights. In the critical case of *Cleburne v Cleburne Living Center* (473 US 432, 1985), for example, the Supreme Court concluded that people with developmental disabilities were not entitled to the benefit of strict standards of adherence to the 'equal protection' clause of the Fourteenth Amendment to the American Constitution. Applying three major tests to determine the guarantees that disabled citizens should be granted under this document, Justice Byron White acknowledged that persons with developmental disabilities have long been subjected to discrimination and that they lack the strength to improve their status through the ordinary means available in political process; but he refused to concede that they were powerless. White cited several state and federal statutes that had been adopted on behalf of this portion of society. The fact that these policies were not actively endorsed by persons who bear the label of retardation did not appear to trouble White. He even asserted that 'because both State and Federal governments have recently committed themselves to assisting the retarded, we will not presume that any legislative action, even one that disadvantages retarded individuals, is rooted in considerations that the Constitution will not tolerate' (p. 446). Apparently White felt that even if these disabled people were harmed, the Court should refrain from intervening to prevent the violation of their constitutional rights. In another preemptive holding, Chief Justice William Rehnquist concluded that the Developmentally Disabled Assistance and Bill of Rights Act of 1975 was merely a federal state spending measure and not a bill of rights after all (*Pennhurst v Halderman*, 451 US 1, 1981). In another statement that seemed to have frightening – as well as confusing – implications, Justice Lewis Powell added in *Youngberg v Romeo* (457 US 307, 1982) that a 'decision, if made by a professional, is presumptively valid; liability may be imposed only when the decision by the professional is such a substantial departure from accepted professional judgment, practice, or standard as to demonstrate that the person responsible actually did not base the decision on such a judgment' (p. 323). Citizens with disabilities, therefore, might be advised to exercise caution in seeking judicial support for their claims unless they are entirely satisfied with paternalistic benefactors.

Who is entitled to speak for the disability movement? The question is crucial not only because of the danger that their opinions can be distorted but also because a possible transfer of leadership almost always entails the reassignment of political power. One source of the difficulties surrounding this can be traced to the law itself. A primary initial goal of any social movement, especially by persons who have formerly been excluded from the governmental process, is to place one of their own members into a prominent position of authority. This objective seems completely understandable both to ensure the authenticity of their voice and to enhance the status of the group. Yet, in the realm of disability, the struggle between rank-and-file citizens and professional 'experts' seems especially intense. Non-disabled specialists appear to be unusually threatened by the prospect of relinquishing even a minor amount of authority to their former clients or 'consumers'. Perhaps they fear that the value of their professional training might be diminished or that their control might be undermined. In any event, disabled people may encounter substantial resistance in their efforts to determine their own destinies, and they are not apt to receive much help from the courts in the event of such conflict.

Judges have also concentrated on the impairments of disabled plaintiffs as a rationale for denying them the protection of anti-discrimination measures. In the first case to reach the US Supreme Court after the approval of section 504, a majority of the justices refused to apply this law to a nurse who was refused admission to an educational program solely because of her hearing impairment (*Southeastern Community College v Davis*, 442 US 397, 1979). The controversy has been reviewed in the following analysis (Hahn 2000a: 186). Justice Powell, speaking for the majority, claimed that her admission to the college might produce a 'fundamental alteration' of the instructional curriculum. America's highest court seemed to conclude that even a slight departure from college classes designed exclusively for non-disabled students could be construed as a special favour for disabled applicants (Hahn 2000a: 186).

In many cases, judges have refused to extend civil rights to plaintiffs by portraying them, solely on the basis of their impairments, as either incompetent or lacking a disability. In disputes involving employees who were fired because they were misperceived as having AIDS, appellate courts have declined to enforce the ADA because the plaintiffs were asymptomatic (Mello 1995). Much of the confusion about the meaning of the ADA probably can be ascribed to the prevalent acceptance by the judiciary of a traditional framework within which disability was viewed primarily as a personal difficulty produced by functional limitations rather than as a social problem stemming from prejudice and discrimination. The courts had apparently failed to read or to comprehend the extensive legislative history accompanying the ADA that contained a detailed explanation of the social model of disability. In any event, without a massive campaign to re-educate judges and lawyers, the likelihood that the disability movement can achieve significant progress through litigation now appear relatively remote.

To some observers, this conclusion might seem surprising or even shocking. Bickenbach *et al.* (1999: 1180) comment on my publications by saying:

He argues that 'the primary problems confronting citizens with disabilities are bias, prejudice, segregation, and discrimination that can be eradicated through policies designed to guarantee them equal rights'. As a result, Hahn puts his faith in the legal protection of rights, and in particular, the legal protection that antidiscrimination law provides. Hahn does not opt for the civil rights approaches because he believes that court and judges are somehow immune to the effects of 'disabling images' and attitudes; instead he believes that, more than any other political or social institution, the law stands the best chance of guaranteeing the basic individual rights of disabled people.

Yet, this restatement of the argument does not take into account the inalienable right of any analyst, including me, to change my mind. The summary of the principal problems facing disabled people still seems accurate, but Bickenbach's report on the possible conclusions that can be derived from these findings is clearly subject to revision. I certainly am not enamored with the law. Although I received high marks in law school, I never received a degree. In fact, I left twice because I become convinced that the logic prescribed by the discipline was restrictive and unethical. My earlier hope that the legal prohibition of discrimination might be helpful to the disability movement was founded primarily on my firm belief, after almost 30 years of experience with disability, that the principal problems faced by disabled people were prejudice and discrimination rather than functional impairments. I still believe that this analysis is correct. But, perhaps unfortunately, I no longer think that the bigotry and bias of dominant non-disabled segments of society can be effectively ameliorated by judicial interpretations of the law. My prior faith in anti-discrimination laws was fueled by my involvement in the civil rights movement and by the dramatic changes in the American South that I had witnessed after the adoption of the Civil Rights Act of 1964. Obviously this statute did not solve all of the problems plaguing racial or ethnic minorities in the US. But it did make an observable difference; and I was then certain that legislation forbidding discrimination on the basis of disability would have a similar effect. Nonetheless, for reasons that I still must admit I do not fully understand, the American public – and perhaps non-disabled people elsewhere – have displayed an increased unwillingness to accept – or to comply with – comparable measures such as the ADA. Perhaps this culture has such a strong investment in the subjugation of disabled people that laws banning disability discrimination are a hopelessly inadequate defense. And I resent the attempt by the WHO cohort to force me into a position I do not support.

Nor should Bickenbach, *et al.* be allowed to use a mistaken appraisal of the issue to create false divisions in the disability movement. They proceed to assert (1999: 1180):

A few advocates of the minority group analysis demur from Hahn's enthusiasm with the law and wholly legal solutions (sic). M. Oliver, for instance, though firmly committed to political activism has not always been keen on using the law as a political tool, believing that this approach reflects the peculiarly American penchant for seeing all social problems in terms of legally enforceable individual rights … In his view, disabled people are an oppressed group who cannot expect emancipation by appealing to one of the many social institutions that oppress them.

In reality, I fully concur with Oliver on these – and many other – questions. The reasons for the change in my opinion reflect, in part, the conduct of lawyers and judges who have betrayed the trust that was placed in them by the disability movement. This judgment must not be misconstrued to imply that people with disabilities should be advised to abandon their attempts to extend and expand the meaning of equal rights through any means possible, including litigation. Nor has the effort to explain the parallels between disabled persons and other disadvantaged minorities been entirely futile. Hopefully, political debates – and the parameters of the dialogue – about disability will be altered significantly and irrevocably by the contributions of the modern disability movement. The defeats that disabled litigants have suffered in American courts, which may offer a valuable lesson to their counterparts in the UK and elsewhere, also indicate the vast distance that remains to be travelled before the major goals of the disability movement can be reached. Perhaps the principle advice that can be offered to citizens with disabilities based on what has happened in US courts is that exclusive reliance must not be placed on anti-discrimination statutes – or any other single method – of achieving their objectives. In fact, this juncture in the history of the movement would seem to provide an appropriate point at which to investigate structural or systemic changes in the economy and society instead of simple modifications and reforms in laws or policy.

Perhaps the most pivotal controversy in the debate concerning disability rights continues to revolve about the idea of equality. There are, of course, many different conceptualisations of this principle, including the notions of 'equality before the law' and 'equal opportunity'. In another study, I applied these standards to the education of disabled individuals (Hahn 1997b: 326–7):

> Perhaps the most appropriate standard for assessing an educational milieu fitted to the interests and needs of students with disabilities is equality of results. Assuming the possibility of defining the skills and knowledge … [needed] to flourish in a suitable environment beyond the classroom, education would continue until each student meets the required criteria. Teaching would be … adapted to the pace at which youngsters with different developmental patterns learn. This procedure would … focus on … evaluations of demonstrated performance and on the identification of necessary or essential requirements for participation in a democratic society. This approach is based on the radical assumption that all human beings have equal dignity and worth. In many respects, an even more desirable proposal is embodied in the idea of equal shares, which could be pursued by mobilizing educational and other resources to combat poverty and to ensure that every body can secure an acceptable measure of … material success. Implementation of the concepts of equal … shares, however, would probably necessitate a substantial redistribution of financial revenue … As a result, both concepts are likely to arouse intense political resistance among adults who believe … they are entitled to [be]… the beneficiaries of social and economic privileges without paying for them.

Freire (1970) has proposed a method of fulfilling these goals. The principal US Supreme Court decision that examined disability and the concept of equality directly, however, seemed to endorse a normative standard far below the level of any of these formulations (*Rowley v Hendrik Hudson Central District Board of Education*, 458 US 176, 1982). The dispute involved an eight-year-old girl with a hearing impairment whose parents had asked the school to provide a sign language interpreter in her classes. In this type of school where teachers seldom even know the most rudimentary elements of signed communication (Lane 1992), Amy Rowley probably had few means of developing her intellectual skills, even though she was given a passing report card and advanced from grade to grade. Speaking for a majority of the Court, the Chief Justice held that a 1975 law guaranteeing disabled students 'a free appropriate public education' established nothing more than a 'basic floor of opportunity' (p. 201). Rehnquist asserted that 'the right of access to free public education … is significantly different from any notion of absolute equality of opportunity regardless of capacity' (p. 199). He even claimed that the law required only 'that the education to which access is provided be sufficient to confer some education benefit upon the handicapped child' (p. 200). The four justices who disagreed noted that the measure of equality should be evaluated by commensurate education for disabled and non-disabled young people. (Without drawing invidious comparisons, such attitudes seem remarkably different from the position taken by a unanimous Supreme Court in the historic 1954 decisions outlawing racial segregation in public schools [*Brown v Topeka Board of Education*, 347 US 483]). In the later opinion, which was issued at the same time that schools first began to approve so-called 'special education' classes for disabled students, the Court declared, 'Separate educational facilities are inherently unequal' (p. 495). Yet 17 years would elapse before the courts finally ruled that disabled children could not be prevented from gaining any education whatsoever (*Pennsylvania Association of Retarded Citizens (PARC) v Commonwealth of Pennsylvania*, 334 F. Supp. 1257, 1971); 21 years ensued before the first major law was passed to encourage 'mainstreaming' or the desegregation of disabled and non-disabled students (see Levine and Wexler 1981); and such plans still have not been implemented in many US school districts. Similarly, beginning with the simple example of chairs which are demanded by non-disabled individuals but viewed as superfluous by wheelchair users, I have proposed that the meaning of 'reasonable accommodations' in the ADA might be determined by the standard of Equal Environmental Accommodations (Hahn 1993a). After many years, I finally gained the realisation that the non-disabled usually are not considerate enough to bring their own chairs. In fact, the built environment has been designed exclusively for their use. A true standard of equality, therefore, would grant disabled people the same benefits that have always been enjoyed by the non-disabled majority.

For non-disabled legal commentators, who commonly approach equality and disability within a peculiar sort of liberal quasi-utilitarian framework, the conundrum may be transformed into a simple problem involving the distribution of resources. This assessment frequently is accompanied by an allegation that a remedy cannot be readily devised to combat discrimination against individuals with many different types of impairments. One law professor (Krieger 2000: 504), for example, sought to employ this specious logic to distinguish her position from a viewpoint espoused by many members of the disability movement – and not just me, even though I am identified as the primary target of her criticism:

At the outset, I should explain why in examining the Americans with Disabilities Act, I should be discussing distributive justice at all. Harlan Hahn has forcefully argued … that the ADA in not about distributive justice; it is about corrective justice. The non-disabled majority simply has trouble understanding this, Hahn maintains, because its members are so inured to the prejudice against the disabled manifested in the … physical environment. Professor Hahn's point is … well-taken, especially in relation to certain disabilities and corresponding accommodations. Admittedly, a legal mandate … has distributive implications. There is only so much money to spend. But such a mandate also provides an easily recognizable correction to an earlier decision … whether conscious or simply uncaring, to minimize costs at a stigmatized group's expense. However, it is harder to argue that accommodation lacks distributive justice implications where the disability category is broad or contested.

Krieger follows this statement with a simplistic anecdote about a senior professional who is deprived of a luxuriant and spacious office suite by a 'not particularly productive' disabled employee. Like other lawyers and economists, she does not formulate a measure of the 'taken-for-granted' aspects of the usual environment that bestows advantages on non-disabled individuals and corresponding disadvantages on disabled people (Hahn 2000a). She discusses such issues only within a narrow distributive framework that excludes any moral obligation to fulfil the principle of equality. Hence, she also manages to avoid consideration of the possibilities of redistributive politics or continuous economic expansion.

These considerations demonstrate that institutions controlled by non-disabled authorities, especially from the legal profession, cannot be expected to serve as significant or dependable allies to the disability movement. When attorneys were asked about representing plaintiffs with disabilities in anti-discrimination cases, the reply frequently was honest but dampening, 'There's not enough in it for me' (personal communications, 15 July 1998; 19 March 1999; 25 March 1999; 5 July 1999; 6 September 1999; 2 December 1999; 15 December 1999; 23 March 2000; 12 June 2000). Another lawyer, who was commonly portrayed as a disability rights advocate, explained with equal candor, 'I am only interested in going after defendants with deep pockets' (personal communication, 12 March 1999). Despite the exorbitant hourly fees charged by attorneys, some of the most successful litigators in the USA have concentrated on so-called 'class action' suits filed on behalf of a large number of disabled persons, which may permit them to obtain a percentage of huge settlements. People with disabilities, therefore, might be appropriately advised to avoid depending on legal, medical, or other professionals in the pursuit of their goals.

Bickenbach *et al.* (1999: 1181), who also approaches the issue of equal rights within a quasi-utilitarian framework, eventually arrives at some unique and surprising conclusions:

> The salient feature of the condition of inequality among people with disabilities is that it typically consists of limitations on their freedom to participate in the full range of social rules and ways of living.... The of denial opportunities and resources is an issue, not of discrimination, but of distributive injustice – an unfair distribution of societies (sic) resources and opportunities.... These allocations create a distributive imbalance, unfairly disadvantaging some people. This accounts for the fact that the most accurate indicator of the social status of being a person with disabilities is poverty.... Distributional injustice is created, not intentionally by those in power; but systemically; institutionally, structurally, as a product of impersonal economic forces.

Bickenbach and his colleagues (1999) confess that the outcomes of capitalism usually mean that serious chronic health conditions may often be neglected, while 'more trivial and more common impairment needs ... tend to be catered to' (p. 1181); and they proceed to endorse a 'universalizing' concept of disability first developed by Zola (1989). Like many other non-disabled lawyers and professionals, they did not refer to the overwhelming evidence of adverse social attitudes or the history of subjugation, which ought to be more significant considerations in litigation concerning discrimination than abstract theorising about 'allocations' or 'distribution'. But the comments about systemic influences and the consequences of a capitalist economy underscore the need to move beyond individualistic legal perspectives and to explore interpretations of disability based on concepts of historical materialism.

Theories and definitions of disability

The failure of US courts to provide effective leadership in the implementation of anti-discrimination laws seems to mark a pivotal phase in the disability movement, which seems to be underscored by adoption of the 1999 Disability Discrimination Act in the UK (Corker 2000: 357–70) and the passage of similar legislation in other countries. Activists in Britain, the USA, and elsewhere must make vital decisions about coming plans and strategies. In many respects, perhaps valuable guidance about future challenges can be gleaned from a brief review of the history of disabled persons. The evolution of western societies, for example, has revealed continuous variations in hegemonic concepts of the nature of disability. In addition, the remedies devised to ameliorate the problems of disabled people have not been consistent or universal. Such changes have usually reflected the impact of prevalent social and economic influences.

Historically, the interpretation of disability in the western world was long dominated by Judeo-Christian principles from Biblical times (Kokaska *et al.* 1984), when it was often described either as a curse from God or the work of the devil, to the Medieval period, when responsibility for abandoned disabled children was increasingly assumed by religious charities (Boswell 1988). Throughout this era, holidays such as the Roman Saturnalia and the Christian Feast of Fools marked a brief reversal of the social order which people with disabilities occupied an ascendant position while dominant elites were thrust into a subservient role. The vocations of entertainers and beggars were virtually reserved for disabled adults to the extent that others were prohibited from disabling themselves to pursue those endeavors (Finkelstein 1980: 8–9). Moreover prior to the separation of home and work, disabled members of families may have made an important contribution to the household economy, especially in peasant cottages and farms (Hahn 1987b). During this era, disabled infants and adults were commonly classified as 'monsters' (Pare, tr. 1982).

Perhaps the most dramatic shift in perceptions of disability, however, occurred as a result of the transition during the Enlightenment from a predominantly spiritual to a secular, and especially a scientific, model for the explanation of human traits. In fact, adherence to a biological or medical model of disability became so intense and so pervasive that disabled people have not yet joined the ranks of other groups which finally succeeded in refuting the claim that they were biologically inferior (Hahn 1985a, 1985b, 1985c, 1993a, 1993b, 1994b). From the 18th to the second half of the 20th century, disability was regarded primarily as a personal deficiency; and almost the only possible remedy was the effort by health professionals to 'fix' the imperfection to whatever extent possible. The principal barriers encountered by disabled individuals, therefore, were attributed to defects within the human body; and little thought was given to obstacles in the attitudinal or the built environment.

The increasing emphasis on functional limitations seemed to support a corresponding tendency to regard disabled people as persons who are unable to work (Berkowitz 1987). In fact, the notion of 'work disability', or an inability to 'engage in substantial gainful activity', became the most common definition in US policy and the basis for major social welfare programmes in the second half of the 20th century (Hahn 1983). The origins of this trend can be traced back to the transition from feudalism to capitalism and to the effects of the so-called 'industrial revolution'. As jobs moved from homes and farms to factories, workers were increasingly regarded as interchangeable parts. An emphasis on uniform physical standards seemed to preclude any accommodations for disabled people. Consequently, unemployment among disabled workers soared to a rate of almost two-thirds in most industrialised nations of the world. Part of the explanation can be attributed to what Marx called 'the industrial reserve army' which has moderated the demand for employment by excluding certain groups, such as housewives, minorities, and disabled people, from the labour force, except when they are needed. During World War II, when most young non-disabled American males were engaged in military service abroad, many people with disabilities became employed through the simple device of waiving the requirement that they must pass a medical exam in order to be employed. When non-disabled veterans returned from the war, however, this waiver was rescinded; employees were again compelled to pass physical exams that were not considered necessary during the war.

Capitalism has favored the non-disabled not only by granting them almost exclusive entry into the workforce but also by manufacturing products for the largest share of the market, which generally excludes consumers with disabilities. Thus, disabled persons cannot readily find vehicles that they can drive, residences where they can live, or even stores where they can shop. (In fact, I ascribe my own capacity to withstand the poverty that accompanied many years of my education to the steps in front of most retail stores that prevented me from shopping in them or acquiring a taste for excessive material goods.) The environment has always seemed to be created for a mythical human being who is not only devoid of any disabilities; but also a male, not a female, at the peak of his physical powers.

In order to explore the economic dimension of disability fully, however, it may be helpful to return to ideas originally conceived in the study of political economy. For Marx, the functional capabilities of the human body seemed to play a major role both in the labour theory of value and in the eventual alienation of workers. As Scarry (1985: 250) has written:

> It is the identification of the materials of earth as a 'prolongation' of the worker's body that leads Marx to designate 'private property' as a key problem for civilization: through private property, the maker is separated from the materials of earth, from the inorganic prolongation of his own activity, and therefore enters into the processes of artifice as one who cannot sell what he makes ... but can only sell his own now truncated activity of making.... Thus the disturbingly graphic concepts of the severing of the worker from his own extended body becomes central to Capital, though it usually occurs in the more abstract phrasing of 'the separation of the worker from the means of production' and as a difference between the capacity to 'sell the products of labour' and to sell 'labour power.'

The principal factor which interferes with the capacity of disabled workers to reap the rewards of their labour cannot be ascribed to organic impairments; instead, it can be traced to a capitalist economic system that divorces everyone from goods that are a natural extension of their bodies. Hence, elimination of the exploitation of labour under capitalism could provide significant remedies for the oppression of disabled workers. Relatively little research has been conducted on the effects of 'aesthetic anxiety', or the tendency to avoid persons with physical appearances that are perceived as unattractive or unpleasant, and 'existential anxiety', or the fear of the eventuality of an immobilising debility; but both factors may be at the roots of discrimination against disabled people (Hahn 1988c). Marx certainly appeared to be aware of these phenomena. He traced both the source and the remedy for both tendencies to the influence of money (Marx 1979: 45):

> That which is for me through the medium of money — that for which I can pay (i.e., which money can buy) — that am I, the possessor of money. The extent of the power of money is the extent of my power. Money's properties are my properties and essential powers — the properties and powers of its possessor. Thus, what I am and am capable of is by no means determined by my individuality. I am ugly, but I can buy for myself the most beautiful of women. Therefore I am not ugly, for the effect of ugliness — its deterrent power — is nullified by money. I, in my character as an individual, am lame, but money furnishes me with twenty-four feet. Therefore I am not lame.

Embedded in this statement is a comprehensive understanding of the extent to which economic forces shape the surrounding world. Even social perceptions of bodily characteristics that are viewed as physically unattractive or functionally debilitating can be ameliorated directly through the reallocation of resources. Since disabled residents of the US and many other countries confront extraordinarily high rates of unemployment, welfare dependency, and poverty (Bowe 1978; Shapiro 1993), the difficulties associated with disability can also be viewed as problems related to social class (Russell 1998). Thus, the search for solutions to the persistent inequality that continues to plague disabled women and men must include careful scrutiny of capitalist economies that have often left them without the means of support necessary to gain what Broek (1966) called 'the right to live in the world'.

These broad analyses of economic forces may also lead to a resolution of many controversies that have emerged about the definition of disability. At least part of the failure of courts to comprehend the Americans with Disabilities Act, for example, can be attributed to a fundamental misinterpretation of the legal definition of disability. The ADA stipulates a three-pronged definition that includes either (a) a physical or mental impairment that substantially limits one or more 'major life activities'; or (b) a record of such a impairment; or (c) being regarded as having such an impairment. To many members of the disability movement in the USA, the interpretation of these clauses seemed relatively straightforward: (a) was viewed as referring to the performance of routine acts in everyday life. Although many authors of this provision thought that bodily traits might be viewed as the initial cause of such limitations, they also felt that the meaning of this clause could be expanded to include environmental configurations that impose restrictions on disabled citizens; (b) seemingly focused on the biases or stereotypes that might be exerted on people with so-called 'hidden' disabilities through the process of labeling; and (c) apparently centered on attitudinal prejudice against persons with obvious or visible disabilities. Hence, they were shocked when the judiciary adopted a traditional and outmoded understanding of disability based on a 'functional limitations' model that seemed to make the claim for equal rights contingent upon a finding about whether or not a specific impairment interfered with 'major life activities'. In addition, a preliminary judgement that plaintiffs had standing to file a case under the ADA sometimes appeared to undermine arguments about employment or other forms of discrimination. Although non-disabled professionals act as though the disadvantages of disability in external surroundings were first discovered in the original draft of the International Classification of Impairments, Disabilities, and Handicaps (1980), the concepts needed to analyse this phenomenon had been implicit for a longer time in the 'social model' that formed the basis for the international disability movement. Advocates in the USA and elsewhere could still try to persuade courts to apply a simple standard for disability determination founded on concepts such as 'existential' or 'aesthetic' anxiety or visibility and labelling. Such a reorientation would permit judges and researchers to assess the prejudice that results from the appearance of visible physical differences as well as the biases that stem from personal fears about the inevitable fate of disablement. But, in all candor, the reluctance with which judges may slowly change their own misconceptions about an issue indicates that such efforts may not provide a viable means by which disabled people can achieve justice.

Increasingly, definitional controversies have tended to center on proposals to revise the International Classification of Impairments, Disabilities, and Handicaps (1980). The three principal paradigms that appear to have remained in consideration in this process are the universalization of disability, the minority group model, and the human rights approach. The notion of universalization, which has been actively promoted by Bickenbach and his cohort at WHO (Bickenbach *et al.* 1999), is founded on the fundamentally accurate premise that nearly everybody now has or will experience some form of disability during their lifetimes. In the short term, this definition could increase the percentage of disabled persons in society. But this sort of expansion could also dilute the message of the disability movement. The orientation might reinforce political support for the principles of universal design by augmenting the size of the disabled community, but it may also result in additional neglect of the interests and needs of citizens with major disabilities. Finally, measurements based on this kind of categorisation can only indicate the prevalence of disabilities and not the number of disabled persons in the population.

Another important conceptual framework is the human rights approach (Rioux 1997) which focuses on the rights to which all people are entitled. This view offers the advantage of re-emphasizing standards of equality to assess discrepancies between the situation in which disabled persons find themselves and the circumstances enjoyed by others. In addition, it seems to make ample provision for the realisation that barriers which have a prejudicial impact on disabled citizens are often the product of aversive biases and attitudes instead of mere happenstance or coincidence. As noted in a draft report (2000: 56–60) concerning disability and international norms and standards:

> By addressing the rights of all people, the definition is founded in the breach of the rights rather than the delineation of characteristics of the person, consequently reducing the need for a specific definition. This makes people uncomfortable because in the law there is a tradition of using 'protected classes' as a unit of analysis or the way in which rights of vulnerable groups are protected in domestic legal systems. The other problem is that if the class is undefined it makes governments uneasy about the scope of their financial obligations.

Perhaps the principal disadvantage of 'the human rights approach', however, is its reliance on litigation and the judicial process to identify the rights available to everyone and to assess the extent to which citizens with disabilities have been subjected to departures from the rights. This problem might be particularly critical because many of the discriminatory barriers encountered by disabled persons represent aspects of the so-called 'taken-for-granted' environment (Hahn 2000a) which have never been thoroughly investigated or recognized in legal doctrines. A brief example may help to explain the point. Although the practice under apartheid which required black individuals to travel through white areas of South Africa would never be tolerated by courts in other countries, judges may have difficulty in grasping the virtual incarceration of disabled persons who are confined, not to their wheelchairs, but to residential locations or even 'back bedrooms' by lack of public transportation, the failure of manufacturers to design vehicles that they can drive, the absence of curbcuts, as well as the inaccessibility of stores, meeting places, and public accommodations. The solution to this situation is apt to require the exercise of political influence that extends beyond an appeal only to the courts.

The third major perspective which has been proposed as a basis for changing the ICIDH as well as other purposes is, of course, "the minority group model", which examines the parallels between people with disabilities and other disadvantaged groups. Despite the fact that the plans to revise the ICIDH were adopted in part to expand the social model of disability by including measures of the environment and participation, Ustun *et al.* (1998: 830) asserted that 'the ICIDH-2 … does not conform to the "minority group" paradigm;…we flatly reject this paradigm in favor of a universal approach to disability'. This statement was not accompanied by any explanation or justification for the decision to 'flatly reject' the model. In fact, there does not appear to be a legitimate reason to dismiss and theoretical orientation arbitrarily without at least consulting a representative group of the persons who have devoted themselves to the task of devising a valid instrument. Nonetheless, Bickenbach *et al.* (1999: 1181) later pressed their attack on the idea that disabled people constitute a minority group:

> Not only are the social responses to different forms of mental and physical impairments vastly different, … there is almost no commonality of experience, or feelings of solidarity, between people with diverse disabilities. There is no unifying culture, language or set of experiences; people with disabilities are not homogeneous, nor is there much prospect for transdisability solidarity.

Perhaps there is little to note about this statement except that it is just wrong. The professionals at WHO appear to be remarkably unaware of the composition of the international disability movement which has for decades included people with a wide range of impairments. The allegation that disabled people are only active within groups defined by their specific impairments is patently absurd. In fact, the principal question that has been debated within the movement for several years is the topic of 'disability culture'. They have been exploring the commonality of their experiences and similarities in the social responses they received from the nondisabled, even though there has been hardly any support from funding agencies for research on these subjects.

In addition, Bickenbach (1999: 1181) attempted to dismiss the 'minority group model' by resorting to abstract philosophical arguments:

People with disabilities face nonaccommodating physical and organizational environments, lack of educational or training programming, impoverished or nonexistent employment prospects, confused and inadequate income support programs, underfinanced research for assistive device technologies, lack of resources to meet impairment-related needs, policy neglect and minimal political influence. These are all social ills brought about by a maldistribution of power and resource. However, they are not forms of discrimination.

In fact, most of these assessments could also be applied to other minority groups. Another striking feature of this contention is embodied in the concept of presentism. There appears to be a somewhat inflexible refusal to recognise that these problems are the product of historical processes. More importantly, there seems to be a reluctance to acknowledge that the source of these conditions can be traced to the prevalence during many eras of unfavorable sentiments regarding disabled people. Admittedly, 'the minority group model' was originally conceived both because it comprised the most accurate framework for the study of disability and because it might help the courts comprehend arguments about disability discrimination. But the fact that judges decided instead to embrace the traditional notion of disability as a 'functional limitation' does not comprise an excuse to abandon the paradigm. The model can be employed to promote political mobilisation that might eventually contribute to the growth of a disability constituency that could supplement the quest for civil rights with the exercise of significant political influence in the democratic process. Like many other movements that furnished the major impetus for social change in the second half of the 20th century, women and men with disabilities can transform physical characteristics that were once devalued into a positive source of personal and political identity (Hahn 1997a). Disability may no longer be concealed or denied. Bickenbach *et al.* (1999: 1182) claim that people 'cannot engage in identity politics without establishing clear eligibility requirements for membership in the group'. But again this assertion is untrue. Most persons align themselves with political movements or segments of the electorate through a process of affiliation. Like many other portions of the population, disabled people are merely seeking the right to define themselves. Since disability laws and polices are designed primarily to affect a particular group of people rather than intangible entities, however, they must be allowed to play a decisive role in formulating such measures.

The quest for empowerment

Due to the failure of courts to comprehend the social origins of disability discrimination and the resulting lack of success with civil rights litigation, the disability movement may want to consider additional methods of achieving their objectives such as the alternatives encompassed by the concept of empowerment (Rappaport 1987; Robertson and Minkler 1994). Part of these strategies may entail efforts to organise a permanent disability constituency capable of exerting decisive influence on crucial political decisions. This plan would impose a major responsibility on disabled citizens themselves to join other movements that have embraced identity politics by transforming a personal attribute which was previously viewed as stigmatising and shameful into a positive source of dignity and pride. The defining element of disability is 'difference'. This approach would seek to translate disability into a kind of difference that can be honoured and even celebrated. The imperative need for this transition is indicated by projects currently promoted by the World Bank and the World Health Organization to develop the measure of health as 'Disability-Adjusted Life Years' (DALYS), which is life expectancy subtracted by the number of years spent in the supposedly 'unhealthy' state of disablement (Groce *et al.* 1998). In a world fully adapted to the wishes of disabled residents, the supposition that disability is always a disadvantage might even be exposed as a self-serving stereotype perpetuated by the non-disabled. A survey of the members of ADAPT, a US organisation that engages in civil disobedience about disability issues found, for example, that more than half would not choose a cure for their disabilities (Hahn and Beaulaurier 2001). The challenges posed by a transformative perspective on disability, however, may not be met without both institutional support and alliances with other deprived groups that might be fostered by an increased emphasis on class analysis.

Fundamentally, the struggle to attain the objectives of the disability movement may depend on innovative systemic or structural changes in society. As part of this project, attempts to alleviate the economic oppression of disabled people must be granted a major initial priority. Efforts might be launched in the USA, for instance, to end the exploitation and indignity imposed on disabled persons who receive far less than the minimum wage in so-called 'sheltered workshops', which are supposed to prepare the most productive workers to enter the competitive labour market but which often try to retain these same workers to maintain the operation of the workshop. Moreover, investigations of job qualifications and the unemployment of disabled adults need to extend beyond the assessment of personal capabilities to explore the extent to which an employer's definition of the physical or mental abilities required for a particular job are really necessary for the routine performance of the work. This type of study could expose the common knowledge that employers frequently use evidence of disability obtained from interviews or application forms merely as a 'sorting device' in order to reduce the pool of potential candidates for an available position to a more manageable number. These plans need to become part of a larger agenda to expand research concerning the impact of capitalism on the problems confronting disabled persons which, at least in the USA, has received relatively little prior attention.

Another important dimension of endeavours to enhance the influence of people with disabilities might appropriately focus on civic institutions. These activities must be founded on a careful scrutiny of existing political conditions. The interests of disabled citizens obviously would not be served, for example, by attempts to promote their empowerment in governmental jurisdictions controlled by corrupt or dictatorial politicians. Similar doubts may be expressed about the value of these activities in areas where the political process is dominated by wealthy campaign contributors. In governmental jurisdictions that reflect democratic principles, however, the traditional authority of non-disabled professionals must yield to the influence of disabled residents themselves. While some of these endeavours might focus on the formation of an expanded disability constituency through methods that have emerged from prior social movements and identity politics, another critical component of plans to enhance the strength of disabled citizens – as well as other vulnerable and powerless minorities – may include major systemic changes in political institutions. In the USA, for example, discussions have been held on many such methods of augmenting the power of African-Americans through proportional representation, cumulative voting, and similar proposals (Guinier 1994). Studies also have found a link between the adoption of statutes forbidding disability discrimination and local measures of economic resources and party competition (Holbrook and Percy 1992), but these issues have not been examined in detail. Perhaps the most effective means of ensuring that the voices of disadvantaged groups such as disabled people are heard continuously in decision-making bodies would involve permanent systemic changes in the political process. The nations of South Africa and Uganda have demonstrated outstanding leadership in the representation of disabled people on local councils that needs to be emulated by western countries. There is also a pressing imperative for additional qualitative as well as quantitative studies of political variables affecting people with disabilities in various countries.

Perhaps some of the most promising developments in the continuing struggles of the disability movement, however, have occurred as a result of research. Increasingly, investigators from many disciplines have begun to expand theoretical paradigms for disability research beyond the clinical confines of the medical model in order to encompass environmental considerations (Fougeyrollas *et al*. 1998; Brandt and Pope 1997). These perspectives may eventually lead to the construction, for example, of a community index not only of the relative influence of disabled residents but also of governmental compliance with policies such as barrier removal. Such projects must be carefully designed to avoid both the dangers of professional intimidation embedded in many forms of participatory action research. A brief glimpse of local responses to the goals of disabled people cannot provide a comprehensive understanding of the struggles of the disability movement at the local or national level; but, in the absence of extensive control of the economic and political apparatus, they may yield some of the leverage needed to facilitate the process of social change.

Concluding comments

The disability movement in the United States and the United Kingdom originated at approximately the same time in the final quarter of the 20th century. Both struggles were based upon a 'social model' of disability that delineated prejudice and discrimination as the principal barriers facing disabled people. In contrast to the medical or 'functional limitations' paradigm that had dominated the study of disability for many years, the goals of disabled people in both countries have focused on efforts to change a disabling environment rather than to 'fix' disabled individuals. Although this analysis of the problems confronted by disabled people resulted in a common understanding of core issues in both nations, the British formulation of the objectives of the disability movement contained a reference to 'oppression' that was missing in most American statements about the subject.

This seemingly minor deviation appeared to reflect a deep chasm between conceptual legacies in these countries. The British emphasis on 'oppression' seemed to indicate the importance of exploring the complex institutional arrangements that tend to instill and reinforce patterns of dominance and subordination between different sectors of society. The notion of 'oppression' implies that a solution to pervasive inequalities might be found by overturning this system: and this remedy obviously requires a full comprehension of the complexity of these interlocking arrangements. The stress on 'oppression', therefore, also permitted researchers in Britain to explore the deep theoretical heritage nourished by the study of political economy as well as other conceptual orientations. By contrast, disabled Americans searched for answers to similar problems by the passage of laws prohibiting discrimination within an individualistic legal system. This pursuit yielded some major victories such as the Americans with Disabilities Act, but it also resulted in numerous defeats in the appellate courts. The use of the law in the USA may have resulted in actions that were quicker but more superficial. The treatment of disabled people by lawyers and judges also seems to indicate that the disability movement might appropriately refrain from placing additional reliance on the legal system.

In contrast to the British plan that was drafted and adopted by disabled people themselves, the first major effort to embrace the 'social model' of disability in the USA was copied and promoted by Congressional staff members, who advocated for section 504 as an incidental part of the Rehabilitation Act of 1973. The major opposition to the quest by the disability movement in the USA for equal rights did not emerge until after the passage of the Rehabilitation Act on the floor of Congress, where legislators would have had to state a public position on their attitudes toward disabled people. Instead, when administrators calculated the potential expense of modifying the built environment and complying with other provisions of the clause forbidding discrimination on the basis of disability, they attempted to 'stonewall' the issue by failing to place their signatures on the regulations to implement section 504. The delay mobilised disabled people to participate in sit-ins and demonstrations at government offices and elsewhere that produced the birth of the modern disability movement in America. The momentum of these acts eventually led to even more civil disobedience protests in numerous cities by ADAPT and to the adoption of the Americans with Disabilities Act in 1990. Many disabled people in the UK have held or joined in comparable demonstrations to gain equal rights.

Early judicial decisions indicated, however, that the courts were not prepared to become an ally of the disability movement in the USA. In the first case brought to the Supreme Court under section 504, a majority of the justices held that a community college was not required to offer an accommodation to the needs of a hearing-impaired student that might contribute to a 'fundamental alternation' of the educational program. Similarly, this Court said that judgements under laws banning discrimination on the basis of disability were not to be held to the strict standards under the 'equal protection' clause of the Fourteenth Amendment to the US Constitution that would be applied to cases involving racial or ethnic minorities. Chief Justice William Rehnquist also stated that a Bill of Rights Act for developmentally disabled citizens was not really a bill of rights after all and that a hearing-impaired student who probably heard little of what the teacher was saying actually had an equal educational opportunity by virtue of being passed from one grade to the next. The lack of success that disabled plaintiffs have encountered in the courts strongly indicate the need to find a new strategy to fulfil the goals of the disability movement.

Meanwhile, the writings of researchers in England, which were frequently informed by the rich theoretical legacy of studies in political economy, began to uncover the complex array of economic and social forces that have kept disabled people in an inferior and unequal position in most industrialised societies. Further examination of Marxist ideas such as the 'industrial reserve army' and 'commodity fetishism' may produce fresh insights about the sources of the extraordinarily high unemployment rates of disabled workers in western countries. In addition, Marx's comments about the effects of money could be employed to launch a new investigation of the 'aesthetic' and 'existential' anxieties that may fuel unfavourable attitudes toward disabled people. Many of the legal briefs filed in American courts seem to avoid such issues which may yet lead to a new understanding of disability discrimination by judges and lawyers. Perhaps most importantly, the intellectual legacies that seem to have flourished in the UK may contribute more to a solid foundation for research and teaching in disability studies. At the end of the day, this contribution to academic endeavours may be an even more significant achievement than temporary wins or losses in the courts.

Disabled people must not abandon the possibility of achieving progress through litigation; but they also need to explore alternative strategies to attain their objectives. Perhaps the most fruitful of these approaches is represented by the concept of empowerment. Permanent systemic changes need to be made to give disabled people increased influence in the decision-making process in communities as well as nations. In particular, attention might be devoted to the possibility of granting disabled residents as well as other disadvantaged minorities continuing representation on local councils. Authoritative bodies at this level would also be able to monitor compliance with statutes such as the ADA that many of the non-disabled treat as laws they do not have to obey. Not all policies should be shaped exclusively by the will of the majority. The interests as well as the rights of minorities must be respected in such deliberations. By exploring innovative changes in the economic and political system, disabled people may still be able to provide innovative leadership that other social movements can follow.

Questions

- What does the USA experience with anti-discrimination measures suggest about the potential effectiveness of such laws in the UK?
- Is the pursuit of empowerment a viable alternative to litigation?

Note

1. This study was supported, in part, by a Mary Switzer Distinguished Rehabilitation Research Fellowship from the National Institute on Disability and Rehabilitation Research (NIDRR).

CHAPTER 7

Out of the cellars. Disability, politics and the struggle for change: the Maltese experience

Joseph Camilleri and Anne-Marie Callus

Introduction: providing a context

Although Malta has a European culture and identity, its size, history and geographical location help make it very different from other European countries in a number of ways. These three factors inevitably impinge on the way Maltese society has evolved, including the growth and development of the disability movement. This chapter looks at the significant changes that took place in the Maltese disability sector from the late 1940s to the present day. It looks at the main agents that brought change and argues that the most significant change originated from above, that it was instigated by a small nucleus of people who struggled to bring about change by obtaining the blessing of the government of the day (or individuals who were part of that government) rather than through the establishment of a grassroots movement made up of disabled people who pushed for that change. We argue in this chapter that this happened time and again over the past six decades and that it is still happening today, although perhaps the voice of disabled people is now growing louder. Finally, the chapter conjectures about what might be the future of the disability movement in Malta given its history and present trends.

Before starting, we felt it would be useful for our readers to have an idea, however sketchy, of the Maltese geographical, historical and political context referred to above. The Maltese archipelago is made up of five small islands, two of which, Malta and Gozo, are inhabited. Malta covers an area of 316km^2 and Gozo 162km^2. Malta's geographical location, approximately 97km to the south west of the island of Sicily and 360km to the northeastern coast of Libya, place it almost at the very centre of the Mediterranean Sea, making it a strategic bridge between northern Africa and southern Europe and a prime target for colonisers throughout history. At some time or another Malta has been a colony of the Phoenicians, the Romans, the Arabs, the Normans, the Knights of St John, the French and the British. And although not itself a coloniser in the strict sense, the Roman Catholic Church has exerted a profound influence on every aspect of Maltese life.

In 1998, the total population of the Maltese Islands was 378,518, of which 349,338 lived in Malta and 29,180 in Gozo (Central Office of Statistics 1998: 8–9). Of these, according to the *National Disability Survey 1999* (NCPD 1999: 2), 1.6 per cent are registered as having a disability. Since the second world war, politics have been dominated by two parties, the right-of-centre Nationalist party and the leftist Malta Labour Party. General elections, held once every five years, are closely run affairs. There is a very high turnout (around 97 per cent) and the party that wins usually does so with a few percentage points, which in reality represent just a few thousand voters. This means that the two parties are very careful about safeguarding voter loyalty, which sometimes leads to the deferral of necessary but unpopular decisions. It also means that politics creates a lot of polarisation and social division which in turn fosters the perception that protesting against the government of the time immediately brands you as a supporter of the party in opposition.

Many of the changes in services for disabled people and in disability awareness and activism were influenced by various factors, such as Malta's colonial ties with Britain, the influence of the family and the Catholic Church on all aspects of everyday life, post-colonial development, the gradual establishment of services by both state and church authorities and, recently, the proliferation of non-government organisations of various shapes and sizes.

One final introductory note concerns the methods used to collect the information for this chapter. We sent out a questionnaire to all non-governmental and voluntary organisations with the aim of collecting data about the way they were set up, the reasons behind their setting-up, their views about disability and the way they look at the future. We also interviewed people who played a key role in the changes that were wrought over the past 50 years. A list of their names appears at the end of the chapter. Information about dates when various services or organisations were set up was mainly taken from a list compiled by Mr Fred Bezzina, Executive Director of the National Commission Persons with Disability (NCPD) and himself the parent of a disabled person and a disability activist.

Out of the cellars (1945–1969)

Unlike larger, more affluent European countries, interest in the lives of disabled persons, or their families, in Malta does not date back to more than 50 years or so (Campbell and Oliver 1996: 15). Major charitable institutions which appeared during the period between 1890 to 1920 were set up exclusively by the Catholic Church and tended to focus their attention on social problems of a 'moral' nature. Such initiatives were usually inspired by the wish to save the souls of those perceived in danger of moral degradation – orphaned children and 'wayward' girls are cases in point.

On a small island where people knew or could easily get to know intimate details about one another, it was vital that families maintained a façade of normality and that any perceived form of 'deviance' was kept well hidden away. In this way it was perfectly acceptable on the part of Maltese families (at every social level) to ensure that disabled members disappeared completely from view. Besides casting a veil of shame on their families, their presence could ruin the chances of any non-disabled siblings of marriageable age. This attitude was set in the permafrost of tradition and a slow thaw would not begin to set in until after the second world war when more efficient communications systems began to open up the islands to external influences.

Until the mid-1960s, disabled persons themselves were not accorded intrinsic value, but, within the prevailing religious environment, they were seen as burdens one had to bear; they were the instruments by which non-disabled persons were tested and spiritually purified. People who were visibly different in body or behaviour were considered impure on a moral level by the general population and on a cultic level by the church (Bishop 1995: 8). Religious imagery and scriptural texts also ensured in a multiplicity of ways that disability in the family was seen as an indelible stigma which affected all members of the family and not just the 'afflicted' individual (Camilleri 1999: 848).

During the late 1940s and 1950s a gradual shift began to take place, away from traditional attitudes which equated disability with sin and punishment, towards a more empirical, positivist approach based upon what is now called the medical model of disability. It was during this time that the first non-government organisations for disabled persons began to be established and the education sector began to lay the foundations of what was to become the special education sector. Since Malta was a British colony between 1800 and 1964, it is hardly surprising that these and subsequent innovations were very closely based on equivalent British models.

For instance, 1947 saw the establishment of the Polio Fund (which later changed its name to the Physically Handicapped Rehabilitation Fund (PHRF)). This was set up by a small group of Maltese people and British expatriates and was originally aimed at alleviating the effects of the serious polio epidemic which hit the islands after the 1939 to 1945 war. Over the years, the PHRF developed into a traditional charity, focusing on fundraising, projecting physical impairment as a personal tragedy and with the stated aim of normalising its members in order to re-integrate them into society. None of the original committee members were themselves disabled persons, nor were the latter ever part of the organisation's decision-making process. For a brief period of time, one of the present writers did serve on this committee, but soon resigned in disgust when it became clear that the opinions and voices of disabled persons carried no weight whatsoever. Significantly, and in spite of repeated calls for change, the PHRF still continues to identify itself with the terms 'handicapped' and 'rehabilitation'.

The year of 1947 also saw the setting up of a Commission for the Sick and the Handicapped (CSH) which was one of the first initiatives of Monsignor Michael Azzopardi, who pioneered a number of services for Maltese disabled people. The CSH was to bring disabled people into public focus in two ways: firstly, through its weekly radio programme; and secondly through the establishment of the first residential complex for severely disabled persons in 1965. The CSH eventually changed its name to The National Commission for the Sick and the Handicapped and finally The National Commission for Sick and Persons with Disability. However, despite the use of more modern terminology, the correlation between sickness and disability has persisted. In their questionnaire, the CSH stated their aim to be 'to provide spiritual and material solace for sick and disabled persons and their families'. Its weekly radio programme, originally entitled *A Call to the Sick and the Handicapped*, offers an unvarying mix of light entertainment and spiritual comfort in the face of personal tragedy. After five decades, and following pressure from the National Commission Persons with Disability (NCPD), the name of the programme was changed to *A Call to the Sick and to Persons with Disability* and introduced a news slot which features items related to the social model of disability and which is compiled by NCPD's Executive Director.

Until 1965, with the establishment of Id-Dar tal-Providenza (Providence House) by Mgr Azzopardi, there was no residential service of any description for Maltese disabled persons. They lived with their families, sometimes hidden away in appalling conditions. There were instances of people having lived 20 years and more chained up in windowless cellars, or hidden in byres and stables in the countryside, by families fearful of the shame and stigma associated with disability (Cuschieri 1995: ix). According to its answers to the questionnaire, Id-Dar tal-Providenza was founded with three services in mind: long-term housing for disabled people whose families could no longer take care of them; a temporary respite service; and occasional activities for disabled people and their families. Today, it is mainly a long-term residential institution for people with intellectual disabilities. Ironically, the set-up occurred at a time when similar services were coming under attack in Scandinavian countries through the work of N. Bank-Mikkelsen and Bengt Nirje, by Wolf Wolfensberger in the United States and by other advocates of the normalisation principle. What is even more ironic is that, at the time, Mgr Azzopardi's work was innovative in Malta and created a revolution in people's attitudes towards those who had a disability, especially those who had intellectual disabilities. According to John Micallef, the present administrator of Dar tal-Providenza, 'Mgr. Azzopardi's aim was integration from the very beginning'. He first sought to acquire a building in two different desirable residential areas, but without success. In 1965, he was given a building which is completely cut off from the surrounding villages. Although the 1968 statute of Dar tal-Providenza states that integration is one of the main aims of the service, the physical isolation of the residential complex, and its present size, militate against this aim. A recent change has seen some residents grouped into 'flatlets', rather than large dormitories and the setting-up of a house for five residents in the heart of a neighbouring village. However, with the exception of these five, residents still live in what is effectively an institution in a remote location. Moreover, Dar tal-Providenza depends for its day-to-day running on the charity of benefactors and handouts from the general public. This need to raise funds constantly leads to the portrayal of residents as pathetic objects of charity. The main fundraising event is a high-profile annual volleyball marathon which is successful in raising scores of thousands of Maltese liri and in breaking world volleyball marathon records, but does little to raise the profile of people with disabilities who do not play any active role in the activities organised, nor are they part of the decision-making process of the organising committee.

Conscious of the deep-rooted and widespread demonisation of disabled people in the Maltese culture, Mgr Azzopardi had also sought to bring about a positive change in this respect by inverting the language normally used when referring to anyone with an impairment. In his vocabulary they became 'angels'. However, by referring to disabled people as 'angels' he gave rise to new stereotypes of untouchability which, over the years, have themselves become powerful instruments of oppression.

From today's viewpoint, this could hardly be considered progress, but in the context of the time, the developments mentioned above were regarded as revolutionary and indeed they represented a terrific improvement on an immediate past overshadowed by rampant superstition, blind prejudice and violent suppression. Therefore, the medical model was enthusiastically espoused as a more humane, 'modern' and pragmatic approach to the problem of disability and 'reforms' based upon these new assumptions were espoused with sincere intentions and generally looked upon favourably where funding was concerned.

Education and employment: rights denied

By the mid-1950s government was beginning to concern itself with the issue of educating disabled children. The need for specialised provision was felt after the introduction of compulsory primary schooling in 1954. Students with a hearing impairment were the first to be identified as needing special provision. According to Mr George Samuel, former Education Officer for Special Educational Needs, they were a challenge to schools, since teachers found it difficult to communicate with them. In fact, provision for students with disabilities started in 1956, when two special classes for hearing-impaired children were set up within the local primary school in Paola, a town in the southern part of Malta. In 1957 the two special classes increased to five and were transferred to another school in Gzira, which is situated more centrally. This meant that these students could be integrated for most of the school day and then be withdrawn from their classes for daily sessions with a peripatetic teacher (Bezzina and Camilleri 1996: 35–6). Unfortunately, this model became a victim of its own success and by the next year enough students with a hearing impairment had been identified to warrant the setting up of a special, that is segregated, school, the Deaf Unit. The perceived success of this model led to the opening of more segregated schools, especially since children with mild learning difficulties began to be considered as being able to benefit from schooling. The first school, the ESN Unit which is today called Santa Maria Day School, for children with mild to moderate intellectual disabilities opened in 1963 and the next year another one, the Guardian Angel School was set up for children with severe intellectual disabilities. This was followed two years later with a special school for boys with emotional difficulties, Mater Dei. It is not surprising that, in a Catholic country, schools that were perceived to have a social role to play were given religious names.

Soon after its establishment in the 1950s, the special education sector rapidly became the Cinderella of the education division, attracting less and less resources: human, financial and technological. In many instances, teaching curricula existed only on a notional plane, with the same simple lessons being repeated *ad nauseum* for years on end, with no 'real preparation to enable students ... to develop the ability to live and work as part of the community' (Galea-Curmi *et al.* 1997: 232). Children with impairment (particularly an intellectual impairment) were not expected to function properly in the adult world and it was thus considered legitimate to provide them with the lowest common denominators of functionality and leave it at that (Galea-Curmi *et al.* 1997: 232).

In 1970, secondary-level education was made compulsory for all. This development was complemented by an expansion in special education provision with a school being set up in Gozo, as an annex to a local primary school, to cater for students with severe disabilities, and an increase in the population of the special schools in Malta. A second school catering for students with mild intellectual disabilities in Malta, Dun Manwel Attard, was inaugurated in 1982.

Throughout the 1950s and 1960s it was considered inconceivable to educate disabled children in the mainstream, and equally inconceivable was the prospect of disabled children continuing with their studies at secondary, or tertiary, level. In 1973, one of the present authors has vivid memories of being the only disabled person out of a total student body of 1,500 at the University of Malta. Naturally, single individuals did occasionally slip through this system of oppression, but they were usually schooled to deny their impairments and strongly pressured into functioning in the same way as their non-disabled peers. This subtle form of brainwashing made these 'supercrips' avoid contact with their disabled peers and avoid any mention of the existence of disability as an individual or national reality (Camilleri 1999: 846).

Something of a sea change occurred in the education sector in the early 1990s with a move away from segregated 'special' education provision and the government of the day espousing a policy of mainstream schooling for all students. Ironically, this change occurred in tandem with the opening of three new special schools. In 1989, a school (San Miguel Febres Cordero) for students with severe physical and intellectual disabilities was opened. This was followed in 1992 with a new school that integrated services for students with visual and auditory impairments. It was named Helen Keller School, making it the only special school whose name does not have any religious connection.

In 1993, NCPD published a report about special education in Malta that recommended the adoption of an inclusive education policy. Up till then, only some students with physical or with sensory impairments had been accepted in mainstream schools. The new policy advocated that even students with intellectual disabilities be included in mainstream education and that they are supported by facilitators. According to Paul Bartolo (2000), the term 'facilitator' was imported from Canada 'because there more emphasis is put on teacher-facilitator collaboration' (p. 81). *Inclusion and Special Education*, a report presented at the National Minimum Curriculum conference this year, states that today there are over 600 students who attend school under this system (*Inclusion and Special Education* 2000: 2).

Although the term 'inclusive education' is now used widely in Malta, it should be pointed out that a revision of the curriculum for mainstream schools is still being carried out and that it is only expected to be implemented within a few years' time. This means that, while efforts are made to help students with disabilities become part of their local mainstream schools, the latter operate within a highly selective system. In state schools, students are streamed for the last two years of primary schooling in preparation for an 11-plus examination that selects students for grammar or area secondary schools. Needless to say, inclusion and selection are contradictory. This paradox is now being addressed in the new national minimum curriculum (NMC 2000).

Along with NCPD, a major factor in the introduction of an inclusive education policy was The Eden Foundation. Set up in 1993, Eden has since introduced a wide spectrum of innovative services to Malta and has also helped to raise the profile of persons with intellectual disabilities. Part of its operation is the provision of services for children that focus on early intervention and on psychological assessment and therapeutic services (according to its responses to the questionnaire). The other work is carried out with adults with mild to moderate intellectual disabilities for whom it provides job-related training. However, although this is a relatively recent organisation it has developed all the characteristics of a traditional charity: a medical model approach. Among other things, this is clearly reflected in very limited involvement by disabled persons and parents in the decision-making process and a perpetuation of negative stereotypes in its fundraising campaigns.

Since educational provision for severely disabled individuals has been driven by very low expectations, it is hardly surprising that schooling has focused at best on 'giving them the basic three Rs' (reading, writing and a little arithmetic) and at worst providing a respite-cum-custodial service. Until quite recently, disabled people were not specifically prepared either for employment or for adult life.

Vocational and careers counselling were, of course, non-existent (Galea-Curmi *et al.* 1997: 230). Disabled people's subsequent inability to achieve a high quality of life in the 'big' world was put down to the nature of their impairments, not to the complete failure of the system to provide them with a basic civil right: an adequate education. Inadequate educational provision has been one of the major factors contributing to the continued oppression of Maltese disabled people, robbing them not only of their potential leaders, but repeatedly preventing them from even comprehending, let alone articulating and struggling against, patterns of oppression when and where these continue to manifest themselves (Camilleri 1999: 846).

In the same way that changes in educational practices were not comprehensive and were sometimes downright contradictory, the move towards training people with intellectual disability for work was not accompanied by an across the board change in day services for adults. In fact, during 1993, two of the existing day care centres for people with intellectual disability (where care and respite, not vocational training, were the priorities) moved to larger premises, while a new centre, run on the same lines as the others, opened in 1998. From their inception, these centres have been chronically under-resourced and their development has been seriously hampered by the absence of clear policy guidelines. It is hardly surprising then that they have been largely ineffective and unable to offer quality services. Nor have the intellectually disabled persons who make up the majority of the clientele been able to maximise their individual potential in any way. There are no formal job-related training programmes in place and the only productive work offered by the centres involves wickerwork and pottery, the products of which are then sold.

The employment sector was, and is, another aspect where disabled Maltese citizens continued to lose out. Productive, gainful employment on the open job market was still considered way beyond the aptitudes or aspirations of all disabled persons, irrespective of their proven abilities. Thus this market was largely closed, or offered only the most menial, low-paid, low-status jobs, such as lift attendant, telephone operator, public toilets attendant, messenger, cleaner and so forth. Towards the end of the 1960s, a first effort was made to allow disabled persons access to the job market. This was made possible through the passage into law of Act No. II of 1969, Employment of Disabled Persons Act, a piece of legislation closely modelled on the Disabled Persons (Employment) Act 1944 in Britain. The 1969 Act established:

- vocational guidance and training courses;
- a register of disabled persons;
- a quota system that established that all enterprises employing 20 or more people had to recruit 2 per cent of their workforce from the ranks of people with disability;
- the designation of classes of employment for disabled persons;
- a Disablement Resettlement Advisory Committee;
- the post of Disablement Resettlement Officer.

From the outset this Act was doomed to fail. Firstly, the 2 per cent requirement is notoriously difficult to enforce and secondly no provision was made for the creation of a legal mechanism which would ensure that 2 per cent of employees were in fact disabled persons. In the words of Fred Bezzina, '...the 1969 Employment Act succeeded on an individual level, as a number of people did find a worthwhile job on the strength of the Act; however, it has to be admitted that the Act has failed on a national level'. This seems to tally with the experience of other countries where such a quota was introduced. The Centre for Educational Research and Innovation (1986), focusing on the experiences of young adults, reports that '[t]here appears to be little evidence in many countries that a quota system helps the young disabled school leaver' (p. 23). For example, in the UK the quota system was put into place in 1946 but in 1990 Morell reported that only a quarter of employers met the 3 per cent target (cited in Riddell *et al.* 1993: 69).

The employment sector was given a boost in 1995 when NCPD published a document setting out policy for the employment of persons with disability. As a result of this document, the 1969 Employment Act was amended and the Employment and Training Corporation (ETC) was given responsibility for this work. Nowadays, ETC has a specialist Support Unit that acts as an employment agency for disabled people and also offers life skills courses for persons with a mild to moderate intellectual disability. In 1999, according to the *National Disability Survey*, 10.6 per cent of people registered as disabled were employed. Of these 1.9 per cent were working in a sheltered workshop (Bezzina 1999: 26).

Notwithstanding all these endeavours, since the 1960s disabled persons employed in high-status high-pay jobs can, almost literally, be counted on the fingers of one hand. Since education and gainful employment are generally the cornerstones of an independent adult life, it is clear from the preceding discussion that even today, after 45 years of 'special' educational provision and at least 30 years of statutory employment rights, the majority of Maltese disabled persons remain virtually totally dependent financially and unable to adequately express their own wishes and needs.

A rise in service provision and parent power (1971–1987)

Historically, blind persons in Malta have always been more vocal in their demands, and, until the advent of Id-Dar tal-Providenza, they were at the forefront of fundraising activities. They also advocated the introduction of a non-contributory pension. However, following the pattern of many single-impairment organisations, their lobbying was specific to their own needs and did not benefit the generality of disabled persons. In fact, by 1964 the Department of Social Services had already agreed to provide unemployed, blind adults with a non-contributory pension. Physically and intellectually impaired persons would have to wait until 1974 before the 'Pension for the Blind' was rechristened the 'Handicapped Pension' and was extended to include them (Bezzina 1996). In 1987 an allowance for families who had a disabled child was also introduced. During the 1970s and 1980s other measures were introduced which were aimed at the improvement of disabled persons' quality of life, including tax exemptions on specially adapted cars and subsidies for disabled people to upgrade their homes.

In spite of all these measures, however, the notion that disabled adults wanted to and indeed could lead independent lives was never seriously entertained by the authorities. Family ties in Malta are very strong and the general attitude is that, if all else fails, there is always the family to fall back on. Moreover, the practice of leaving the family home before getting married, even by non-disabled persons, was very rare up to a few years ago, and even today is still relatively uncommon. For adults with a disability who remain single it is considered normal and respectable to go on living with their parents throughout their lives. Not to do so would cast a slur on the family honour, implying that it does not look after its own. Family support is therefore a double-edged sword: at its best it can ensure a high degree of support and encouragement for a disabled person, at its worst it is a life sentence of oppression. Camilleri, one of the present authors, maintains that even when families are very supportive they can manifest a strong reluctance to 'let go' once the disabled individual has decided to live independently. While the family is an integral and often positive part of Maltese culture, in the case of disabled persons, strong family ties have perpetuated the myth of disabled people as eternal children, unable and unwilling to function as adults. This pervasive stereotype has had a disastrous effect on the manner in which financial support is perceived and the degree of financial assistance required to enable disabled persons to enjoy an acceptable quality of life. To date, the state has not felt compelled to facilitate independent living, but only to provide disabled persons and their families with some financial support. The level of the existing Disability Pension can never facilitate independent living (Kinsella 1998) and remains one of the most powerful tools of oppression, condemning Maltese disabled people to a life of dependence and denying them the opportunity for personal development and empowerment. It is very much a part of what Campbell and Oliver (1996) describe as 'a massive infrastructure of complex, confusing and dependency-creating services' which is reinforced by 'the existence of passive and disempowered disabled people' (p. 44).

As has already been pointed out, measures introduced during this period were for the main part instigated by the government of the day or by the church authorities. Inevitably, the changes and services were very much introduced with a top-down approach. Before the introduction of these measures there was practically no service provision of any description for people with disabilities and consequently these changes signalled the beginning of a willingness on the part of the authorities to shoulder some of the responsibility of service provision in this sector. On the other hand, the strength of the family ties and the responsibility of family members, especially parents, means that these same parents have been an important agent for change. Thus, in Malta most of the services now available to disabled persons came about as a result of strong lobbying by different groups of parents, often focusing on single-impairment needs, rather than at the insistence of disabled persons themselves. In 1976, for instance, a group of parents of children with various disabilities joined together to form the Parents' Society for Handicapped Children (a name which was changed in 1994 to the Parents' Society of Persons with Disability). Initially, the Parents' Society lobbied for severely disabled children to be admitted into special schools even if they were incontinent (at the time only children who were toilet trained were allowed to attend school). Their first success in resolving this issue spurred them on to more open criticism of the special education system, which had until then been considered a good thing. Since it was evident that their severely disabled children could never be 'cured', or 'normalised' to any significant degree, it became clear to these and other parents that quality-of-life issues were not the exclusive domain of medicine, where, as one parent succinctly put it: 'there exists a very rich sea for "sharks" … prepared to do everything for the sake of financial profit' (Bezzina 1989). It was thus that a small nucleus of parents began to shift their focus away from the medical model of disability and to look for more enduring solutions through social change.

The advent of the social model and the establishment of the National Commission Persons with Disability (NCPD)

Perhaps the most momentous outcome of parent power and the growing disillusionment with the medical model of disability was the establishment of the National Commission for the Handicapped (NCH) in 1987. From a political point of view the establishment of the NCH was a direct response to the United Nations' document *World Programme of Action Concerning Disabled Persons* (WPA), which urged governments to:

> ... establish a focal point (for example, a national commission, committee or similar body) to look into and follow the activities related to the World Programme of Action of various ministries, of other government agencies and of non-governmental organizations. Any mechanism set up should involve all parties concerned, including organizations of disabled persons. The body should have access to decision-makers at the highest level. (United Nations 1988 para. 89)

However, the establishment of NCH was not in itself an indicator that there was a ground swell for change as a result of lobbying from an increasingly self-aware disability movement. On the contrary, the commission's genesis was brought about by a small core of people putting their heads together and pushing for change themselves while the majority of disabled people remained voiceless and virtually invisible. The fact that NCPD was set up by government meant that change could proceed without political opposition. But there was also the realisation by politicians that disabled people and their families formed a significant constituency. One respondent to the questionnaires wrote that 'holier than thou attitudes by MPs' was a major factor in bringing about change. This change, however, occurred mostly in the decision-making processes of ministerial and departmental offices. The continued absence of a strong grass-roots movement has made it all the more difficult to change mentalities and attitudes at a more popular level.

Running contrary to current practice, the NCH immediately set itself the task of including a meaningful percentage of disabled people and listening to the voices of disabled persons and parents of disabled youngsters and acting upon their advice. This meant that often the Commission was seriously at odds with established charity-based organisations and the advice of well-known 'experts' in the field. Furthermore, by investing in recent disability literature the NCH became aware of the struggles of disabled persons in other countries and examples of civil rights activism in the United States, Canada and the United Kingdom influenced it to adopt a social model (Oliver 1990), civil rights approach to disability issues quite early on. One of the earliest initiatives was the setting up of the Child Development Advisory Unit (CDAU) whose task it was to identify impairment, offer immediate support, give parents timely information in plain language and recommend future strategies for development (Bezzina 1989). CDAU was emphatically not meant to focus exclusively on the medical aspect. Perhaps it was to be expected that professionals entrenched in the medical model approach would not give up their power base so easily, and indeed today the CDAU offers not only a purely medicalised service, but against advice, its name has been changed to Child Development *Assessment* Unit, thus completely undermining its original *raison d'être* and ensuring that Maltese parents still remain without effective guidance when they most need it. However, other than this foray into the medical sector, NCH's other major campaigns focused on the struggle for equal opportunities in the social field: accessible public transport, inclusive education, ending discriminatory employment practices and the development of community-based services focusing on the specific needs of the individual. Between 1993 and 1995, following consultation with a wide spectrum of individuals and groups, it published its National Policy documents on education and employment.

In keeping with social model definitions, in 1993 NCH changed its name to National Commission Persons with Disability (NCPD). The American usage 'persons with disability' was preferred over the British 'disabled persons' for the following reason: the British phrase simply does not render itself into Maltese, whereas the American phrase translates perfectly into the Maltese 'persuni b'dizabilità'. It is in using the social model as a standard that NCPD has brought about the greatest changes. By doing so it has brought about a change in definitions, in language usage and more slowly in perceptions. We cannot delude ourselves into thinking that the changes wrought in the last 13 years have brought about a complete and lasting transformation, but without doubt, the influence of NCPD has forced government, the two main political parties, the civil service, some traditional charities and an increasing proportion of key individuals to redefine their approach to disability and to disabled people as a group.

NCPD organises regular seminars on areas of national priority, mainly during Disability Week which centres around the International Day of Persons with Disability (3 December). In 1993, it began offering a credit course on Disability Issues to students at the Institute of Health Care. Over the years the credit has become compulsory in courses in Health, Education, Social Work and Social Administration. Modified versions of the course are also given to students at the Faculty of Engineering, the Faculty of Management Studies, and latterly disability awareness lectures have been extended to private and parastatal companies. These lectures treat disability as essentially a civil rights issue and are thus firmly based on the social model. They are coordinated by a disabled person and include a high proportion of speakers who are either disabled or closely related to disabled persons (NCPD 2000a). In 1996 NCPD established the PEKTUR Programme, a continuing education, research and training initiative which aims at funding research in areas considered a priority by NCPD. The principle aim of PEKTUR is to actively encourage research based on the social model of disability and in areas considered a priority by disabled persons themselves. (NCPD 2000b).

By 1990 there was a growing realisation that awareness campaigns and social pressure alone would not bring about the radical and lasting changes required to ensure both an acceptable quality of life and the safeguarding of disabled persons' civil rights. A small number of disabled activists began to lobby for the introduction of anti-discriminatory legislation, along the lines of the 1990 Americans with Disabilities Act (ADA) and the original, pre-1995 draft of the British Disability Discrimination Act (DDA). A national seminar organised by the NCPD in 1992 set the agenda and in 1996, after a long process of consultation with disabled persons' organisations and other interested parties, the final draft was completed and presented to the Maltese parliament. Unfortunately, a general election was called on the very day the bill was to have its first reading. A subsequent change in administration resulted in the publication of a White Paper with the aim of completely reviewing the draft bill. For the second time, when the bill came up for its first reading in 1998, Parliament was dissolved and an early election called!

In January 2000, the Equal Opportunities (Persons with Disability) Act finally passed into law as Act I of 2000. NCPD has been given the responsibility of ensuring that the provisions of the Act are adhered to and, to this end, it has set up an Equal Opportunities Compliance Unit, which by 1 October of this year will begin functioning as an Ombudsman for disability matters, with the power to investigate and sue if and when necessary.

The first glimmers of identity: the road ahead

There has been considerable progress in areas of service provision, educational policy and legislation. Providing services *for* disabled people is 'in'. This is exemplified in a report in *The Times* (Malta) (2000) that the local council of the town of Cospicua objected to plans by the Church to build a home for battered men and women. The mayor was quoted as saying:

> We believe that there are more urgent things required in Cottonera [the town of Cospicua forms part of a largely socially depressed district known as Cottonera], such as a respite centre for the handicapped.
>
> Moreover, battered men and women would continue to add to the stigma that already exists in the area. (p. 4, our emphasis)

This mayor does not see 'the handicapped', as he calls them, as carrying a stigma. However, like so many other people in Malta he does not take into consideration the ability of Maltese disabled persons to fend for themselves. In fact, the latter still remain largely passive and silent in the face of oppressive disabling barriers.

One may at this stage ask: what was the role of disabled people themselves in all these changes? The short answer is 'not extensive'. Both Eden and NCPD were founded and are still run by small core groups which have continued to use the top-down approach when it comes to changing attitudes. One thing in their favour is the fact that they have been endorsed by the relevant authorities and, to a large extent, had backing from above in order to bring about the changes they have in a relatively short time span. They have also presented people with a different mindset and started to foster a culture of self-determination. The questionnaires returned indicate that many NGOs working in the area of disability were set up during the past four years. The majority of them involve disabled people in the main committee. However, the main aim of these organisations is to offer support to its members and to lobby for small changes in areas that affect its members directly. Consequently, despite their existence, there was, and there still is, no widespread movement lobbying for change at a lower level; none of the public outcries and mass demonstrations that helped bring about a societal change of attitude in other developed countries. The emergence of the disability movement as a social movement, as described by British authors such as Campbell and Oliver (1996) and Oliver and Zarb (1997) has not yet taken place in Malta.

The reasons for this are many and complex. Part of it may be the fact that, as was pointed out in the Introduction, the bipartite political system in Malta makes for a rather polarised environment in which protest does not simply place you as being anti-government but also as being firmly in the opposition's camp. Despite the fact that there is no curtailment of the right to freedom of speech, many may feel constrained from exercising this right because of their political allegiances. Thus, if you are a keen supporter of the party in power you might think twice before protesting publicly and loudly because you may be seen as an agitator. If, on the other hand, you support the opposition party, your involvement in protests may brand you as a puppet of that party. Such attitudes add to the existing fragmentation within the disability sector, and of course, this works in favour of better established groups with their own agendas.

A palpable sense of vulnerability also militates against Maltese disabled persons speaking their minds and demanding their rights assertively. Unless the disabled individual finds support from their family, or other (usually voluntary) means of assistance (MSU 1999: ii), there are no alternatives to institutionalisation in its crudest form. In Malta, at the time of writing, this means a 'choice' between a residence for the elderly, or a mental hospital. Thus, disabled persons are extremely reluctant to voice real frustration when they experience overt, or covert, injustice. The pre-eminence of paternalism, through the family networks, serves to reinforce passivity and to ingrain a sense of over-riding gratitude and a 'can't complain' attitude.

We began this paper by referring to Malta's geographical size, a fact which, at the outset may seem to bear no direct relevance to the present argument. However, we believe that limitations of size and population is a significant element in hampering the development of a Maltese disability movement, by making it that much more difficult to achieve a critical mass of disability activists working together for a common goal. In Malta, the loss of a single individual who carries their disability with pride and who projects disability as essentially a civil rights struggle can have a devastating effect on the development of the whole sector. Furthermore, as stated earlier, the long-term neglect of educational and employment provision has robbed disabled persons of potential thinkers and leaders, making the disability sector overly dependent on traditional charities and individuals, who repeatedly put personal agendas before the interests of the disabled people they purport to represent.

Another serious constraint which stifles activism is the sheer amount of energy many disabled Maltese expend just struggling to get through the day. Despite the growth and improvement of services in general, the absence of basic services geared specifically towards independent living: schemes for residential support, personal assistance schemes, realistic disability income and an efficient and accessible transport system, Maltese disabled people complain that they spend all their time struggling to survive from day to day, so that they cannot afford the time to organise themselves into an effective movement. Anger, where it exists, is kept firmly under control and is seen as a negative force. On the other hand, one realises that the majority of these constraints had to be confronted and, if not overcome, at least come to terms with in every country where disabled people have sought to grasp and control their own destinies. The struggles are no different here. The truth of this came out clearly during a five-day workshop entitled 'Back to Our Roots' and held in October 1999 during which a significant number of disabled people in the audience voiced their frustration and anger at the *status quo*, first steps, we hope, towards more assertive action.

Conclusion

The disability movement in Malta may still be in its infancy. But, when one looks back to the 1940s and the dearth of disability awareness then, one realises that disabled people in Malta have in fact come a long way in the past 50 years or so. From a struggle against blind prejudice and superstition, we have moved on to challenge the charity-based services that had evolved as a result of that initial struggle. The task for the immediate future must be to raise the stakes of that challenge by creating a critical mass of activists, a strong, independent movement of disabled persons.

Because of the hold political parties have over the Maltese electorate, lobbying politicians will continue to play an important part in the activities of this emergent movement. There cannot, however, continue to be a dependence on anti-discriminatory legislation on its own or on the blessing of politicians to safeguard the rights of disabled people and to dismantle the disabling barriers created by society.

There needs to be a movement that is made up of disabled people who are conscious of the fact that it is not enough for them to fight their corner to make their lives marginally better in material terms. They have to realise the need to raise the consciousness of the public in general, and of decision-makers, employers, educators, and service-providers in particular. Similarly, the increasingly vocal parents' lobby also needs to realise the importance of getting together and fighting for the rights of their disabled offspring to access the same resources and services as their non-disabled peers. No lasting change can come about if it is not founded upon, and safeguarded by, a strong, independent movement of disabled persons.

Questions

- In your opinion, what concerns should an emergent disability movement address and act upon?
- In this chapter, the mayor of the town of Cospicua is quoted as saying that a home for disabled people is preferable to one for battered men and women since the latter 'would continue to add to the stigma that already exists in the area'. Do you think that this type of attitude indicates that disabled people's status in Malta is secure or that they are still considered as objects of charity, albeit worthy ones?

Note

Interviews with:
- Mr Fred Bezzina, Executive Director, National Commission Persons with Disability
- Mr George Samuel, former Education Officer, Special Educational Needs
- Mr John Micallef, Administrator, Dar il-Providenza

Many of the Maltese references in this paper can be downloaded from the National Commission Persons with Disability's website: http://www.knpd.org/.

CHAPTER 8

Disabled people and the politics of partnership in Aotoaroa New Zealand

Martin Sullivan

and I'll tell it and think it and
speak it and breathe it
and reflect from the mountains so all
souls can see it
and I'll stand on the ocean until I
start sinking
and I'll know my song well before I
start singing
and it's a hard, it's a hard, and it's a hard,
it's a hard rain's a gonna fall

In the four decades since Bob Dylan wrote *A Hard Rain's A-gonna Fall,* a social movement of disabled people struggling against the oppressive conditions under which they are forced to live has emerged throughout the western world. Written at the time of the Cuban missile crisis (1962), the closing stanza quoted above could easily have been written as a recipe for that struggle upon which disabled people were about to embark. Of the ingredients listed – passion, pride, fearlessness, a clear analysis, tenacity in the face of huge odds and continual setbacks – perhaps the most important is that of having a clear analysis as this is the precursor, the vanguard of struggle. Unless the pride, passion and tenacity are focused by a clear understanding of the problem, all this energy will scatter and dissipate. In other words, a social movement for change must be underpinned by a clearly articulated and agreed upon analysis and strategy for change if it is to succeed. Most importantly, the analysis will give a sense of right and justice to the cause, elements so necessary in sustaining the self-belief, fearsomeness, tenacity and sheer hard work throughout the campaign.

Most importantly the analysis will shape the political strategy of the campaign, will give rise to a politics of struggle. By 'political' I mean a particular course of action designed to achieve specific outcomes. That course of action is driven by a commitment to a particular ethic or set of moral principles which produces a particular point of view or position and ways of doing and being. Whereas the British disability movement has been characterised by self-determination and self-organisation, the politics of partnership adopted in Aotoaroa New Zealand has resulted in structures and policies that have more often than not developed as a result of political compromise. This raises a whole series of questions about the nature of partnerships, when and on what grounds disabled people should enter them and the potential conflicts of interests between disabled people, their families and service providers.

This chapter is presented in three parts. The first examines the theoretical and ideological underpinnings of the disability struggle as they emerged in Britain.[1] Part two will provide an explication of the nature and politics of the disability movement in Aotoaroa New Zealand, the role of disability theory in shaping that movement and an evaluation of the struggle thus far. Part three provides an insight into the way Maori perceive disability and how this differs from Pakeha (white man, Europeans) perceptions.

PART 1: UNDERSTANDING DISABILITY: SETTING THE AGENDA FOR STRUGGLE AND CHANGE

It would have been in the mid-1980s when I picked up Vic Finkelstein's (1980) *Attitudes and Disabled People* and the words I'd heard some 15 years earlier from other disabled people came flooding back to me. I'd just had my accident and as part of my rehabilitation would do sports with other disabled people, some of whom worked in the community. These people, who had known the reality of disablism and the disabling society from birth, made it clear to me that it was not their impairments which had stopped them from achieving all they were capable of achieving, but the attitudes of 'normal' society. What Finkelstein provided was a framework for me to think more structurally about disability in general and my experiences in particular. His analysis also prompted me to the conclusion that many disabled people have an inherent understanding of what has become known as the 'social model' of disability.

It is not surprising, therefore, that it was a group of disabled people, the Union of the Physically Impaired Against Segregation (UPIAS), who first articulated a radical new understanding of disability by separating impairment (body deficits people have) from disability (the social oppression impaired people experience). Other writers (e.g. Abberley 1987, 1993; Barnes 1991; Finkelstein 1980; Oliver 1986, 1990, 1996a, 1996b), starting with UPIAS and drawing mainly on historical materialism, went on to explain the particular form disability takes in modern, capitalist societies. From this perspective disability is located unequivocally outside the body:

> …In our view, it is society which disables … Disability is something imposed on top of our impairments… . (UPIAS 1976: 3)

The social model, thus, provides a highly politicised account of disability which acts both as a counter-hegemony to medicalisation and as an agenda for the elimination of disability: the social model is a manifesto for change (Sullivan 1999). As such, it has been incredibly important in identifying barrier removal as a political strategy and in liberating disabled people from medicalised conceptions of themselves over the past two decades (Shakespeare and Watson 2000).

However, it would be misleading not to acknowledge the growing struggle over the adequacy of the social model when it comes to impaired people defining themselves in light of their multiple experiences of disability and oppression. Writers such as Crow (1996), French (1993) and Morris (1991) have argued that impairment is a major factor in disability while others have explored the 'simultaneous oppression' of disability and sexism (Fine and Asch 1988; Lloyd 1992; Morris 1989, 1991, 1996), racism (Begum 1992; Stuart 1992, 1993) and heterosexism (Corbett 1994; Hearn 1988, 1991) and found the social model wanting. For Vernon (1996a, 1996b, 1998), the social model is silent, unable to account for the multiple oppression experienced by disabled women, blacks and ethnic minorities, gay men and lesbians. Corker and French (1999), drawing on the ideas of post-structuralism and post-modernism, provide a compelling argument for a reclaiming of discourse in disability studies and the need for disability theory 'to conceptualize a mutually constitutive relationship between impairment and disability which is both materially and discursively (socially) produced' (p. 6). Unlike UPIAS and others, these writers place the body at the centre of understanding disability.

These debates within disability studies have been touched on here because they have relevance in Aotoaroa New Zealand and will be returned to later.

PART 2: THE DISABILITY MOVEMENT IN AOTOAROA NEW ZEALAND

In this section the way history and culture has shaped the politics of the disabled people's movement and the ongoing struggle for disability rights in Aotoaroa New Zealand is examined. To understand the culture and nature of our society one has to first understand the relationship between Maori, the tangata whenua (local people, indigenous) and Pakeha. This relationship was formalised in the Treaty of Waitangi under which Britain annexed New Zealand as a colony in 1840 and was subsequently forged in the struggle by the colonised to have the Treaty recognised in law and honoured by the coloniser. It will be argued that not only are there many parallels between the respective struggles of Maori and disabled people to have equal access to and full participation in Pakeha society, but that the former has profoundly influenced the latter in a number of ways. It will also be argued that population and geography have played a vital role in shaping the politics of the disability movement and the way the struggle has unfolded. A critical assessment of the umbrella organisation of disabled people, Disabled Persons Assembly (DPA), its successes and failures, will also be provided.

The Treaty of Waitangi

The Treaty of Waitangi constitutes the founding document of Aotoaroa New Zealand. While a short document, its meaning is highly contested. In the English text Maori cede sovereignty to the Crown in return for the 'full exclusive and undisturbed possession of their Lands and Estates, Forests, Fisheries and other properties' and 'all the Rights and Privileges of British Subjects'. Under the Maori text, Maori grant the Queen *kawanatanga* or governance over the land (thus making the unruly settlers subject to British law) but retain *tino rangatiratanga* or absolute chieftainship over their lands, villages and all their treasures while granting pre-emption to the Crown and gaining English citizenship. The discrepancies between the two texts is clearly evident: *kawanatanga* does not convey the meaning of sovereignty and *tino rangatiratanga* implies that Maori will be subject to customary lore not British law. This is reflected in the fact that only 39 chiefs signed the English text and a little over 500 signed the Maori text (Binney 1989).

Notwithstanding, the English text took precedence and colonisation proceeded with the Treaty being more honoured in the breach than in fact. By the end of the 19th century, the majority of Maori land had been alienated and with it the economic and spiritual base of Maori culture and society. Until the urban migrations of the mid-20th century, Maori, for the most, lived in rural poverty working as farm labourers or eking out an existence on marginal land. As a result of the urban Maori protest movement of the 1970s and the cultural renaissance of Maori, the Waitangi Tribunal was established in 1975 as a forum for the airing of contemporary Treaty grievances and for making non-binding recommendations for compensation to the Crown (government) in an effort to redress past injustices. By 1980, the policy of assimilation had been abandoned and biculturalism[2] adopted by government as the basis of Maori policy (Durie 1994). In 1985, the powers and personnel of the Waitangi Tribunal were extended by granting it and the Crown retrospective jurisdiction to 1840 giving Maori a far more effective mechanism for resolving grievances. By the late 1980s a legal revolution was underway with references to the Treaty and Treaty 'principles' making their way into New Zealand law by way of combination of statute, the findings and recommendations of the Waitangi Tribunal and the courts (Sharp 1992).

Partnership consciousness?

In the spirit of biculturalism all departments of state, ministries and agencies were required to include clauses in their mission statements expressing commitment to the Treaty and protocols in place for establishing a partnership relationship with local iwi (tribe). In turn, government agencies required the providers and voluntary agencies they contracted to show how they were giving effect to the Treaty outlining the partnership protocols they had in place with local iwi. In short time, a 'partnership' consciousness spread throughout Aotoaroa New Zealand with many organisations, especially human service organisations, inserting a Treaty clause in their constitutions and talking more openly about developing partnerships not only with local iwi but also with their employees, customers, clients and beneficiaries.

For Maori, 'partnership' is an expectation of a relationship based on good faith, mutual respect and understanding, and shared decision making in both policy making and resource allocation. However, when it came to powerful service provider organisations for disabled people (e.g. CCS and IHC – formerly the Crippled Children Society and Intellectually Handicapped Children), which traditionally had, at best, a paternalistic relationship with their members, any talk of partnership was highly ideological; more often than not it was aimed more at defusing incipient demands from members for a greater say in running 'their' organisations than in seeking a true partnership. For disabled people in Aotoaroa New Zealand, a true partnership with the state and service providers is preferable by far to the client relationship which currently prevails. Moreover, we have the model of biculturalism between Maori and the Crown to emulate when seeking such partnerships.

However, there is one major difference when it comes to disabled people entering partnership relationships: we inevitably enter from a position of weakness whereas Maori enter from a position of moral strength. Maori have the Treaty on their side whereas disabled people have only the good intentions of the people for whom they are a source of income and career opportunity and on whom many depend. Most importantly, Maori are united in their struggle by a clear analysis of the cause of their dispossession, namely the Crown's refusal to honour the Treaty of Waitangi. It is this component, a clear analysis of what disability is, which is missing from the disability movement in Aotaroa New Zealand and which places us in a position of weakness in our struggle against oppression and when entering partnerships with the state and/or service providers. A review of the formation of the umbrella organisation for disabled people, DPA, shows how, in the absense of a clearly articulated analysis of disabilty, a politics of 'partnership' and cooperation with service providers was idealistically chosen as the way forward rather than forming an organisation made up exclusively of disabled people to go head to head with the disabling society.

The Disabled Persons Assembly

In 1972, Coordinating Councils for the Disabled were set up in the four main centres: Auckland, Christchurch, Dunedin and Wellington. As the name suggests, the aim of these councils was to coordinate the responses of the various groups of and for disabled people on issues such as education and access. In 1978 they combined to become the New Zealand Coordinating Council for the Disabled (NZCD) and were soon at loggerheads with CCS and IHC who blocked their attempts to become the New Zealand representative on Rehabilitation International because they were 'too much influenced by consumer interests' (Georgeson 2000: 56). This should have served as an early warning of the entrenched and hostile attitudes of traditional organisations towards their 'children' when they start talking and organising for themselves. But, it did not.

At one of the many meetings set up to discuss issues facing disabled people during the International Year of Disabled Persons (IYDP) (1981), it was proposed that a cross-disability organisation be formed to continue the work of IYDP. In 1983, at an Extraordinary General Meeting of NZDC a resolution to change its name to the Disabled Persons Assembly (New Zealand) was passed.

Organisational structure: enter a politics of partnership

From its inception, DPA aimed to be as inclusive as possible by creating categories of membership which would draw recruits from across the disability spectrum: individual, family, corporate and associate memberships. The vehicle chosen for achieving inclusion was the partnership model. It was hoped that partnerships would develop between all these categories of members: together they would work to achieve DPA's vision for New Zealand society to be one 'which provides both equity and maximum opportunity to participate for all people' (DPA cited in Georgeson 2000: 65).

While there is nothing inherently wrong with developing partnerships with various groups to achieve one's end, it is crucial for the protagonist to be careful about the partnerships it enters into and the way that partnership is structured. For example, it would be foolish to enter a partnership with a far more powerful group, whose world view is ultimately diametrically opposed to your ends. It would be even more foolish to give that partner a dominant position on the governing body of the partnership/organisation.

DPA membership is open to both disabled and non-disabled people alike, including family and corporate membership. Corporate organisations are defined as any non-profitable, charitable or welfare organisation whose objects are similar to DPA's or who work in any way for the benefit of 'people with disabilities'. At any general meetings or national and regional assemblies, family members are entitled to two votes and corporates to a number proportional to their membership. Moreover, the Constitution requires corporate members to be in the majority on the ruling National Executive Committee and the Regional Executive Committees operating at the local level! When one considers that corporates such as CCS and IHC, with histories of running archipelagos of sheltered workshops and mini-institutions masquerading as 'community homes' are required to be in majority on the NEC and RECs, then it is difficult to understand why the constitution was written in such a way. Even more so given that some astute thinkers like Quentin Angus, Don McKenzie and Byron Buick-Constable (all disabled people) were at the helm at the time. They must have reasoned, however, that this set of arrangements would represent a true and equal partnership between disabled people and service providers within the organisations. They also hoped that disabled people within the corporates would be nominated as their representatives (Georgeson 2000). Today, this reasoning appears naïve given that, apart from appearances and the public relations angle, service organisations really had nothing to gain from a 'true' partnership with their client populations. Equally naïve is the belief that 'people with disabilities' will represent anything other than their employer's interests when a choice has to be made.

Many of the organisations involved in DPA adopt a traditional model of service delivery. Such a model has been criticised by Munford and Sullivan (1997) as promoting an image of disabled people as 'passive, dependent, powerless and requiring nondisabled people to do things for them' (p. 18). Similar criticisms of traditional charities in the UK have been raised by Hevey (1992). It is inevitable that such service providers will come into conflict with disabled people who wish to advocate for themselves. Self-organisation involves the development and empowerment of disabled people but it can also mean disempowerment for people and organisations with a vested interest in keeping disabled people dependant and powerless.

It can also be argued that a number of other cultural and social factors may well have influenced DPA in adopting a politics of partnership. First, in the 1970s Maori militancy had burned issues surrounding the Treaty of Waitangi deep into the national psyche as matters of honour and social justice (see Awatere 1984), biculturalism had been adopted as official government policy in 1980 and talk of partnership was thick in the air. Second, the wounds from the anti-tour demonstrations of the 1981 Springbok rugby tour which had torn the country apart – dividing friends and families alike – were still fresh: partnership must have been far more appealing than 'in your face' tactics. Third, the Disabled Persons Community Welfare Act 1975 (DCPW) had clearly signalled the state's intention to hasten the process of deinstitutionalisation by putting in place a range of services to facilitate supported living in the community. It had been in operation for eight years, and it may have seemed an obvious choice to enter partnership arrangements with service providers in this policy environment. Fourth, although the economy had been in decline since the late 1960s and unemployment was rising, remnants of the equalitarian ethos which had dominated the national psyche since 1935 when the first Labour government had proclaimed that 'Jack was as good as his master' and that 'all should be given a fair go', still persisted. No doubt the persistence of these cultural icons played a part in persuading DPA that the time had finally arrived for disabled people to enter a new relationship, a partnership with their former masters. Finally, population and geography had a part to play. In Aotoaroa New Zealand, with a highly mobile population of approximately 3.5 million people spread throughout two long (each 1,000km) islands covering in total roughly the same area as the UK, there is a tendency to get to know people throughout the country working in the same sector. In the disability sector, the same faces, often wearing different hats, keep appearing so networks develop and we get to know one another well. Hence, the rationale may well have been that it is better to be nice to these people, to be in partnership with the service providers and influential people, than to be at loggerheads with them. Indeed, John Stott, past president of DPA, argued 'Disabled people are not as successful when acting alone as when collaborating with other groups…' (Beatson 1998: 11). Who knows, its best to be nice to these people – you might be sharing an office with them sometime in the future!

But, for me, the real reason for DPA opting for a consensual politics of partnership rather than a confrontational politics of self-determination, was their failure to do the intellectual work necessary for them to arrive at a clearly articulated position on what disability actually is. A space was never created in which disabled people could define and work out their own position on disability.[3] I find this rather surprising given the example of other oppressed groups who separated themselves from their oppressors in order to work out their analysis and strategy for action. In the Treaty workshops of the late 1970s, part of the process was for Pakeha to be separated from Maori so that each could do their own work on coming to terms with their distinct culture, to discover their own turangawaewae (home turf, standing ground) as part of the decolonisation process and as a prerequisite to becoming truly bicultural. A part of the reason that DPA never engaged in the intellectual work, can probably be traced to New Zealand's closeness to our colonial and largely rural past in which a culture of rejecting things intellectual in favour of just getting 'stuck in' and getting things done with resources at hand emerged; of our pride in ourselves as a nation of do-it-yourselfers where give the average person a bit of number 8 fencing wire and s/he can fix anything. Under this scenario, a pragmatic approach by DPA of just getting on with our new 'partners' and doing 'it' seems highly plausible.

An eschewal of separation and intellectual work could also be partly attributed to fear, embarrassment and unwillingness to cause offence. Earlier I argued that disabled people have an inherent understanding of what disability is by virtue of their lived experience of impairment. However, in a country where we are so nice and tolerant of each other, it is very difficult to unpack the immediate elements of the disabling society when those who are part of it – your service provider, sometimes your parents or helpers on whom you depend – are taking part in the same debate! It is a risky and embarrassing business to cause offence to such powerful people. Who knows what political strategy may have emerged in Aotoaroa New Zealand if disabled people had drawn aside to debate disability in their own space, had arrived at their own position free from those most threatened by their so doing?

The example of blind people

For a possible outcome of what may have happened, one needs to look no further than the New Zealand Association of the Blind and Partially Blind. The New Zealand Institute for the

Blind (NZIB) had been operating for 55 years in an autocratic and paternalistic way before the Dominion Association of the Blind (DAB) was formed to give an organised voice to blind people. Newbold (1995) outlines the struggle beginning with about 100 blind people who met in Auckland in 1945 to form their own association to advance the interests of blind persons. Membership was to be restricted to blind people aged 18 and over. In 1958, after a systematic campaign to recruit and register DAB members for voting in the annual election of NZIB governing board of trustees, DAB members or sympathisers won and occupied the five seats on the board which were up for election that year (the other four were government appointees) (see Newbold 1995: 84–8 for a detailed account).

By 1975, the détente was at an end and the Association became locked into one of its 'most protracted and bitter' disputes with the Foundation in its history.[4] At issue was, *inter alia*, representation on the RNZFB board of trustees and policy committees (see Newbold 1955: 123–47). In 1979, Association member Don McKenzie was appointed to the board and the following year he was elected as the first blind chairman. Of the 14 trustees, five were members of the Association and the rest were sympathisers: the Association, once again, had effective control of the Foundation board of trustees.

It seems, however, that struggle between the Association and the sighted leaders of the Foundation is on a 20-year cycle. In 1999 the struggle appears to have entered its endgame, with the Association seeking changes to the Act which governs the Foundation so that only blind members of the Foundation would be eligible to vote for trustees. Quite simply, the blind want to control the organisation dedicated to blind well-being, i.e. their organisation. According to Beatson (2000), this stand-off is even more confrontational than the 'bad old days' of the late 1970s.

The Association and DPA

The Association has been a corporate member of DPA since its inception with Don McKenzie, a prominent blind activist, serving as DPA's first vice president. Two Association members also served on the first national executive committee of DPA. However, in 1996 the Association withdrew because it felt that DPA was not using the Association correctly as a consultative part of DPA's corporate membership, and withdrew from the organisation. It was felt that compliant blind people were being chosen by the chief executive of DPA to promote the interests of DPA before those of the Association and blind people generally. At that time, the Association had more individual members than DPA, many of whom were opposed to the corporate membership system, believing it devalued their vote to the same worth as some of the more oppressive service-orientated corporate members (Dodd personal communication). Moreover, history had shown that the interests of the blind are better served by their own organisation; an organisation which is not compromised by having service providers on its governing body.

Lessons to be learned from the blind experience of self-organisation

In his history of the NZABPB, Newbold (1995) notes how soon after its inception the Association had transformed into 'a co-ordinated and strategic force' (p. 195) engaging in vigorous campaigns against foundation policy for the greater part of its history. He concludes:

> Without the DAB's vigorous and sustained lobbying, some of the improvements which later occurred in blind welfare would have been much longer coming, and many would not have come at all. … over the past 50 years, at all levels and in all areas in blind service provision, there has been hardly a single decision taken which has not been influenced by association input. (pp. 195–6)

This is significant. But what is most instructive about this history is that the Association has always been able to represent the interests of blind people unequivocally precisely because only blind people can be members and because it has always maintained a critical relationship with the Foundation. From this position the Association has won many important victories, the most notable being the abolition of the means test in 1958 for blind people when applying for the invalids benefit. This has created some divisiveness and jealousy within the broader disability movement where, instead of looking at how their own organisations are structured and their interests represented as a consequence, there has been a tendency to individualise and personalise the problem and thereby miss the most obvious lesson of self-organisation and self-advocacy.

The Association has also been remarkably successful in its advocacy for the creation of talking book libraries, instruction in occupational therapy and piano tuning for its members, the training and provision of guide dogs and improved educational facilities for blind people. By the late 1950s it had won concessions on domestic and international air postage, and 50 per cent subsidies on internal air, sea and rail travel by the mid 1960s. These concessions were expanded in 1970 to include sighted guides. In terms of information access the Association established talking book services, radio for the blind, and magazine taping (eventually taken over by the Foundation when demands outstripped the Association's resources). Similarly, with IT the Association has successfully lobbied for the provision and training of its members in the use of computers so they may have print, speech and Braille access to information via computer. In terms of funding, the Association won its struggle in 1983 to have its funding based on a set percentage of the Foundation's annual Braille Week appeal and general purpose donations rather than the grant basis which had existed since 1961 (Newbold 1995).

Cultural benefits in terms of consciousness and conscientisation have also emerged from the blind's self-organisation and 50-year struggle for equity with the Foundation. This struggle has been predicated on a structural analysis of blindness providing a counter-hegemony to the medicalisation which engenders self-blame on the part of blind people for the poverty of exclusion as well as a collective identity as an oppressed minority and the need for collective struggle for inclusion. As battles were won the collective and individual sense of dignity and self-worth on the part of Association members was generated and enhanced as was their sense of solidarity and purpose.

Newbold's statement that 'hardly a single decision' (1995: 196) affecting services for the blind in the past half-century has been made without input from the Association bears testimony to the effectiveness of self-organisation and serves as an object lesson to DPA and the broader disability movement in Aotoaroa New Zealand.

How effective the struggle for change?

It would be churlish not to acknowledge that a great deal of positive change has occurred for disabled people over the past 30 years in Aotoaroa New Zealand. It would be Pollyannaish, however, to suggest that that change has progressed anywhere near as fast or gone as far as disabled people would like. The foregoing suggests that the politics of disablement adopted by the NZABPB has been a far more successful strategy for blind people than the partnership strategy adopted by DPA to advance the interests of disabled people generally.

However, this is not to say that DPA has had no successes. Rather, it is to say that while DPA has had one or two major successes at a national level the effectiveness of its overall contribution to the struggle for change in Aotoaroa New Zealand is not always clear. This is partly because at a national level a lot of energy goes into administrating the organisation and being the 'official' voice of disabled people in a variety of settings such as parliamentary and select committees, lobbying politicians and bureaucrats, consultation in the private and voluntary sectors and monitoring and evaluating government disability support services. This is predominately 'behind-the-scenes' work, the effectiveness of which is difficult to evaluate because the extent to which DPA perspectives are incorporated in policy development and implementation is always dependent upon wider ideological concerns, political feasibility and the fiscal implications of the measures proposed. Positive change has been mostly incremental rather than fundamental in Aotoaroa New Zealand and, in frequently going only part of the way, politicians and the political process has often left disabled people in, arguably, a worse position than when they started.

The Building Act 1991 (BA) and the Human Rights Act 1993 (HRA), for which DPA lobbied hard, are cases in point. Both are equivocal about compliance and both are in keeping with the flexible regulations which had emerged with the ascendancy of neoliberal politics in 1984. For example, the BA does not specify design standards in any detailed way nor require on-site inspection during construction. It also contains let-out clauses such as 'as nearly as reasonably practicable' (section 46(2)(a)) for alterations, and grants Authorities the right to waiver or modify the Code. This has been happening regularly and disabled people have been up in arms throughout the country over non-compliance with the Code. Similarly, the HRA prohibits rather than outlaws discrimination on the basis of disability, the state is not covered by the Act until 2000 at the earliest and there is a list of exceptions where discrimination is permitted. For example, where it would 'not be reasonable' to provide facilities to allow access to public space or where it would be too expensive or too difficult to provide 'reasonable accommodation' in areas such as employment or housing, discrimination would be allowed (see Gleeson 1999: 178–94 for a good discussion of both acts).

Although both acts can be seen as partial victories for DPA, one could also argue that disabled people are worst off under these statutes. Purists would argue that it would be better to have no legislation on access or human rights than to have legislation which is either not enforced or is filled with holes so large a bus could be, and has been, driven through (see Beatson 2000 for an account of the Accessible Bus Campaign). The current legislation serves disablist interests and reflects a situation where the prerequisites for a non-disabling society are subverted by politicians in the interests of capital and political expediency.

While DPA has won partial victories on some of the macro issues, it has failed dismally to effect change where it really counts for most disabled people: at the micro level in the home. Throughout the 1990s the National government undertook a massive restructuring of welfare, including health and disability support services. Qualifying thresholds for home help and attendant care were raised and the hours available cut. Many lost out completely or had their hours cut so dramatically that the say and control these people had over their lives was severely restricted. DPA, however, was remarkably quiet over these events. This can be partly attributed to structural factors whereby the national office is largely dependent on receiving information from the regional assemblies if it is to lobby effectively at the centre. Messages were sent out to the regions requesting anecdotal and actual accounts of the effects the cuts were having. However no information was returned, suggesting that the evidence did not exist (highly unlikely), members were thin on the ground (likely) or that members were just so demoralised by the vicious onslaught of new right ideologies since 1984 that they had become either fatalistic or had little energy left to complain. Further, why bother complaining anyway? DPA's position was so compromised with first, service providers, the hard edge of the cuts, making up the majority of the governing executive and second, the person who held the vice-presidency and presidency of DPA during this era also being employed as the manager of Disability Support Services – the department of state implementing these cuts. While it can be argued that she was in a good position to resist, to ameliorate the worst excesses of the cutbacks, it was still not a good look for the rank and file of DPA.

On the other hand, the structure of a national office located in the capital close to government with relatively autonomous regional assemblies throughout the country, does have advantages. First, as the 'official' voice of disabled people, the regional DPAs are routinely called upon by regional and city councils, hospital boards, schools, community services, etc. to provide the perspectives of disabled people on a variety of local policy and planning issues. The regional assemblies also provide a network for the distribution of information, policy discussion documents, bills before select committees and the like for comment, feedback and submissions from disabled people around the country. The regional assemblies, even if somewhat hollow in terms of active membership, thus provide a mechanism for the mobilisation of disabled people around issues when they arise.

Such an occasion arose with the release of *Making a World of Difference: Whakanui Oranga. The New Zealand Disability Strategy Discussion Document* (NZDS) in September 2000. Utilising its regional network, DPA was in a position to co-host with the Ministry of Health 41 workshops around the country to discuss the document. That these were well attended by disabled people is probably due to the fact that DPA insisted that separate workshops be held at each venue for disabled people to ensure that their feedback was recorded 'uncontaminated' by the presence of service providers and medical professionals. This in itself marks a small but significant advance in first, the struggle for change and second, thinking at national executive level of DPA.

The NZDS can also be seen as a significant advance in the struggle for DPA. Leading up to the 1999 election, DPA released *Our Vision* its disability policy platform in which it called for the development of a 'strategic vision and plan for future support and independence of people with disabilities' (p. 3) as well as a Minister of Disability within cabinet to advocate the vision (p. 19). DPA, under the more progressive presidency of Paul Gibson, also did a lot of 'behind the scenes' work with the opposition spokesperson on disability issues, Ruth Dyson, in the 12 months leading up to the election. Dyson was subsequently appointed Minister of Disability Issues and charged with developing a disability strategy in 'Partnership with the voluntary sector and with the community of people with disabilities' (*Able Update*, August 1999: 5). A 14-member (nine disabled people) Disability Strategy Sector Reference Group was assembled and delivered the NZDS discussion document. It is intended that the *Strategy* in its final form will act as a blueprint for disability policy and, perhaps more importantly, provide a set of overarching principles to which all policy must adhere. For a government policy document on disability this is quite remarkable insofar as it states that it is clearly based on a social model, focuses on the 'disabling society' (p. 1) and seeks to create a 'non-disabling society' (p. 4) in which disabled people 'are integrated into community life on their own terms' (p. vii). However, whether or not these concepts and aims are included in the final NZDS that is presented to cabinet for adoption remains to be seen.

PART 3: MAORI PERCEPTIONS OF DISABILITY

I began this chapter by arguing that to understand the politics of the disability struggle in Aotoaroa New Zealand, one has to understand our history and culture in light of the Treaty of Waitangi and the relationship between Maori and Pakeha. One has also to understand the way Maori perceive disability and what it means to them. As a Pakeha I am reluctant to speak for Maori, but I can refer to what Maori have written on the subject. Unfortunately little has been written by Maori on disability and what follows has been drawn from three sources so it must be read with caution. As a qualification, I quote from one of those sources, *Maori Concepts of Disability*:

> The research outcome has been the revelation of 'a' Maori world view of disability. This cannot be regarded as 'the' world Maori view of disability, if in fact such a view exists. (Kingi and Bray 2000: 5)

When Jo Kingi asked Maori what the word 'disability' or the concept of disability meant to them, they generally saw it in terms of the effect of colonisation:

> It's disability to have your land taken off you, it's a disability to have your family dissolved and shifted to an urban environment where you've never been before. It's a disability to be told that you can no longer grow your own food so you have to get a job in a system that has been set up by white people for white people.... (Kingi and Bray 2000: 8)

> Maoris are being brainwashed into doing things the Pakeha way – that's disability – it's got to be done the Pakeha way – brainwashed. (*ibid*)

We are disabled in the Pakeha world – in our world we're not. (Kingi and Bray 2000: 21)

Poverty was seen as more disabling than any physical, psychiatric or sensory impairment. Drugs, alcohol and tobacco use by Maori were issues that were also perceived as disabilities by Maori (Kingi and Bray 2000: 12). Policies of assimilation, especially the legislation which made the teaching of te reo Maori (language) in primary schools illegal and which remained in force until 1967 were seen as very disabling. One person spoke of his loss of language as his disability. Most spoke of the process of colonisation and its particular effect on identity and self-worth as a disability:

We have a tendency to think of people in wheelchairs but I think from my understanding, and no doubt others, that disabilities is that people have lost their knowledge of whakapapa [genealogy] and how they are related to whanau, hapu and iwi [family, sub-tribe and tribe]. (Kingi and Bray 2000: 18)

When asked if they thought there was a difference between Maori and Pakeha concepts of disability, many commented on just how different the world views actually are:

Well I think the Maori health view is far more holistic than the pakeha health view – it takes into account the whole being and I believe the pakeha health view separates it – fixes one thing. (Kingi and Bray 2000: 22)

Well I know we are different because we accept people as they are. (*ibid*)

There was no such things as manic-depressives or schizophrenic in Maoridom…. (*ibid*)

A real difficulty with Kingi and Bray's study is that we cannot guage the degree to which it represents the views of disabled Maori as it does not provide a breakdown of its sample in terms of disabled/non-disabled. The 1995 report, *He Anga Whakamana. A Framework for the Delivery of Disability Support Services to Maori,* by Ratima *et al.* is based, however, on a sample of 30 consumers, 24 providers and 13 caregivers, giving confidence that the views contained in the report are those of either disabled Maori or their support workers. The framework for culturally appropriate services developed in *He Anga Whakamana* support Kingi and Bray's findings insofar as they are designed to address not only the effects of impairment but also those of colonisation and assimilation. These services will:

- actively promote opportunities for disabled Maori to participate in both mainstream New Zealand society and in Maori society by providing access to Maori institutions such as marae (meeting house), kohanga reo (language nests), Maori sports teams or culture groups;
- encourage initiative by enabling disabled Maori to develop abilities relating to 'being Maori';
- educate Maori communities not to impose limitations on disabled Maori who are often more ready than the community for participation in community life;
- develop links with Maori institutions which provide a source of identity, self-determination and empowerment;

- provide a workforce which is professionally qualified and competent in enhancing cultural understandings to better equip disabled Maori to meet Maori needs (Ratima *et al.* 1995).

In summary, it is evident that disabled Maori see themselves as Maori first and as disabled people second. This has huge implications for the disability movement in terms of developing a true partnership with Maori if it is to have any relevance for Maori. It is also apparent that while Maori have a different perspective on disability from Pakeha, and additional expectations of what Disability Support Services (DSS) should provide for disabled Maori, there are parallels between Maori perspectives and those of disabled Pakeha who operate from a social model framework. Many Maori see disability as an effect of the colonisation of Aotoaroa whereas many disabled Pakeha see disability as the effect of medical hegemony and the colonising tendencies of the medical professions. Both Maori and Pakeha are seeking *rangatiratanga* in their lives and demand DSS which increase their choices, control and participation in their respective communities. However, Maori and Pakeha experiences of disability diverge as Maori may be subject to multiple oppression within mainstream society (where they are subject to racism) as well as within both the disability and Maori communities. Maori are marginalised in the former when their specific needs and world view are not recognised and catered for, and in the latter when cultural imperatives create dependence. The latter occurs if, for example, Maori communities insist on 'taking care' of their impaired members rather than enabling them to assume more control in their own lives and to participate in their communities (see Ratima *et al.* 1995: 40).

Conclusion

In this chapter I have shown how history and culture have shaped the politics of the disability movement in Aotoaroa New Zealand. At the centre is the Treaty of Waitangi, the foundation document of New Zealand, based on the principles of partnership, participation and protection between the Crown and Maori. More honoured in the breach than in fact, Maori have struggled throughout the past 160 years to have the Crown honour the Treaty and restore their *tino rangatiratanga* via policies of biculturalism and partnership. The Disabled Persons Assembly, the umbrella organisation for disabled people, having not done the intellectual work and, hence, bereft of a clearly articulated structural analysis of disability, was influenced by the principle of partnership and welcomed non-disabled people and service providers as full members. This politics of partnership has subsequently resulted in political compromise and produced a polite, timid and generally apathetic disability movement which seeks approval and acceptance rather than radical change.

In contradistinction, blind people adopted a politics of self-determination and only accept blind or partially blind people in their organisation. They have since won many concessions from the state with the Foundation for the Blind exercising considerable influence over the great majority of decisions made which have affected them in the past 50 years. Also, there have been spin-offs in terms of conscientisation, self-advocacy and blind pride. Clearly, a politics of self-determination has borne more fruit for blind people then the politics of partnership has for DPA and the wider disability community in Aotoaroa New Zealand.

This has profound implications for the disability movement if it is to continue with its politics of partnership. First, it must clearly define what it means by and expects from the notion of 'partnership'. In doing this we have much to learn from Maori in their struggle to have the Treaty honoured in both word and deed and then in the working out of their relationship with the Crown. Many tribes refused to engage with government in its 'practical partnerships' (involving consultation with *iwi* and government agencies over policies of concern) and instead opted for 'a parallel partnership plan' (as adopted by the united tribes of the Bay of Plenty and the Area Health Board) of shared decision making, policy development and service provision for Maori client groups. In other words, two partners working together to achieve mutually acceptable goals (see Durie 1994: 87–8). For the disability movement this means no longer colluding with the state in its endless rounds of consultation over issues about which decisions have already been made; it means ongoing struggle with the state (and service providers) to accept us and include us as respected partners in the creation of a non-disabling society.

Second, for DPA, the example of the Association of the Blind and Partially Sighted raises questions about membership and the nature of the partnership between disabled and non-disabled members, especially service providers. During the writing of this paper this issue was addressed at DPA's biennial conference and it was decided to ballot the membership about investigating four new membership categories: disabled individuals, organisations of disabled people, non-disabled individuals, non-disabled corporates. Only the first two categories would have full voting rights with associate status and no voting rights attending the remaining categories. The outcome of the vote will act as a weathervane for judging the tenor and direction of the struggle in Aotaroa New Zealand.

Parallels have been drawn between the respective struggles of Maori and disabled people. Just as Maori had *tino rangatiratanga* denied and were made subject to British law, disabled people have had their humanity denied and made subject to charity, medical science and welfare. In both instances the outcomes have been the same: a systematic exclusion from participating in the dominant Pakeha society and economy to their fullest ability. It is not surprising, therefore, that many Maori see disability as an effect of colonisation and policies of assimilation; the loss of their land, language and cultural knowledge are the impairments which alienate Maori from what it is to be Maori. It follows that these spiritual and socio-cultural impairments must be addressed by disability support services alongside sensory, physical or psychiatric impairments to enable Maori to participate in both mainstream and Maori society. More importantly, if the disability movement in Aotaroa New Zealand is to have any relevance for Maori it must become truly bicultural. This will mean honouring the Treaty of Waitangi in deed as well as word and developing structures and policies which reflect a true partnership between its *tangata whenua* and *tauiwi* (non-Maori) memberships.

In our struggle for a non-disabling society, further insights can be drawn from the way disability is understood and dealt with in Maori society. These include struggle and inclusion. First, as a consequence of the Crown not honouring the Treaty, the relationship between the two Treaty partners has been very disabling for Maori. But Maori have struggled long and hard to turn this relationship around so that it becomes non-disabling, becomes one of mutual respect and shared decision making. And this struggle is beginning to bear fruit in terms of the settlement of Treaty of Waitangi claims, compensation, policies of biculturalism and the return to *iwi* of *tino rangatiratanga* over their traditional resources and in the implementation of government policy. We can learn from this struggle: the inherent justice of our cause, to not become defeatist, to never give up. Perhaps we need to redirect our struggle for some sort of Treaty with the state to include disabled people as respected partners in all decisions made about us? That the NZDS, *Whakanui Oranga,* does attempt this in a not entirely oblique way (p. iv), is a cause for hope.

Another insight to be drawn from Maori society is the way in which it deals with difference and diversity, with disability: '...we accept people as they are'; '...no such thing as manic-depressives or schizophrenic in Maoridom' (Kingi and Bray 2000: 22). Thus, within Maoridom, individuals identify and are identified first as being or belonging to a particular *iwi* rather than in terms of individual characteristics. Hence, an individual is, say, Tainui, before s/he is a para-plegic, blind etc. In other words, difference and diversity is accepted and included within but subordinate to *iwi* identity, to the collective. This approach to difference and inclusion has implications for not only the disability movement in Aotoaroa New Zealand but for the disability movement worldwide.

Just as the disability movement in Britain is being challenged by the particular issues of women, ethnic minorities, gays and lesbians (see above), so too is it being challenged here. These issues are about being marginalised within the disability movement or being fully included. How DPA responds to this challenge to become a wholly inclusive movement is crucial. Ignore this challenge and it won't go away: it will destroy us. It presents the opportunity, however, for us to become an example to other minority group movements on how to celebrate difference and diversity as opposed to being threatened by it. The trick, however, will be in achieving this without subordinating the political imperative of the social model to those of liberal, identity politics.

Finally, no one promised disabled people that the struggle for change was going to be an easy road to travel. Indeed, it will be a matter of maintaining the heart to 'tell it and think it and speak it and breathe it'; the pride to 'reflect it from the mountains so all souls can see it'; the fearlessness to 'stand on the oceans until we start sinking'; the analysis so that we 'know our song well before we start singing', and the tenacity to keep going because the hard rain of small victories and large setbacks is gonna fall for some time yet.

Questions

- Think about the partnerships you or your group are in and score them in terms of how they are operating, the power relationships between partners, their goals, their effectiveness, what you are gaining/have gained from them personally and how they might be better structured.
- Keeping in mind the experience of the politics of partnership in Aotoaroa New Zealand, which of the following scenarios do you prefer? Disabled people and their organisations:

  a) go it alone in their struggle for a non-disabling society;

  b) enter partnerships with non-disabled individuals and groups in their struggle.

Why do you prefer the scenario you have chosen?

Acknowledgements

I would like to thank Mark Sherry, Maureen West, John Walton and Robyn Munford for their constructive comments on various drafts of this paper. Responsibility for final content, however, rests solely with me.

Notes

1. These have explanatory power in Aotoaroa New Zealand, a former British colony with a population of mostly Anglo-Celtic heritage, a Westminster parliamentary system, a welfare state and a treaty with the indigenous population, the Treaty of Waitangi, giving legitimacy to these circumstances.
2. Defined as 'cultural pluralism characterised by two, rather than several, partners' (Durie 1994: 100) and adopted by all departments of state by 1985. It implies a partnership between the state and local *iwi* in developing and implementing policy with elements of equality and enhanced service delivery.
3. Both Campbell and Oliver (1996) and Oliver and Zarb (1997) stress the crucial importance of doing this if disabled people are to successfully self organise.
4. NZIB became the Royal New Zealand Foundation for the Blind in 1955 and DAB changed its name to the New Zealand Association of the Blind and Partially Blind in 1976.

CHAPTER 9

The process of change and the politics of resistance in educational contexts: the case of disability

Anastasia Vlachou-Balafouti

This chapter is based on the belief that the process of change in education demands inclusion policies to be considered with respect to the larger education policy context. Inclusive policy practices and discourses strike at the heart of the endemic tensions and contradictions inherent within mass education as a whole and this is one of the many reasons of explaining why the process of change towards more inclusive schooling practices has proved to be an extremely complex task.

While 'the only way forward in the struggle for equality for all is through a struggle against *all* forms of discrimination for *all* groups and individuals in society rather than focusing attention on groups identified on the basis of official and institutionalized categorizations' (Armstrong *et al.* 2000: 8), at the same time the notion of 'societal change' for all forms of discrimination can be very abstract and vague. Thus, I will concentrate the analysis of this paper in the area of education for two main reasons:

Firstly, in modern societies

> education is one social context, if not the social context, wherein the tension, the dialogue and the politics of the self and others unfolds. The role that education plays in socialization, in citizenship formation, in making available the intellectual, cultural and recreational heritage of a society, in the provision of the resources of social imagination, and creativity, and in enhancing one's vocational opportunities, all point to the significance of education in shaping both the self and society. (Isaacs 1996: 38; see also Wexler 1992)

Education is an 'enabling good' in the sense that it is required to obtain other social goods, such as income, employment and self-esteem. Discrimination, marginalisation and exclusion from this social context can have direct effects on other contexts, including the formation of 'identity'. From this perspective, schools are important places for the playing out of struggles and conflicts which can only be understood in their wider social context (Armstrong *et al.* 2000). Thus,

> the extent to which schools both contribute to the legitimation and exacerbation of existing inequalities and exclusions, as well as simultaneously challenging those factors within the school/the wider society, is a topic of enormous importance. (Barton and Slee 1999: 6)

Secondly, specifying the context of analysis enables us to identify specific contending socio-political factors that impinge upon the creation of more inclusive practices and at the same time to provide indicators for approaching inclusive education. One such indicator emerges out of the fact that over the last 30 years we have seen that different interest groups struggle over the definition of disability and, as Fulcher (1989: 24) strongly indicates, disability is disputed. This is because much hinges on it politically, socially and economically. Proposing that definitions over disability entail struggles means that disability is political.

Disability and exclusion in a political context

Impairment is a personal trouble and to deny its consequences on people means denying 'the personal experiences of impairment', including the psycho-emotional and psycho-somatic dimension of impairment (see Thomas 1999; Morris 1992c, 1995, 1996). However, what is usually being ignored in most social contexts is that within many of our personal troubles reside compelling public issues (Mills 1963). Mills (1963) has persuasively argued that the challenge is to illuminate the connection between those two. We cannot make any difference at the interpersonal level unless both problems and solutions are enlarged to encompass the conditions that surrounds them (Fullan 1993).

In the area of disability, Thomas (1999) argues that the personal is simultaneously political as the 'micro' is constitutive of the 'macro'. As individuals do not exist except as socially located beings, 'experience' itself speaks of the composition of the social formation and enables us to understand the material, ideological and discursive contexts in which life is lived out. The study of experience can be a very powerful way to understand the world – a precondition for changing it. This proposition of political is different from what Finkelstein (1980, Finkelstein and French 1993) and others have proposed, according to which the emphasis should be on challenging the *social* causes of disability, through a critical examination of the macro-societal structures that create disability. This implies that disabled people experience disability as social restriction, whether or not those restrictions occur as a consequence of attitudinal, ideological, material, architectural and structural barriers, connected with the willingness of society to include or exclude the needs of disabled persons. Both ways of approaching disability raise a series of central issues, relating to the political origins of exclusion.

The personal political stance reminds us that the issue is not that society ignores disabled people but how it takes them into account. One of the most disturbing elements is the absence of the voices of disabled people themselves, even in committees that claim efforts to create more inclusive structures in societal contexts, such as education, employment, health, even in architectural designs. For instance, in 1975 in Greece, a Review Committee was formed for the Organization and Planning of Special Education, directed by the Ministry of Education. The work of this committee was very important considering that historically it has been the first major official attempt to organise the area of special education while the Report produced by this committee was the basis for the first major Legislative Act (1143/1981) concerning the aims, the role and functioning of special education. The membership of the Review Committee, by and large, represented administration, teachers and health professionals mainly psychologists and psychiatrists. Disabled people's voices were absent. The absence of disabled people's voices is a political act that denies access to particular decision-making processes for services that affect first and foremost their lives. This absence can be found in many different contexts (i.e. designing legislation, policies, public buildings, research proposals and/or organising different forms of school settings, classrooms, curricula and methods of teaching). This political act is based on the assumption that disabled people's definitions, opinions, suggestions and experiences are not in any sense valuable. In the area of special education, and more recently in promoting inclusive education, disabled people are excluded from decision-making processes, since professionals assume and at times publicly claim, that only they can legitimately interpret the true nature of 'the problem' or 'need', that only they can speak with authority about what is in the individual's best interests, and that they carry out these responsibilities in a context of 'care', 'treatment' and 'intervention' (see McDonnell 2001). It is indicative that in Greece the main state care facilities concerning disabled children are: *institutions* (day-care centres, long-term care centres), *diagnostic centres* (usually special units in paediatric hospitals), *special education units* (consisting of entire school units or special classes) and *associations* (consisting of parents' leagues with regard to institutions and schools). From the above facilities, the medico-pedagogical diagnostic centres are the only agencies with the official authority to define needs, to categorise children and to indicate what they do consider as 'the appropriate' educational placement. Within this context, expertism is based on

> a particular kind of social *authority*, characteristically deployed around *problems*, exercising a certain *diagnostic* gaze, grounded in a claim to *truth,* asserting technical *efficiency*, and avowing *humane* ethical virtues. (Rose 1999: 86)

It is this presumption of authority that gives exclusionary practices their political dimension as:

a) it does not allow disabled people to have the chance to control aspects of the services affecting their lives and even more it leaves little space to have control over their own self and self-identity; and
b) it implies 'that there can be one "right" answer and that those who raise objections are either whingers or pessimists. This is a dangerous attitude for any society to adopt, as history has repeatedly demonstrated'. (Mortimore 1997 in Barton and Slee 1999: 10)

From this perspective, disability is a political issue and it is fundamentally about unequal social relations and conditions and the ways in which *power* is exercised. In the process of challenging these oppressive power relationships we can realise our (the non-disabled) responsibility by critically examining questions such as how relations of position and power (as a teacher, a doctor, a researcher, a parent, a 'carer', a non-disabled citizen) influence our relations with disabled people by reproducing disablist images and discriminations.

In education, disability has been de-politicised, as the focus has been towards an individualistic approach to the education of children, who have been characterised as having special educational needs. Within the Greek educational context, we have witnessed an extremely strong emphasis on individualism at a number of educational policy-practices: diagnosis, educational evaluation, placements, educational provision, organisation of the class, differentiation at the level of curriculum, notions of excellence, ability and of course notions of failure and disability.

Individualised procedures perpetuate practices which focus on *managing* and *controlling* difference within a system, where promoting homogeneity, competition and selection are the main characteristics. The increasing tendency of developing special classes within Greek ordinary schools (there were only seven such classes only ten years ago, and increased to 602 in 1992) is indicative of a) the strong tendency of medicalisation of the difficulties caused by an underprivileged social and economic background, and b) the dominant efforts to protect the homogeneity and smooth functioning of ordinary classes. Currently, special classes in Greece consist of disabled children, children from socially disadvantaged family environments, immigrant children, 'street'-children, children who are characterised by their teachers as having emotional, behavioural and learning difficulties and children belonging to gypsy communities.

Even though stated and written governmental policies refer to efforts for promoting 'one school for all', at the same time unsupportive teachers refer to their inability to cope with the demands that they have to deal with in an everyday educational setting (Vlachou 1999, 2000).

It seems that, schools have been entrapped at the intersection of society and government policies and are increasingly at a loss to find ways of meeting the demands of both, especially in times of fiscal stringency, when economic rationalism rules social policy formulation and implementation. As we learn from a preliminary study concerning disabled children and their families in Mediterranean countries, conducted by the Greek National Centre for Social Research (1998);

> concerning financing for special education which is the responsibility of the Ministry of Education the available data on the budget show that the budget allotted to Special Education Units corresponds to only 1% of the total budget for education in Greece. (p. 22)

Juggling with funding constraints, schools and teachers have to face a number of practical contradictions and dilemmas as a result of the contradictory educational policy directives of competition and selection on the one hand (Education Act 2525/1997) and a contradicting – quite confusing – notion of inclusion on the other (Education Act 2817/2000). It is important also to mention that teachers have to respond to increasing numbers of children which represent social problems, that are more numerous, more complex and qualitatively different from those of 20 years ago (Vlachou 1997: 199). In particular, in the last two decades Greece has had to face an increasing number of refuges as well as both legal and illegal immigration from countries (i.e. Albania, Yugoslavia) that have gone under tremendous political, social and economic turmoil. If the novelty of the phenomenon is taken into consideration, the presence of immigrant population finds Greek schools and teachers totally unprepared to deal with children of other languages and cultures. Greece, for historical and socio-political reasons, has traditionally been a country exporting human labour. For the same social and economic reasons, Greece has never up to now experienced the presence of 'other' people. Thus, it can be claimed that it has been a country with relatively very high cultural, linguistic and religious homogeneity. The historically constructed relatively high homogeneity has been accompanied by a highly ethnocentric policy concerning ethnic and religious minorities. An assimilation policy was characteristic of education since 1930s. The only exception has been the Moslem minority of mainly Turkish ethnic background, living in the east-northern province of Thrace. For this particular minority education is regulated by international agreements and Greek laws.

The new school populations of children of other languages and cultures have created more complex dilemmas and contradictions that the Greek school has to deal with (Tsiakalos 1999). Research shows that an important part (40 per cent) of in-service nursery and primary school teachers is found to be in disagreement with the official stated ideological goals of school, regretting the loss of the values of the triptych 'fatherland–religion–family', which they consider as the foundation of all education. A majority of 55 per cent of teachers adhere to the new values and practices, and they are open to reforms and modern approaches of teaching, however, they claim that they lack the knowledge and skills necessary to apply other than traditional discipline and other than memory exercises. A minority of 5 per cent among teachers are facing critically the educational reality and try to innovate their teaching approaches (Frederikou and Folerou 1991). The above example indicates that the politics of exclusion and inclusion extends well beyond disability issues and has little to do with 'impairments'. Even in cases where teachers are aware of what constitutes 'good practice' under the increasingly complex conditions of their work, 'good practice for *all* children' will remain on its rhetorical basis. At the same time, an emphasis on only the social and moral benefits of inclusion as a way of giving voice to a charitable type of humanism is likely to hinder the translation of this moral commitment into an assertion of rights.

Rights and tensions

Over the last 30 years, the notion of 'equal opportunities' based on statements of 'human rights' have had a high profile both at the level of government policies and at the level of institutions in many westernised countries, including Greece. Further, there are numerous declarations of international organisations concerning the issue of human rights. Just to name some we have: 'The Declaration of Children's Rights' (1386/1959); 'The Declaration of The Rights of Mentally Disabled People' (2856/1971); 'The Declaration of Disabled People's Rights' (3447/1975); 'The Declaration of SUNBERG for Disabled People' (1981); 'The Salamanga Declaration for Special/Inclusive Education' (1994) and so on. The numerous declarations of the rights of disabled people mean that there was and still is a violation of rights for specific groups of people, and in this case violation of disabled people's rights. On the one hand, declarations may create conditions for policy practices (i.e. legislation) but they do not determine them. On the other hand, the notion of 'rights' seems to be highly problematic in the way it has been used by the stated, written and enacted policies and the contradictions that this triptych entails.

Fulcher (2001) indicates that the idea of human rights can be deployed in struggles at whatever level, but the outcome of these struggles cannot be guaranteed. She goes further by stating that the attempt to challenge the politics of needs and exclusion via a discourse on rights has failed.

Cooney (1995, in McDonnell 2001) argues that if statements of rights and entitlements are to be meaningful they must be enforceable and must be underwritten by appropriate sanctions if they are breached.

However, as Armstrong *et al.* (2000) point out, rights are being approached in such an abstract-ethical way that they are in danger of remaining at the level of rhetoric:

Whilst [the concept of human rights is being] articulated as an abstract principle it is limited in its impact, and in particular may be constrained within the bounds of an ethical critique of exclusion which offers no strategies for bringing about change... The language of rights may obscure their political origin. Through their abstraction from real historical and social contexts, 'rights' may be represented as 'given' rather than as secured through a continuous struggles between contending social factors. (Armstrong et al. 2000: 9)

This is particularly true of the rights of disabled people in the context of education. An official discourse on rights for promoting inclusive education has failed to address the inherent tensions within dilemmatic situations and the inevitable instability of attempted resolutions of those dilemmas that both teachers and pupils have to deal with in specific contexts (Clark *et al.* 1995).

Clark and others (Clark *et al.* 1999), by using a case study of an apparently inclusive school in Britain, have so powerfully demonstrated, that schools are characterised by a number of complex dilemmas:

Mass (let alone universal) education systems seek to reconcile the essentially individualized processes and outcomes of learning on the one hand, and the delivery of 'education' as a social good in a universal form, that is common to all learners, on the other hand. This contradiction generates a series of dilemmas: how to devise a common curriculum which meets individual needs; how to resource all learners equally while responding to their individual characteristics differently; and how to develop individual autonomy while inducing learners into common social values and norms? (p. 46)

We need also to remind ourselves that the school was largely a 19th-century invention sharing many characteristics with workhouses, factories and prisons, and was essentially about a large number of inmates being controlled by a small number of supervisors (see Lawton 1997). Lawton (1997) questions whether schools have changed enough to meet current needs and describes schools as being 'wracked' with contradictory aims.

These contradictions, tensions and dilemmas become more acute as differences between learners become more marked and begin to require resolutions at all levels of the education system. As Clark and others illustrate (Clark *et al.* 1999) teachers in their endeavour to promote more inclusive practices can identify a number of such tensions:

They would like to work in a mixed-ability groups, but the pressures of the curriculum and raising achievement push them towards ability grouping; They would like to accept all children and young people into the school, but some students are too problematic for them to work with effectively; They are committed to in-class support as a major plank of their inclusion strategy, but its practical difficulties drive them towards withdrawal... (pp. 45–6).

The following example given by Tilstone and Rose (2001) indicates the complexity of the issues involved even in the cases where it is assumed that a consensus of the rights of disabled people to mainstream education has been gained:

Teachers are increasingly expressing the need for practical advice on the management of pupils with complex needs in their classrooms and whilst a consensus about the rights of pupils with special needs to be educated alongside their peers is being gained, there remains an uncertainty about the ways in which this may best be achieved. (p. 9)

Within an inclusive discourse, assertions for the rights of disabled people to equal opportunities can have meaning only when they:

a) link the project of inclusion to wider educational dilemmas and contradictions;
b) challenge the specific conditions, practices and relations that discriminate and exclude certain groups of people within different contexts; and
c) are related to strategies for change in terms of creating these specific conditions, practices and relations that are necessary for the promotion of a more inclusive society.

Thus, as Clark *et al.* (1999) argue:

we should begin to see inclusion as a resolution of dilemmas which extend well beyond the boundaries of traditional special education and are endemic within mass education as a whole. The dilemmas generated by diversity do not arise simply in respect to students with 'disabilities' or 'special educational needs'. Rather they point to fundamental issues of values and purposes in mass education systems. The 'ghettoization' of inclusion as a disability or special education issue is a missed opportunity to address these issues. (p. 48)

Every attempt to promote 'effective schools for all' (Ainscow 1991, 1995, 1999) should be engaged with the tensions created within and by these existing structures of thought and (policy) practices that render education contradictory in its nature and structure. At the same time, however, we cannot expect to solve problems within existing structures of thought and practices (Branson and Miller 1989). The experience of integration illustrates the dead-ends that follow efforts to implement – or better to 'fit' – new and simultaneously complex ideas within unchanged structures. Such practices have led to further political, ideological and practical contradictions and confusions and to the adoption of systems which can segregate children within a mainstream school by creating new forms of oppression. In Greece, placing pupils in mainstream schools, where they need to fit into existing inflexible curricula and teaching practices, often without any support, has led to an extreme form of marginalisation. Currently, to compensate with the lack of specialised teaching personnel there is a great emphasis on specialisation and the development of a strong network of special teachers and other specialised personnel within ordinary schools. Even though there is a need for further support, we must remind ourselves that placing pupils in mainstream schools, where they need to fit into existing practices, often requires one-to-one sessions with a support/special teacher for most of the day, which tends to segregate and isolate them from the rest of the class (Farell 1997). As Tilstone and Rose (2001) point out:

such systems may in fact be seen to create dependencies, as well as drawing attention to the inability of a pupil to function adequately alongside his or her peers. We may also question the notion that any child should spend the entire school day with a personal 'minder' encroaching upon their personal space, and preventing them from behaving in the same ways as other pupils in the class.

A strong emphasis on specialisation means that students 'with special educational needs' will become the subject of a uniquely rigorous and concentrated professional 'gaze' (see McDonnell 2001), they will be 'marked as "cases"' (Foucault 1977) and will be the subjects of 'perpetual surveillance throughout the remainder of their school career and beyond (Allan 1999). Such individualistic dependency-oriented practices leave little space for societal and educational changes.

Educational policies and dominant ideological formations

The analysis of policies concerning education, including integration, indicates that there are particular predominant ideologies and conceptual frameworks which have been taken to be unproblematic. These ideologies are so deeply embedded in social consciousness generally that they become 'facts'. In other words, they become naturalised. For instance, in Greece, according to the Law number 1566, chapter I, number 32(2):

> Individuals with special needs are considered those who, due to physical, mental or social causes appear to suffer from retardation, disabilities or disorders of their general psychosomatic condition or in their different functions and to a degree that it is difficult or seriously impeded for them to attend the general and professional education, to participate in the labour process and to adjust and be accepted by their social environment. (*Government Gazette*, Athens 30 September 1985, vol. I, No. 167)

Thus, the underlying ideology is that impairment is the direct cause of disability and social exclusion, without any consideration of the relative nature of 'special needs' and the importance of socio-political factors that construct the mechanisms of exclusion. If these ideologies are not recognised and transformed, segregative relations within education will be reproduced even under well-resourced administrative structures and pedagogical practices which set out to be reforming and attempt to be more 'inclusive'. We have numerous examples that demonstrate the above. For instance, as politics shift the terms deployed shift as well. Thus, in Greece there has been a shift in terminology. The terms 'handicapped or abnormal children' were replaced by terms such as 'children with developmental disabilities' or 'children with particular abilities', with the intention to express the potential of children rather than their limitations.

However, a shift in terminology without a shift in the ideological and educational policy-practices that render school exclusionary in its nature and structure will bear little impact on promoting more inclusive school communities. It seems that most educational policy-practices are underpinned by a number of implicit ideological perspectives. As McDonnell (2001) and Drudy and Lynch (1993) so powerfully have shown, the three most prominent perspectives are:

firstly, a particular conception of society itself which has been identified as consensualism; secondly, a particular conception of the individual which has been referred to as essentialism, and thirdly, a particular conception of the relationship between the individual and society which has been identified as meritocratic individualism. (McDonnell 2001: 2)

In the emerging era of educational transformation (in both 'developed' and 'developing' countries) we witness a fourth perspective which can be identified as market thinking or economic rationalism. McDonnell's (2001) reference to the above three most prominent perspectives will be used as analytical tools in the following discussion, as they provide the basis for identifying, analysing and contextualising some of the issues that we have to engage with in the process for change.

Consensualism

Consensualism represents society as an undifferentiated whole and assumes that there is a general agreement about what constitutes the public or collective interest (McDonnell 2001). For instance, the language of economic rationalism has no necessary content or substance. Terms such as cost-effective, efficiency, objective, goal, performance, performance indicator are abstract terms. However, in a consensualist context, those who deploy the language of economic rationalism present these abstract terms as though there are no dilemmas about what these terms might mean, as though everyone agrees on particular goals (see Fulcher 2001).

In the context of everyday educational practices, consensualism takes the form of 'common-sense logic'. According to this logic, it is common sense that disability is a personal tragedy in the same way as it is common sense that some groups of children are uneducable. In these terms, it is again common sense that disabled children cannot be educated in ordinary schools, due to their inability to respond to the demands of an ordinary environment. From this perspective special schooling is essential in order to provide *the type* of education these children need. Within the Greek educational context, however, it is often forgotten that special schooling might not be the 'right' type of education for disabled children since, as we are informed by the Information Bulletin of the Directorate of Special Education, Ministry of Education (1994), to date there have not been developed any specific educational programmes for disabled children attending special schools. Therefore, the teachers, who work at special schools, try to adjust the official programmes, without any support, to the needs and abilities of their students. This problem becomes even more acute with the secondary special education programmes where teachers are obliged to teach the one-third of the regular curriculum which is characterised as strongly subject-oriented and very abstract in its structure. Additionally, the increasing trend of establishing more special classes in ordinary schools is based on a 'common-sense' belief that this is the best way for promoting the socialisation and integration of all students. It is usually forgotten that, up to now, we do not have any data concerning the effects of special classes on the cognitive, social, emotional and academic development of the child. It is also forgotten that, very often, placement in special classes takes place on the basis of the subjective unofficial criteria used by the ordinary teacher while even today, it is not yet clear what makes special classes so 'special' apart from the fact that they consist of a very small number of students and that they allow the smooth functioning of the ordinary classes.

Questions of 'Who has the power to create definitions with "sticability"?' (Abberley 1989: 57), 'Who is involved in the agreement and in what basis?', 'Who defines interests and for whom?', 'Why some are considered eligible to define interests and others are not?', and in any case 'For whose best interest?' are not being seriously addressed.

The perspective of consensualism through the language of policy principles remain silent on its politics and morality. It also remains silent on the struggles of different interest groups to promote their objectives within unequal power relationships. It claims consensus when in fact every policy meaning is contested, complex, is made at various levels and by different actors, involving action and conflicts (Fulcher 1989, 1993) For instance, the formation of the current Act 2817/2000 concerning the Education of Persons with Special Educational Needs involved serious conflicts among different interest groups; it took five years before being submitted to the Greek Parliament and at the end it was an effort to compromise different conflicting interests among different groups surrounding the area of special education. However, the Act was presented as a 'consensus' regarding the meaning, aims and functions of special education without any official reference to the politics involved in forming policies. This is a serious [political] omission as it allows little space for understanding the complexity of issues involved in education.

In reality, it is due to lack of consensus and the existence of conflicts as well as efforts to resolve conflicts and tensions that create space for change. Efforts towards the creation of more inclusive social contexts must resist consensualist ideologies even if that means that:

> we should be prepared both to commit ourselves to what seems the best option at a particular time (and inclusion has some claims to this status) and be prepared to engage in the critical deconstruction of that option, so that some 'better' alternative may emerge. (Clark *et al.* 1999: 48)

Essentialism

Essentialism, defines individuals in terms of attributes which they are deemed to possess in greater or lesser amounts (McDonnell 2001). The most valuable attributes are the ones that are considered to be essential to our culture. It is assumed that such attributes are formulable and should be taught to all alike by certain time-tested methods. Since both schools (including teachers) and society are steeped in this assumption the essentialist perspective has dominated different educational policies and practices. Essentialist ideology has created a number of dilemmas and tensions as it responds to multiple differences through the language and practices of sameness.

For instance, the Greek educational system is very centralised. That means, that there are no flexible teaching materials. School textbooks are written according to a strict application of the curriculum which is developed by the Ministry of Education and becomes a law of the state. There is one single textbook for each course, identical for all the schools of the country, including special schools, which is distributed to the children free of charge, and a corresponding manual for the teacher. Teaching methods and the organisation of the class are still very traditional. Pupils sit in rows from primary school. Teachers are mainly teaching by narrating knowledge they are supposed to transmit, and by examining through questioning the pupils. The main source of knowledge is the school textbook. There is a lot of emphasis on rote memory, and less emphasis on comprehension, thus, excluding a critical approach to different kinds of knowledge (Fragoudaki, unpublished paper). The above are relevant to the understanding of how Greek teachers conceive of 'normal' school procedures and methods of teaching. Teachers of both primary and secondary school perceive the school class as a homogeneous group of pupils and are both untrained and even unwilling to deal without support with individuals considered to be different. For instance, as Fragoudaki (1987) showed, teachers do not recognise (because they have never been taught so) the existence of local and social dialects of Greek, which differ in various degrees from the phonological and grammatical structure of the school linguistic norm. This attitude in conjunction with the fact that writing and reading is taught through textbooks (written in the standard linguistic norm) results in an appropriate differentiation in pupils as to the speed with which they learn how to read and write. Since the difference in maternal language of the pupils that are natural speakers of local or social dialects is not acknowledged, these pupils are classified as having 'learning difficulties', and are often through their placement in 'special classes' oriented towards general school failure.

It is even more difficult for teachers to face new phenomena such as the new school populations of children of other languages and cultures as well as the complexities originating from promoting inclusive education in terms of cognitive differences. Even though Greek teachers have a greater degree of autonomy, compared to teachers of other European countries (i.e. Britain), in terms of adjusting the official curriculum to children's needs and abilities, they feel that they lack the necessary skills.

The new law (June 1996) on intercultural education is only starting to organise a new approach of viewing all school classes as non-homogeneous entities, and searching pedagogical methods and teaching techniques for a response to the heterogeneity of the needs presented in the class. At the same time, in-service training programmes on new teaching approaches and pedagogical methods are starting to be experimented with. For instance, a very interesting programme called 'Melina' has been addressed to primary school teachers in order to help them apply arts in the service of knowledge.

However, pedagogical methods and teaching techniques for responding to differences impinge upon the cultural context of education in which 'ability' has been the most valued attribute. Ability implies normality and in education there seems to be an overriding attachment to normality: normality is being perceived as an attribute that exists and can be defined. Children are valued not on the basis of their difference, and of who they are, but rather on their struggle to become the same as the majority of the other children: to become 'as normal as possible' or to be viewed as 'normal'. That struggle, in itself, can be debilitating and frustrating, creating additional disadvantages to those already marginalised within the system.

Where the concept of 'inclusion' differs significantly from the concept of 'integration' is 'in its shift of emphasis from the individuals' efforts to integrate themselves into the mainstream culture to the institutions' efforts to create a climate of receptivity, flexibility and sensitivity' (Corbett 1999: 59).

The social conditions and discourses that reconstruct difference as disadvantage have been challenged along with the social relations of a professional practice which reinforces disabling identities through the ideology of 'care' and 'treatment' (Abberley 1992; Barnes 1992).

However, at the level of many social organisations, there seems to be a continuous stubbornness in understanding that there are particular relations and practices that legitimise discrimination via a deficient perspective to difference. As Morris (1991) argues:

> ...the non disabled world assumes that we wish to be normal or treated as if we were. From this follows the view that it is progressive and liberating to ignore our differences because these differences have such negative meanings for disabled people. But we are different. (pp. 16–17)

The stubbornness on the perpetuation of deficient approaches to difference implies that other, more prevailing, interests-at-hand are at stake. The notion of interest-at-hand is important for understanding 'how priorities are perceived as classroom processes evolve' (Woods 1981: 283). For instance, educational practitioners often vacillate between an ideology of valuing difference, a liberal humanist ideology of tolerating difference and a prevailing practical perception which demands conformity.

Conformity is a key interest-at-hand in the context of education and it is part of a regulatory discourse involving power and control on the part of professionals and government agencies (Slee 1995). Children are supposed to be liberated by education but they are also compelled to attend school (Lawton 1997). Attending school means conforming within a particular set of relations and practices which are connected with the role of schooling to induce learners into common (dominant) social values and norms which very often contradicts the other role of schooling: that of developing individual autonomy. Lack of conformity is a potential threat to systems which base their functioning on multiple ruling practices.

Within an increasingly competitive and instrumentally led system of learning two of the most basic interdependent sub-roles of teaching are negotiating discipline and imparting particular types of information. These sub-roles are stressed at national policies and continue to be constituted in and by the practices of schooling. Thus, conformity to particular notions of discipline and cognitive ability are reinforced to become of high priority in everyday educational practice.

This emphasis on conformity affects first and foremost those groups of children who may not share the dominant value systems (immigrant children's school experiences can be revealing on such affects). In the area of integration, this strong emphasis on conformity can be tyrannical for the so-called disabled or children with special needs. In practical terms, that means that disabled children have to conform to environments that have been designed without taking seriously into consideration their needs. Within 'a cyclical process, children who are already experiencing discrimination and disadvantage in many forms encounter further practices of exclusion and marginalization within the school situation' (Barton and Slee 1999: 6).

In addition, conformity in education is a very restricted and restrictive parameter, as it is strongly related to a very narrow essentialist sense in which definitions such as 'high ability' and 'low ability' are understood. Schools have not been designed to accommodate multiple intelligence as they value certain forms of competence over others. As Mc Donnell (2001) points:

> The special needs label is applied on the basis of a very narrow definition of 'ability'. As a result, those other talents and abilities which are important in everyday life, but which fall outside this definition, are devalued and marginalized. Secondly, pupils who are believed not

to possess the required abilities, in the required amounts, at the required age, are expected to have limited educational and career prospects. Thirdly, an essentialist outlook provides a convenient device for policy makers and practitioners in education to rationalize failure and underachievement in the student population: lack of success can too easily be attributed to the individual limitations and incapacities of the pupil. (p. 12)

The essentialist ideologies legitimise and are being legitimised by clinical understanding of difference and a discourse of professional expertism; which in turn have been consistently used for securing conformity practices. These two discourses exert a pervasive influence on almost every educational practice such as how pupils are defined, where they should be educated, how they should be treated and by whom, how educational programmes are designed and implemented, and which educational outcomes are evaluated. For instance, in Greece for the last decade the most dominant demands for responding to diversity refer to more extensive clinical practices, greater number of experts and further training and professional development for experts already in the field.

Meritocratic individualism and economic rationalism

Essentialist assumptions are further legitimised by the way meritocratic individualism has been used in an era of economic rationalism. Meritocratic individualism has a profound influence in education. This perspective is based on the assumption that all pupils have equal rights and entitlements in the education system. According to the Greek Constitutional Law (1974):

Every Greek has the right to free of charge public education … The State encourages and promotes the gifted students as well as those who need assistance and special protection in correspondence to their different abilities. (art.16, para. 4)

Despite stated meritocracy, differentiating between people has become increasingly significant as a basis for entitlement and disentitlement. In the area of disability, social inequalities have been justified on the basis of biological inequalities. This can partly explain why the language of entitlements and rights has not been officially based within a context of discrimination. For instance, in regards to ethnic equality, the language of entitlements and rights in Greece have emerged within a context of racism in education and other areas such as employment and health services. In regards to gender equality, the language of rights and entitlements emerged out of acknowledging the existence of gender bias in the educational system even though still there is pronounced gender inequality as to the way educational success is been actualised as there is a comparatively very low percentage of women in the total active population (27 per cent) which affects the economic independence of the female gender. However, in the area of disability, the language of rights, regardless of the struggles of disabled people and their organisations, has remained at the level of a 'benevolent humanitarianism'. Since no structural biases were assumed in relation to disability and education, the official discourse on rights has been restricted around issues of the distribution of scarce resources in a context of needs and deficiencies. This socio-political phenomenon is not a characteristic of Greek society alone. As Barton (2001) argues, by locating the source of the problems within an individualised deficit-model of the person, a powerful legitimation for social inequality and the limiting of entitlements became established (see also Tomlinson 1985).

Merit, worth and rewards in education have been directly connected with an extremely narrowed understanding of individual success. Those who are successful deserve rewarding. Despite the questionable definitions of measurement procedures of intelligence, IQ and other national/norm-based testing procedures have been excessively used for legitimising the limiting of entitlements (see also Troyna and Vincent 1996). Over the last two decades, within the Greek context, we have witnessed an increasing tendency of an extensive use of different IQ and personality tests which are basically a replica of well-known American Tests, adjusted to the Greek culture. Fears are expressed that via the newly introduced Diagnostic, Evaluation and Support Centres (Act 2817/2000) entitlements to educational services will not be provided on the basis of rights of citizenship but on the basis of professional authority who, based upon their 'rational' application of knowledge, and the application of tests, will determine what is in the 'best interest' of the pupil (special issue of the journal *Issues of Special Education* 2000: 79). However, as Armstrong *et al.* (1999) illustrate, rationality in decision making often remains constrained within boundaries determined by the concerns and value-bases of professionals and of the institutions which they service. Thus, educational decisions may be influenced by institutional assumptions that are incongruent with the child's needs resulting in discriminatory practices. Further, where funding and resources are restricted and contested, the issue of entitlement can become one of fighting for individual wants rather than community needs (Corbett 1998). Questions such as how institutional constraints influence efforts to resource all learners equally while responding to their individual characteristics are of immense importance in understanding the manner in which 'entitlements' to education have been conceived and implemented.

In an era of economic rationalism, based on market forces, meritocratic individualism will be further reinforced in the process of justifying failure. Economic rationalism – that habit of thought which excludes consideration of social issues – (see Fulcher 2001) assumes:

> benign quality to the selective precision of the market as it randomly picks and chooses according to 'natural talent' ... Competition as the instrument of selection will include and it will exclude. Markets are thus claimed to be the most efficient mode for allocating scarce resources, more responsive to individual needs. (Barton and Slee 1999: 5)

Terms such as effective, efficient, cost-effective, choice, opportunity, performance, performance indicators, outcomes and excellence have influenced the shift from the classical meaning of the idea of the citizen to the notion of the 'active citizen' (see Fulcher 2001). The active citizen having choices and opportunities (ironies abound) will be accountable for his/her own failure. There is a danger that the child/individual will be represented either as a 'wrongdoer' or as the victim of his or her own failure to adjust to the conditions of competition and selection through which the organisation of rewards and opportunities is managed (Armstrong *et al.* 1999). Contradictions between the political ideology of 'opportunity' in the marketplace and the centralisation of economic power that has marked the globalisation of these markets will create conditions in which the social and economic exclusion of growing numbers of people will be legitimated by reference to their supposed personal inadequacies and lack of marketable skills (Tomlinson 1988).

Conclusion

This chapter has been an attempt to show that the politics of change towards the creation of more inclusive educational contexts necessitate a serious engagement with the specific policies that discriminate and marginalise different groups of people. However, as it was indicated, policies do not exist in a vacuum; they reflect underlying ideologies and assumptions that affect everyday educational practices. The strong emphasis on essentialist ideologies create restrictive practices of understanding and responding to notions of 'ability', 'difference' and 'normality' while the politics of 'meritocratic individualism' mask the structural biases of creating disability, failure and exclusion.

It was also argued that the politics of exclusion and inclusion extend well beyond disability issues and have little to do with 'impairments'. In particular, inclusion refers to the fundamental issues of values and purposes in mass education systems and thus it is about the way ordinary education responds to the problems, tensions and complexities that emerge out of the ongoing and more complex challenges that the school has to face. Hargreaves (1994) has shown, in a very powerful way, some of the complexities involved in education:

> the fundamental problem [in education] is to be found in a confrontation between two powerful forces. On the one hand, there is an increasingly postindustrial, postmodern world, characterized by accelerating change, intense compression of time and space, cultural diversity, technological complexity, national insecurity and scientific uncertainty. Against this, stands a modernistic, monolithic school system, that continues to pursue deeply anachronistic purposes within opaque and inflexible structures. Sometimes school systems actively try to respond with seriousness and sincerity, but they do so with an administrative apparatus, that is cumbersome and unwieldy. Educationally, this central struggle presents itself in a number of ways. (pp. 3–4)

Inclusion is a great and an extremely difficult struggle/challenge for both schools and society. It involves the way different societies secure the implementation of all citizens' rights at all levels, including education. Official assertions for equality and rights to education cannot be conceived as a matter of managing, in a cost-efficient way, the distribution of extra resources to the 'needy'. When this is the case, demands for responding to diversity refer mainly to effective management, more clinical practices, greater number of experts and further professional development for experts already in the field. It is indicative that the new legislation Act of 2817/2000 concerning special education emphasised that the education of disabled people is a matter of rights but at the same time recommended limited forms of integration, and a strong emphasis on normalisation and expertism. The dominant discursive practices have failed to acknowledge that unsupportive teachers, inflexible curricula, conflicting and contradictory educational aims, a political pre-occupation for applying marketing ideologies to education as well as the medicalisation of social difficulties and difference are some of the issues that we have to struggle with in the process of creating more effectively inclusive school communities. Thus, the struggle for promoting inclusive education needs to be intensified as the most outstanding challenges that the school has failed to consider is: a) How educational institutions can create a climate of receptivity, flexibility and responsiveness to difference; and b) What are the necessary strategies for securing the rights of different groups of people through a continuous struggle between contending social factors?

Given that inclusion is a rather recent concept in education and has emerged from historical processes which are of course ongoing (Clark *et al.* 1999), we still have a huge task in front of us.

Questions

- How can inclusive education be used as a means for creating more responsive curricula to difference?
- Explore some of the political, social and economical issues that hinge on defining disability as a political issue.

CHAPTER 10

Inclusive education, politics and the struggle for change

Simone Aspis

Introduction

This chapter will look at why and what disabled young people need to know so that they can be effective with campaigning for inclusive education. In particular disabled young people need to be supported to understand how they are labelled as having learning difficulties and the contradictions between their own and professionals' assessments value put upon their achievements. This enables disabled young people to question the role of assessments and how they are used to legislate and legitimate segregated education or how learning takes place in a mainstream school environment. Understanding assessment models and learning outcomes will enable readers to consider possible changes so that inclusive education for disabled children with learning difficulties is being promoted within the inclusive education model.

Traditionally parents have taken on the struggle for inclusive education both on an individual and collective level. Parents were the ones who have undertaken the advocacy role on behalf of their children. This may include taking appropriate legal action. While parents are active in this way, a question must be asked on what happens to the children during the process? Many parents with good intent often believe it's best to leave children out of the campaign because of the stress that such struggle involves. However, leaving children out of the struggle may have long-term affect especially where they do not have the chance to develop and practice speaking up in an environment where their views could be supported. Thus, what children will be capable of doesn't just depend on their age and abilities. It also depends on their experience – what they know and can do already and how confident they are and how much encouragement and support they receive. To be able to be involved in decision making from the earliest appropriate age they need the opportunity to learn, within the safety of their home, how to exercise their rights.

What parents do not always appreciate is that disabled children with learning difficulties are already aware of being treated unfairly and if left unsupported may internalise the oppression which can be very damaging to their self-esteem and self-identity. So, disabled children must be supported to value their own intellectual ability and to be helped to understand the contradictions between their own and society's idea of what being 'clever' means. This involves being critical of government and schools, especially over the strong emphasis on assessment-led learning. It is the schools who are failing to meet the needs of disabled children.

Disabled children are learning to speak up about inclusive education on both an individual and collective basis. David McKibben is a member of Young and Powerful which is a young people's group campaigning for inclusive education. He was one of the delegation which delivered a letter to the Prime Minister, Tony Blair, at 10 Downing Street, during the first National Day of Action for Inclusive Education. Part of the letter expresses the deep concerns of the group:

> We are a group of disabled and non-disabled young people and supporters who believe we should all have the right to go to our local mainstream school. We feel that children in special schools miss out on a decent academic and social education, and those in mainstream schools, who hardly ever see disabled people, miss out on the opportunity to learn about and appreciate differences, rather than only seeing disabled people through the patronising view of the media.
>
> We feel we deserve each other's friendship and that the segregated education system denies us the chance to be together and see each other for what we really are.
>
> We ask <u>YOU</u> to put an end to compulsory segregation by changing the law.
>
> <u>WE</u> want to be together. (Young and Powerful 1998a)

These concerns were expressed more fully by Young and Powerful (1998b) who were asked to write up an action plan and send it to the Department for Education and Employment which highlights what the barriers to inclusion are and the need for them to be removed. The plan included the following.

Principles

1. Inclusive education is education that disabled and non-disabled children can be part of with the help they need and the right support for their needs.
2. All children, disabled and non-disabled, should be in mainstream schools with their friends, if disabled children and their parents want to be. If they and their parents want a special school they should be able to choose it. We believe that, once inclusion is working properly, very few will choose special schools.
3. We want a *choice* of school for every child and a school with high-standards of education for every child.
4. Non-disabled children and adults benefit from the presence of disabled children. It broadens their experience and gets them used to disabled people being around and so cuts down on prejudice and discrimination both in school and in later adult life.
5. This applies to physically disabled children, deaf children or blind children, children with learning difficulties and children with behaviour problems. The difference is we need different sorts of support.
6. Physically disabled children need to have access to the building, toilets and classrooms including different activities in the curriculum and personal assistance with certain tasks. The young person needs to be in control of this personal assistance.
7. Blind and deaf children need access to different forms of communication – Braille or BSL. Children who can not talk should be taught to use talkers, symbols or computers to communicate.

8. Children with learning difficulties should be given appropriate work at the right speed for them. Everyone learns at different speeds.

9. Children with behaviour problems need extra support staff and a place to go where people will listen to them when they cannot cope in the class.

What is necessary to change an ordinary school into an inclusive school?

1. There should be a ten-year plan to make all schools accessible.

2. There should be an access task force under the New Deal so unemployed young people can learn the skills of making schools accessible. This task force should be able to make an ordinary school accessible in three months when a disabled child wants to go there.

3. Bullying policies should include bullying of disabled people. All the children at the school should be involved in making the policy work and learning to treat each other with respect.

4. Teachers and other staff at the school should get training from young disabled people and Disability Equality Trainers.

5. Parents of disabled children not in school yet or transferring should be able to talk to young disabled people in inclusive schools about why it is important for their children to go to mainstream schools.

6. School trips should be planned to go to places that the whole class can get round. The government should force leisure places to be accessible.

7. Adjustable furniture and equipment should be provided so disabled children can do practical work in science, technology, art and music.

8. Extra exam boards should allow disabled children to take the exam and submit course work even where they have to direct their learning support assistant to physically do it for them. Alternative ways should be found for disabled children to take part. They should be marked on their thinking and not their disability.

9. The school should be given the resources to give disabled children all the help they need.

10. Disabled children should have a say in who is to be their learning support assistant as they often have to give intimate personal assistance. This will be good practice for when we are older and have to employ personal assistants under direct payments.

11. Disabled children should be allowed to choose their friends to go with them in the lift, to lunch or go to SEN resource rooms.

12. SEN teachers should not be able to keep disabled children separated from non-disabled children in the school.

13. All new and trainee teachers should get disability equality training on inclusion and hear groups of children like Young And Powerful talk about their experiences.

14. Children should have rights that are separate to their parents.

15. The government should set up an advisory group of disabled children and their non-disabled friends. Some adults, who act as our facilitators, but we must be able to control what they say in our name (pp. 8–9).

Each of these points do deserve to be seriously engaged with and provide a stimulus for debate and discussion.

Disabled children do express strong preferences over their educational provision, which may or may not be in line with parents' thinking. One of the important points that Young And Powerful have advocated for is that disabled children should have *rights separate* from their parents within the Education Law.

Another very good reason why disabled children should have the legal right to attend a mainstream school is so that those in foster care are protected against local authorities' decisions to place them in a special school against their wishes. These disabled children must enjoy the same legal protection as other children who could be discriminated against on the grounds of gender or race.

Inclusive education

Having the legal right to attend a mainstream school does not mean that disabled children will be included and valued for what they bring to the learning process. There has been much confusion over what is meant by disabled children being truly included in an ordinary school. This is not just related to the physical environment where disabled children are expected to be as mobile as possible without the school buildings being changed or a lack of provision of personal assistants, communication aids, Braille and computer equipment. It is also significantly about how disabled children are valued as learners by non-disabled people. This is what Micheleine Mason (1997) had in mind when she maintained:

> Inclusion – 'All For One and One For All' – A philosophy which views diversity of strengths, abilities and needs as natural and desirable, bringing to any community the opportunity to respond in ways which lead to learning and growth for the whole community, and giving each and every member a valued role. Inclusion requires the restructuring of schools and communities.

Inclusive education should create opportunities for all learners to work together. This requires a recognition that learning is enhanced when individuals of different abilities, skills and aspirations can work together in a joint enterprise. The educational system has a responsibility to create learning environments and provide teachers who are skilled at creating ways in which all contributions are recognised as being of value. The effort of each learner is recognised as being of an equal challenge regardless of the particular area of curriculum in which they are working. It is crucial that we appreciate that fundamental to such a philosophy is the recognition that all learners will require different forms of support at different times of their study. Thus, the educational system should have a responsibility of devising the most effective and appropriate form of support for each individual.

The Duke of Edinburgh Award is an example of a scheme which encourages an approach in which young people are supported to set their own goals and this includes their own self-development plan. The philosophy of the scheme as outlined by HRH Prince Philip (1990) in the Handbook is viewed as:

... neither very profound nor very complicated. It is simply this: a civilized society depends upon the freedom, responsibility, intelligence and standard of behaviour of its individual members, and if society is to continue to be civilized, each succeeding generation must learn to value these qualities and standards ... Above all, it depends on a willingness amongst younger generations to find out for themselves the factors which contribute to freedom, responsibility, intelligence and standards of behaviour. These are all rather abstract concepts. The scheme ... has attempted to bring them down to earth; to give individual young people the opportunity to discover these ideas for themselves through a graduated programme of experience. (p. 9)

Young people are encouraged to keep an account of what they achieve through helping them to define their own achievements and value their own learning. Different levels of skills can be developed and appreciated. For example, Jenny was one of a group of participants who took part in an environmental project in a local park adjacent to their school. In conjunction with the cleansing department, the group undertook to collect and remove litter from the park. A photographic diary of the project was also produced.

This is an example of an approach to collaborative and individual learning that could contribute to the struggle for a more inclusive approach to learning and a more enabling experience of assessment.

A Preston-based parents group called 'All Children Together' (ACT 2000) commissioned a youth and community worker to work alongside learning disabled children and young people (REACT) to find out what some of their disabled peers think about their schooling. These children gave a range of reasons for being excluded:

- They felt it was due to discrimination/prejudice;
- they thought that they were too disabled;
- because they didn't think they were clever enough;
- felt it was because he or she was not liked;
- thought they were not good enough;
- felt they caused trouble;
- because they got blamed for things they haven't done. (pp. 29–31)

This study clearly indicates that barriers to learning included: boring lessons; teachers not understanding their needs; other pupils messing about; and a feeling that no one really expects them to do well.

A powerful barrier to the development of an inclusive culture within schools is the priority that is given to mental ability and the use of various tests and examinations. Success and value are celebrated through individual achievement. Pupils are labelled as 'bright, 'intelligent' or 'thick' and 'slow'. This encourages exclusionary values and practices and is part of a wider set of concerns. The problem is, it is the government and schools who think that learning is based on passing tests. It is the school who cannot give us school work we can do. It is the schools who make children learn at one pace. It is the school who cannot find a way of helping us to learn.

Examinations, testing, the values and assumptions about ability on which they are based, are serious barriers to inclusive learning and social relations (Aspis 2000).

Conclusion

Inclusive education is not an easy option and is part of the struggle to create a culture, an ethos in which all learners are supported to value their achievements. This will mean, in particular, challenging the assumptions and practices associated with standardised tests. It will require the development of forms of assessment that promote a more flexible learning environment and which give greater opportunity for all young people to fulfil their full potential.

If inclusive education is to be realised it will mean abolishing the current assessment and examination system with all its preconceived assumptions about what a young person should be able to do/attain before awarding them with a 'valued' grade, mark or qualification. We need to rethink what it is we value within the current educational system and why?

Questions

- How can we discuss the discriminative practices behind the standardised psychological and scholastic examinations and tests with disabled young people with learning difficulties in an accessible way?
- How can we support the greater involvement of disabled young people with learning difficulties in inclusive education campaign work?

CHAPTER 11

The struggle for inclusion: the growth of a movement

Richard Rieser

Never doubt that a small group of thoughtful committed citizens can change the world: Indeed it's the only thing that ever has. (Margaret Mead)

Introduction

Over the last 12 years a movement has developed in the United Kingdom that struggles for the inclusion of disabled children and students in mainstream schools and colleges as a civil and human right. It has set about changing the thinking throughout the education system; giving a voice to disabled children and their non-disabled peers and allies; supporting parents in coming to know it was the oppressive special educational needs system that was their problem and not their disabled children; changing thinking in the voluntary sector and government; creating a space for all those many professionals who influence the lives of disabled children so they can reconsider their beliefs and practices and thereby improve the life chances of disabled young people.

This has not been easy and even today, as will be shown, there is much resistance which maintains oppressive structures and practices in the education system and beyond. However, real change is occurring in schools and colleges, teacher thinking and government policy.

Here I will examine the development of the thinking, policies, practices and a few of the struggles which shaped the Integration Alliance. From 1989 the Alliance has developed a radical approach to the inclusion which has had impact well beyond the few dozen activists who make up the core of the Alliance. In 1996 the Integration Alliance changed its name to the Alliance for Inclusive Education. This was more than a change in name or image; it came from a growing understanding of the major differences between integration and inclusion. The former is a matter of location; placing a disabled child in a mainstream setting, usually with some additional support to access what was being offered in the school, changing the child to fit in with the social and academic life of the school. The latter is about valuing all children irrespective of their type or degree of impairment; of restructuring the institution to remove barriers so teaching and learning take place so all children can be valued for who they are, participate, interact and develop their potential.

If the thinking of the disabled people's movement was an essential 'hammer' for this process to occur, which led to the analysis of the oppression created for disabled children and adults by 'medical model thinking' and its replacement by 'social model thinking', then the understanding of the need for the intentional building of relationships from North America and the overwhelming desire of parents for their disabled children to be part of their local community was the 'anvil' on which our movement was shaped.

The Movement for Inclusion in the UK grew out of a range of groups and individuals who came from a range of perspectives, but all of them wanted to throw off the shackles of the past with its oppressive treatment of disabled young people, especially within the education system. They were guided by a principle of equality and human rights. For parents this was the idea that their disabled child had a right to belong to their local community and play a full part in their local playgroup, nursery, primary or secondary school and local college. For teachers and other professionals it meant a commitment to equality and civil rights which led them to question current segregative practices and the ideology of special educational needs with its oppressive origins and led to new practices of supporting inclusion. For disabled people the issue was an understanding of the damaging effects of their own schooling and a desire to bring civil rights for disabled people into education so that further generations of disabled young people would not have to undergo the alienation and isolation they had experienced. Civil rights organisations and activists saw the need for greater social justice and equality (Integration Alliance 1989).

The Integration Alliance

The Integration Alliance was set up following a conference in September 1989 of disabled adults, parents of disabled children and professionals and others who allied themselves to getting rid of segregated education for all children.

Parents of disabled children at the conference told of how the current special education legislation, practices and views of professionals prevented the integration of their children.

You're told everyone wants integration, but only in an ideal world, not here and now. But we do want it here and now.

Integrated placements should be a right not a privilege. It really is very odd that we have to go round asking – feeling we are imposing on the school.

Professional advice on statementing is a nation-wide joke: it is always designed to fit the kind of provision available, not the needs of the child.

Who are the most prejudiced people we encounter as parents? Not ordinary people, not other parents, but the providers of services. (Integration Alliance 1989)

The initial impetus for the conference came from a linking up of Parents in Partnership, a Wandsworth, London-based group of parents of disabled children who fought for their belief that their children had a right to go to mainstream schools, with Micheline Mason, a disabled mother of a disabled child who brought the thinking of the disability movement to the question of integration. The Centre for Studies of Integrated Education, a small research and

information-providing charity that had grown out of the Spastics Society but was now independent (CSIE) and Newham Council which since 1984 had been developing integrated
schools and closing special schools were also important early key supporters.

Micheline had been educated at home until she was 14 and then sent to a special boarding
school and was determined her daughter Lucy would not have to undergo the isolation that she
had.

> Children, contrary to the adult view, are not cruel. I have a daughter with a major physical
> disability. She has mixed with able-bodied children all her five years of life and is now in a
> mainstream primary school. The children's problems around her have been very easy to deal
> with. A bit of good information about her disability, a few guidelines about rough games and
> Lucy has been completely absorbed into school life. The children have come up with
> wonderful plans to overcome some of the problems caused by stairs, for example. Our
> problems in securing and keeping the integrated placement have all been with adults, and
> most particularly with bureaucrats, distant from the actual situation. (Micheline Mason, Inte-
> gration Alliance 1989)

Other disabled people attending spoke about the oppressive nature of their schooling.

> Being separated at school was uncomfortable. I was being picked on and bullied quite a lot,
> made fun of, in the special school – which made me very aggressive towards people, even
> teachers. In an ordinary school, I wouldn't have seen the blackboard, but if I had closed
> circuit TV I would. And I would have mixed with ordinary people.... Start young because
> then the kids would accept the other kids with learning difficulties or missing limbs and they
> would grow up with them. (Simon Gardiner Integration Alliance 1989)

The local disability movement in Lambeth – Lambeth Accord – and the London Boroughs
Disability Resource Team who provided advice and training on disability equality across
London, were also at the conference.

> It really is about time you parents joined forces with us disabled activists, and perhaps
> together after sharing our expertise and strengths, we shall be able to blast a hole through
> what has seemed to be an impenetrable barrier of attitudes and inaccessible schools and
> teaching methods, and show what we really want and need, and also how to go about it. (Jane
> Campbell LBDRT Integration Alliance 1989)

Other disabled people at the conference spoke of the deeply harmful effects of being segregated, of not having a peer group, of being isolated. The following are examples of such
perspectives:

> The experience of being isolated from our peer-group, and brothers and sisters, produced
> loneliness and isolation.

> No common schooling meant no common ground for play or association.

We felt we were 'out of sight' Out of mind.

We need more disabled teachers.

We need disability equality training to be built into the training of teachers and educational psychologists.

The difficulties for us in mainstream schools need to be tackled, not avoided. Integration needs to be on our terms! We are not the problem. (Integration Alliance 1989)

The conference was held in the run-up to the break-up of the Inner London Education Authority which although the most segregated education authority in the country, with over 3 per cent of its pupils attending 105 of its own special schools and many others, was committed to developing more integration in the wake of The Fish Report Educational Opportunities for All (ILEA 1985). This document which had argued for structural changes to develop more integration had been largely blocked by the Teachers' Associations and the ILEA Inspectorate, but more and more parents were wanting an integrated school placement for their children. The conference developed and campaigned around the slogan 'Integration Now' to take to the 13 successor Inner London Boroughs and then as the Alliance grew across the whole country.

The trend for integration, had started in the 1960s and 1970s, when more liberal ideas about education began to develop and has continued to the present day among growing numbers of teachers and parents. For example for England and Wales the number of ascertained (equivalent of statemented) pupils in mainstream schools including units and special classes rose from 11,027 (6.8 per cent) in 1973 to 21,245 in 1977, 12 per cent of all children requiring special provision (HMSO 1974 and DES 1977). The percentage of pupils with statements placed in maintained mainstream schools in England has continued to substantially increase, from 54 per cent (113,224) in 1995 to 60 per cent (152,800) in 2000 (Dfee 1999). However, in 2000 there were still 100,066 pupils with statements outside the mainstream in special schools, Pupil Referral Units and independent and non-maintained special schools in England (DfEE 2000).

Also at the founding conference were Linda Jordan and Chris Goodey who were part of a group of parents of disabled children in the London Borough of Newham who had fought since 1984 to close special schools in Newham and develop an integrated system where all children could go to their neighbourhood school:

Newham is no different to anywhere else. We have as many people in Newham who don't agree with it as anywhere else, people who prefer to close their eyes to disability unless it's merely a matter of a charity box. The Council , however, has taken a policy decision: there may be some teachers, parents, officers who disagree but it's policy and that's it. We have brought disability squarely into our equal opportunities principles in education, and the policy is based on the connection between discrimination against disabled people and segregated education ... we have closed our secondary special school for pupils with emotional and behavioural difficulties, and now we have less than 30 of these pupils in residential schools.... Many of our infant and junior age children with severe learning difficulties now attend ordinary schools.... People are now saying Downs Syndrome is not really a handicap, is it … and in the end there will be no such thing as a handicap just children getting extra support. (Linda Jordan parent and Chair of Education, Newham)

Since that time Newham has continued developing its policy for inclusion and now has the lowest number of disabled pupils attending special schools in the whole country. Only 0.33 per cent of all pupils compared with 1.3 per cent as an English average (DfEE 2000 Table 15). More interestingly, Newham schools continue to demonstrate that the changes in teaching and learning style that teachers have had to develop to include the full range of children in their classes has led to a general improvement in educational achievement. Newham secondary schools topped the improvement league tables over the last four years on A*–G GCSE grades (DfEE 1997–2000). In addition exclusion rates are the lowest in London with a growing emphasis on developing the emotional intelligence of all pupils (Jordan and Goodey 1996).

In Canada, Denmark, Sweden, Italy and some parts of the USA integration or main-streaming was well established by this time but in the United Kingdom, which had given birth to the ideology of segregation and the development of special education, the pace of change was very slow especially for children who were described as having severe or complex needs. These were the very children whose parents were most committed to getting their children into local mainstream schools so they could grow up as part of their local community and be accepted for who they were and not be seen as a label or a bunch of special needs.

The prospect of an integrated future for some disabled children had been raised by the Warnock Report (HMSO 1978) with the implementation of its thinking in the 1981 Education Act. However, there was much resistance in the educational and medical worlds to the integra-tion of all children. Indeed the Warnock Report while getting rid of the old categories of 'handicap' linked to particular types of special school introduced the broader concept of 'special educational need' and put forward the idea that there was a continuum of special educa-tional needs, some of which could be met through integration in ordinary schools, but that there were groups of children for whom provision at special school is particularly to be needed in the future (p. 123).:

i) children with severe or complex physical, sensory or intellectual disabilities who require special facilities, teaching methods or expertise that would be impracticable to provide in ordinary schools;

ii) children with severe emotional and behavioural disorders who have very great difficulty in forming relationships with others or whose behaviour is so extreme or unpredictable that it causes severe disruption in an ordinary school or inhibits the educational progress of other children; and

iii) children with less severe disabilities, often in combination, who despite special help do not perform well in an ordinary school and are more likely to thrive in the more intimate communal and educational setting of a special school. (HMSO 1978: 123)

This, together with the recommendation that LEAs should produce a special education review and plan led to a geographically discrete fixed continuum of provision in most Authorities, where pupils with mild impairments or needs were integrated and those with more significant needs were segregated in separate special schools or separated in units attached to mainstream schools (geographic or social integration).

Previously, the 1976 Education Act through section 10, had put on the statute book, as part of a move to wider comprehensive education,

> that subject to certain qualifications and from a date to be approved by the Secretary of State 'handicapped' pupils in England and Wales are to be educated in ordinary schools in preference to special schools.

The qualifications were impracticability, incompatibility with the efficiency of the school or would involve unreasonable public expenditure. However, ministers had given assurances that this was no threat to special schools:

> The new law … does not herald the precipitate dismantling of the very valuable work of special schools, particularly those for children with severe disabilities … a minority of hand-icapped children will always need the help that only a special school can give, and it will be important to ensure that integration does not force them into isolation. (Shirley Williams 1977: 122)

In the event the 1981 Act laid down three caveats which would make integration much harder to achieve as they could be used as hooks on which professional prejudice and fear could be hung.

This was later incorporated into section 316 of the 1996 Education Act is as follows :

(1) Any person exercising any function under this part in respect of a child with special educational needs who should be educated in school shall secure, if the conditions mentioned in sub-section (2) are satisfied, the child is educated in a school which is not a special school unless it is incompatible with the wishes of the parent.
(2) The conditions are that educating the child in a school which is not a special school is compatible with—
a) His receiving the special educational provision which his learning difficulty calls for,
b) The provision of efficient education for the children with whom he is educated, and
c) The efficient use of resources.

The Warnock/1981/1996 approach is fundamentally discriminatory and is based on viewing children with special educational needs as having individual needs which need to be met in the most appropriate setting regardless of how socially isolated this makes them. There is no conception of human rights here. At its heart it viewed children with special educational needs as needing to be subject to a multi-professional assessment which is predominantly based on a 'medical model' approach in which the impairment and fixing it is seen as more important than the ordinary needs of the child to be socially included and be valued for who they are.

Writing in 1989 (Swann 1989) noted it was hard to discern anything that could be termed a national integration strategy policy since 1981. No clear steps had been taken by the DES to reduce the numbers going to special schools. They have not issued guidance to LEAs about

how they should interpret the integration clauses in the 1981 Act. Colin Barnes (1991) undertaking a widespread review of education among other areas for the disability movement
reached the following conclusion:

> From the outset the mainstream education system was not constructed for disabled people
> with 'special educational needs'…. Historically they have been marked out for a particular
> form of 'special' educational provision which in general is both socially and educationally
> inferior. Clearly, traditional attitudes towards the education of disabled children and young
> people have hardly been challenged by recent events. (p. 61)

The Integration Alliance aimed to address this inequity and developing from this conference
has played a key role in developing the struggle for inclusion and its development in the UK.
There isn't space here to recount all the thinking and struggles of the last 11 years so I will select
a cross-section to give the flavour.

The organisation currently has a council which meets quarterly and this is elected at the
AGM. It has an individual membership of around 200 families, individual parents, disabled
people and professionals and some 60 affiliated organisations. A majority of the council are
disabled people. This allows it to be part of the British Council of Disabled People which
today has some 130 organisations which are run by disabled people representing over
300,000 disabled people. This distinction between organisations 'of' and organisations 'for'
disabled people is important. The lives of many disabled people especially in the world of
education have been determined by charities run by non-disabled people. They have often
been patronising and disempowering to the disabled people they claimed to represent.
Secondly, much of the disability movement has tended to be dominated by people with physical or sensory impairments. The Alliance set out to have representation from adults with
learning difficulties on our council. We do not make a distinction between different impairments in defining disabled people because like BCODP we base our thinking on the social
'model of disability'.

Developing our thinking about inclusion

We start from the point of view that there is a real difference between our impairment and our
disablement.

> Impairment is the loss or limitation of physical, mental or sensory function on a long-term,
> or permanent basis.

> Disablement is the loss or limitation of opportunities to take part in the normal life of the
> community on an equal level with others due to physical and social barriers. (Disabled
> People's International 1981 published in Mason 2000: 60).

Much of the confusion parents reported from schools faced with the demand for integration
was based upon the non-appreciation of the difference between these two definitions and the

implications for schools. The traditional thinking which had grown up around the identification and assessment of special educational needs was based upon a 'medical or individual model' of the child. What was needed was to view the child in a whole-school context. To identify and systematically reduce the barriers to their involvement in the full social and academic life of the school by changing the environment, communication, teaching and learning, attitudes and organisation to fully include the child. Our thinking was not as clear as this and it has taken the last ten years of testing our ideas in both training situations in schools and colleges and in struggles for inclusion for individual children to reach our present level of clarity (Table 1) and this process will continue.

Table 1 Medical and social model thinking in schools

MEDICAL MODEL THINKING	SOCIAL MODEL THINKING
Child is faulty	Child is valued
Diagnosis	Strengths and needs defined by self and others
Labelling	Identify barriers and develop solutions
Impairment becomes focus of attention	Outcome-based programme designed
Assessment, monitoring, programmes of therapy imposed	Resources are made available to ordinary services
Segregation and alternative services	Training for parents and professionals
Ordinary needs put on hold	Relationships nurtured
Re-entry if normal enough or permanent exclusion	Diversity welcomed child is included
Society remains unchanged	Society evolves

Source: R.Rieser 2000 adapted from Micheline Mason 1994

I will select a number of key moments to illustrate this development of our thinking.

As a disabled teacher in the 1980s I had become increasingly involved in the struggle to improve equality for disabled teachers (Rieser 1994). At the same time as my involvement in the struggle for greater equality for disabled teachers, I increasingly realised that the oppression we were up against was part of a wider ethos inside education, that did not welcome difference and sought to exclude those who could not be assimilated into schools, as they were currently organised. In addition the curriculum content itself, by either reinforcing negative stereotypes of disabled people or by the absence of the experience of disablement from history, geography, English, science, maths, drama, PHSE, PE, art and music, was neither 'balanced or broadly based' nor was it:

promoting the spiritual, moral, cultural, mental and physical development of pupils at the school and of society, and preparing pupils for the opportunities, responsibilities and experiences of adult life. (Definition of the National Curriculum's purpose, 1988 Education Act)

My work while seconded led me to produce an internal document for the ILEA (Rieser 1989) which raised all these issues. My secondment had arisen from a battle against an unfair decision to force me to move from the school I had taught in for ten years based on my disability. I won my grievance appeal and the ILEA did not know what to do with me so they agreed I could look at disability and the curriculum. At the same time, the parents Consultative Committee for Special Needs, which had one parent from a special school and one from a mainstream in each ILEA area was demanding ILEA did something from an equal opportunities perspective on disability in the last few months before it was disbanded. ILEA brought me together with Micheline Mason, a disabled parent of a disabled child in a mainstream school, and we were given ten weeks to come up with a document. We had never met before and coming from different backgrounds and perspectives we had an intense period of discussion, criticism and argument. Out of this highly charged atmosphere we both gained clarity and the result was not the pamphlet originally planned, but a fully illustrated, 260-page book, *Disability Equality in the Classroom: A Human Rights Issue* (Rieser and Mason 1990/1992).

From this work it became clear that the perspective of the 'social model' of disability and the Disability Equality Training that disabled people had developed themselves to promote this view was urgently needed inside the British education system. In 1991 Micheline and I were approached by Comic Relief to produce a resource and training for teachers for disability equality. We successfully argued that we needed to involve the Disabled Peoples' Movement in this project. With funding and support from Comic Relief we organised and ran two national Training the Trainers for Education courses for 60 disabled trainers. This was followed up by the writing of a booklet and the production of a video which provides ideas, arguments and visuals for the promotion of the 'social model' of disability in schools – *Altogether Better: From 'Special Needs' to Equality in Education* (Mason and Rieser 1994). This has been distributed widely and used to train many thousands of educationalists.

Some of our thinking developed the need to move from a 'medical model and integration/segregation' approach to a 'social model/inclusion approach'.

We try to get people in schools to understand that what we call the 'Medical Model' is more than just what doctors do to us. It started from what doctors do to us because it was looking at our impairment. We were no more than our impairment. In fact many children are still labelled by their impairment. A Down's Syndrome child, a child with spina bifida. However we say: 'they are children first, we are people first'. Traditionally the focus is on the impairment and the cure or if we cannot get the cure we get shunted off to this 'special land' which is a different and parallel system. In fact it is very similar to mainstream in many respects but you are denied the rich social mix of peers available in mainstream. In 'special land' you have hydrotherapy, in mainstream schools we have swimming. In 'special land' you have art therapy, in mainstream art. In mainstream schools you have literacy and language development, in special land you have speech and language therapy. What is the difference between physiotherapy and an individual physical education programme? As integration has developed it is seen as essential that more of these medicalised therapies are made available in mainstream whereas the key issue for inclusion is to develop a diversity of teaching and learning strategies that encompass all pupils' needs.

Once you are in 'special land' you have few skills, you often have no qualifications, you have no self-esteem and no life skills so then you have to be looked after for the rest of your life. More than a million disabled people (1.1 million) in the UK want work and cannot get it (Labour Force Survey DSS 1998). In schools it has led to a geographic development continuum of provision with the rarer your condition the more likely you are to be bussed or sent to board long distances from your home community. These schools are very far flung because that is where the 'expertise' resides. We spend a lot of money with psychologists and other people assessing the 'shape' of the child to slot them like a child's game into the 'right' peg hole.

The Alliance came to the realisation that we need to get rid of that 'fixed continuum' of provision. We need to stop putting the child who is different under the microscope asking 'what can't she/he do?'

In the training we have developed we are saying this approach and treatment of disabled young people is an oppression, it is just as bad as other forms of oppression which have been outlawed and it has to go. The barriers are what disable us not our impairment. It is the lack of access, the lack of communication, the lack of appropriate teaching methods, it is the way we reflect back to you what you do to us which leaves us with no self-esteem (Mason and Rieser 1994). It is the barriers in society which disadvantage and are discriminatory.

Therefore we get schools to identify the barriers which prevent inclusion and develop their practice to eradicate barriers. Barriers of access; barriers to communication arising from lack of British Sign Language, lack of Braille, information not in different formats such as tape, disc, pictogram or plain English; barriers in organisation; barriers in transport; or barriers in attitudes shaped by stereotypes.

We were also influenced a great deal in the early 1990s by the thinking from North America about inclusion and in particular by Marsha Forest, Jack Pierpoint, Herb Lovett, Judith Snow

> who flew in as a team, crashed through our British reserve and, in their generosity, gave us the language and tools of inclusion. (Mason 2000: 1)

Joe Whittaker of Bolton Institute organised four inclusion conferences where they taught us that inclusion was also about the intentional building of relationships, person-centred planning using such techniques as Maps Path and Circles of Friends (Pearpoint et al. 1992).

Our training and campaigning has been further strengthened by investigating and developing materials which expose the history of our oppression in education and society at the hands of the authorities, reformers, charities and eugenicists. Eugenicists who incarcerated many thousands of disabled children and adults for the whole of their life and set the seal on how disabled children should be educated in the first part of the 20th century and thus so influenced the development of special educational needs in the second half (Rieser 2000; Mason 2000). As labels and labelling increased, so has the population of our special schools (see Table 2). There was an inexorable rise in the special school population of England through most of the last century.

Table 2 Number of children in special schools in England and Wales 1897–2000

Date	Number of children
1897	4,739
1909	17,600
1914	28,511
1919	34,478
1929	49,487
1939	59,768
1947	40,252*
1955	51,558*
1965	70,334*
1967	78,256*
1977	135,261*+
1987	107,126*+
2000	105,152@+

*hospital schools not included
+ includes Severe Learning Difficulty

Source: Cole 1989 based on Chief Medical Officer, Ministry of Education, Dept of Education and Science Annual Reports and DfEE Green Paper Oct 97 @ DfEE 09/00 England only including PRU with statements.

Developing training for inclusion

We took a decision early on that our training should be separate from our campaigning work as schools, local authorities and government were often greatly challenged by the Alliances campaigning role. From 1992 to the present we have sought to set up, train, market and develop a national trainers network of disabled disability equality trainers under a separate charity Disability Equality in Education. DEE is as an educational trust, to provide training, consultancy and information and to publish curriculum materials to further develop equality and inclusion. In recent years after a very hard struggle operating from my basement room we have an office with three part-time staff and have trained 160 trainers in England and Wales, over 115 of whom are on our network. DEE is providing training for LEAs, schools and colleges across the country. Our leaflet has gone to every English school and we launched the network at the Department for Education and Employment in November 1999 with a government minister. Our funders have included Comic Relief, Dfee, Barrow Cadbury and the Platinum Trust, but it is still very difficult to get the funding and support we need (DEE 1999).

Every school needs this training and INSET to shake off the shackles of the past, address the genuine issue of ending discrimination against disabled people in education and create more inclusive schools and communities.

During my secondment and since I have worked in a number of different classes in schools and colleges developing strategies for both teachers and children to raise disability awareness. Interesting observations arose from this work once I was talking freely to a group of children about how I was treated by non-disabled children when I was at school. First, they had a great sense of injustice and empathy for me. Secondly, a number of children began to volunteer information about themselves and immediate family who were disabled that the class teachers were very often not aware of.

This is very much backed up by the Office of Population and Censuses Study on Disability in Britain, Vol.6 (Meltzer *et al.* 1989), which shows that 66 per cent of children they define as disabled, some 240,000, are in mainstream classrooms. This is a gross underestimate as it does not include the some 800,000 children with a specific learning difficulty such as dyslexia, many children with emotional and behavioural problems, which create learning difficulties, or large numbers of other children with hidden impairments, such as asthma, diabetes, fragile X, sickle cell anaemia and many others. In a classroom where difference is welcomed and valued, many impairments that have been hidden will be talked about freely and many children will feel happy to 'come out'.

Name calling and bullying will not be acceptable in such schools and classes and their life-threatening consequences and damage to children's self-esteem will be fully taken on-board by teachers and other school staff. However, it is very difficult because people are surrounded with an image environment that is absolutely full of confusing stereotypes and with disabled people there is not one single stereotype. There are at least ten identified by the 1 in 8 Group which the Alliance set up to influence the portrayal of disabled people in the media following a joint conference with Save the Children 'Invisible Children' (Rieser 1995) and you can probably think of more:

> Pitiable and pathetic; an object of violence; sinister or evil; atmosphere; 'Super Crip' or 'Triumph over Tragedy'; laughable; having a chip on their shoulder; a burden/outcast; non-sexual or incapable of having a worthwhile relationship; Incapable of fully participating in everyday life. (1 in 8 Group 1996 in invisible child report, pp. 44–9)

What also became clear from this work was the unchallenging way that negative portrayals of disablement were routinely used in the school curriculum, displays and learning materials. There were very few books about and illustrations of disabled people just getting on with their lives in a non-stereotyped way. Children's book publishers, film and TV producers, writers and directors are still very much in need of re-educating on portrayals of disability. This led to 'Invisible Children: Joint Conference On Children Images and Disability' attended by 70 children's authors and some 100 image makers from radio, TV and Film (Rieser 1995). There was a general consensus that things had to change and that disabled people were generally absent in the media, but when they did appear they were stereotyped. This process was not without resistance, as one children's author was heard to remark 'How can we show evil in our stories now we can't use disabled people'! This led to a number of children's books that just included disabled children, a conference at the BBC, the setting up of the 1 in 8 Group and its Raspberry Ripple Awards 1997–99 and a broadsheet of which 20,000 were distributed throughout the media industry (1 in 8 Group 1996). Progress is slow in this area in the meantime, and as teachers did with books that were sexist and racist, they should be used with a 'health warning' and teachers and children should make their own books, displays and resources which include disabled people in a non-stereotyped way.

The Alliance for Inclusive Education

So our journey to inclusion has involved us in developing training and challenging the media, but the primary role the Alliance played and continues to play is to campaign for inclusion. The Alliance does this through campaigning to change the law and bad practices and supporting a number of high-profile cases to gain publicity, change thinking and achieve inclusion.

In 1996 we realised we could no longer call ourselves the Integration Alliance. We needed to be much clearer about the difference between inclusion and integration. The development of our training and our campaigns had made us understand integration was just a necessary precursor of inclusion. It was just a starting point for a process of whole-school change that needed to identify the barriers that were preventing disabled pupils from accessing the teaching, learning and full social life of the school and to find solutions to overcome those barriers. We also learned that there were no children with categories of impairment or severity of impairment who could not be successfully included in mainstream school where the local authority was prepared to properly resource and the staff were prepared to change their attitudes and practices. 'All does Mean All' to quote People First (the self-advocacy organisation of people with learning difficulties).

We learned that inclusion was a process that started with integration, but went on changing the school so that all children in the local community could be valued and achieve success. This requires both the redistribution of resources from special land, the retraining of staff and the development of a pedagogy capable of meeting these diverse needs.

This thinking was important when members of the Alliance were on the working group which developed the Index for Inclusion (CSIE 2000). The index, which has been distributed by government to all schools in England, is a school self-review tool which encourages schools to ask questions and examine their policies, practices and culture or ethos to become more inclusive. The thinking of the school improvement movement had a synergy with our barriers analysis and this gave the index a firm basis and fitted the government quest to improve performance while developing inclusion (Ainscow and Booth *et al.* 2000). Often viewed as contradictory, there is much evidence to support the view that inclusion can improve the quality of education for all (Sebba and Sachdev 1997).

The Qualifications and Curriculum Authority have taken on board the barriers analysis as the key to delivering Curriculum 2000 in their General Inclusion Guidelines which all teachers are required to have regard to in the delivery of teaching and learning for all pupils.

> In planning and teaching the national curriculum, teachers are required to have due regard to the following principles:- ... Setting suitable learning challenges ... Responding to the diverse needs pupils bring to learning ... Overcoming potential barriers to learning and assessment for individual pupils or groups. (QCA 2000: 1)

In November 2000 OFSTED, despite some resistance, published guidance on inspecting schools for educational inclusion which all inspectors have to have mandatory training on. It lays emphasis on:

> How well does the school recognise and overcome barriers to learning. This is about the schools understanding of how well different groups do in school; the steps taken to make sure particular groups are not disadvantaged in school and to promote their participation and success; its strategies for promoting good relationships and managing behaviour; what the school does specifically to prevent and address racism, sexism and other forms of discrimination And what it does about cases of discrimination that do occur. (p. 6)

The compulsory segregation of disabled pupils against their wishes and those of their parents remains the most obvious denial of human rights against which the Alliance campaigns, both generally and in supporting numerous specific campaigns.

Sometimes we win and sometimes we lose for the individual concerned, but all the time we are shifting the climate of opinion. There have been many battles in our campaign but I will illustrate them with four.

Zahrah Manuel and her mother Preethi struggled for inclusion into both her local primary and secondary school.

It took over three years trying to convince the local authority that Zahrah could go to a mainstream primary school. By this time we'd sold our flat and had used all the money from the sale of the flat towards educating Zahrah at home, we'd even gone to a tribunal and won but the tribunal decision was not legally binding so not much came of that. After lobbying the Council the Alliance organised an occupation of the Education Officers and after some negotiation after three years Zah started at school. Zahrah thrived at primary school. Children would warm towards her and children learnt to communicate with her. Zahrah uses switches to communicate.

Zahrah is a happy thriving child as a result of inclusion. We can go down the street and there'll be a child running up to her 'look there's Zah'.

Recently we had a place for Zahrah at a secondary school which was resourced for £750,000 to include physically disabled children but the school refused to admit Zahrah using the three caveats. We went to court and challenged them with a judicial review. Minutes before the hearing the school agreed to admit her. Now Zahrah has been accepted by Hampstead comprehensive and she started in September 2000. What a contrast. The staff have all had disability equality training from DEE. They have spent £140,000 over the summer holidays making enough of the school accessible for Zahrah to function and more work is planned. Zahrah and I have been made to feel welcome and part of the community. (ISEC 2000)

Maresa MacKeith. We have found that the protest and voice of young disabled people and their peers can in the end be effective in a way that parents and their supporters cannot. The story of how Young and Powerful, a group of disabled and non-disabled young people supported by the Alliance, who campaign for inclusion, supported Maresa MacKeith in being included in a mainstream school is told in detail in 'Young Persons Guide to Changing the World, the Universe and Everything' (Comic Relief 2001). In brief Maresa, who is a non-verbal wheelchair user who has developed using facilitated communication, was categorised as having a 'mental age' of two years by psychologists and sent to a special school for six years, finally was integrated into a mainstream secondary school in Nottinghamshire. Here she was taught in a room on her own and said by the staff not to be ready for social contact with her peers. Young and Powerful as a result occupied the Director of Education's office and with much publicity and a further meeting got an agreement that Maresa would attend regular classes. Later Maresa moved to a different secondary school much more receptive to her needs and with greater understanding of the process of inclusion. Now Maresa has a circle of friends of other girls in her year 'The Girls Gab Gang' and will do her GCSEs this summer (*Flying Pigs*, No.1 1997). Listen to her voice:

> The most important thing is that I want to be part of ordinary life, and I want the same experiences as other kids. Also I want to be allowed to learn things that need thinking about and are challenging.
>
> I want to be able to contribute, and to discuss things that are important to me and other kids. We need to be together to do that.
>
> When we experience things together, we can learn about what we are each interested in, and about each other's life.
>
> It is important to educate schools so they change to make things better for kids who need a lot of help or get very tired. (Maresa MacKeith ISEC 2000)

The segregation of young people with a learning difficulty can often be the hardest to change. The whole education system is structured on a normative model of measured 'intelligence' and narrow academic ability. Many teachers and education officers cannot envisage how pupils with severe learning difficulties can be included in secondary schools. In other LEAs, however, such as Newham, Stockport or Barnsley, they are automatically included in mainstream secondary schools.

Chloe McCollum and Zelda, her mum and her family were supported by the Alliance with high-profile lobbying of Lewisham Council and a picket outside the town hall but in this case we were unable to convince the council that this was a case of disability discrimination and they insisted upon placing Chloe in a special school most of the week using the efficient use of resources and appropriate education caveats. Listen to her voice:

> My name is Chloe McCollum. I am 16 years old and have Down's Syndrome. I love parties, having drinks going to the market, stories and E.T.
>
> I went to Lucas Vale, an ordinary primary school. I liked it there. I had many friends especially Nejula, Siobahn and Ellie. When I left Lucas Vale (after nine years) I wasn't allowed to go to ordinary secondary school with my friends. I campaigned to go, but the education authority said no. I stayed at home and my daddy taught me reading. He took me to museums and we had picnics together. I now go to Greenvale special school with kids my own age. I go to Deptford Green one day a week too.
>
> Deptford Green is a mainstream secondary school with lots of children in it. I love it because it is good there. I like reading especially a book called 'Underground to Canada'. I like writing, Science, Maths, English and Humanities. I like the experiments best. I play with everyone in the playground. Its great to go to an ordinary school and I like both my schools.
>
> I wish I went to Deptford Green after Lucas Vale and there wasn't such bother. I hope there won't be such bother for other children in the future. (Chloe McCollum Nov 1998 in Comic Relief 1999)

Anthony Ford's mother and father believed strongly that Anthony should go to his local primary school. Eventually through their campaigning Camden Council put in a lift and accessible toilet. However when it came to transfer, the local secondary school said they couldn't manage having

Anthony even though they demonstrated a stair climbing wheelchair would work. So the family moved to Harrow where Anthony is now attending Whitmore High School which is accessible.

I went to Beckford Primary School in Camden from my first year of school. For two years first my mother and then a school assistant carried me up and down about one thousand steps a week to lessons. This was because the school refused to keep my classroom on the ground floor. I hated being carried because it made me very nervous. Eventually the school got a lift. This meant I could go in the lift to lessons. I was delighted.

At the end of my time at Beckford I wanted to go to Hampstead School, but the school refused to let me use a stair climbing wheelchair to go up and down the stairs. This stopped me going to the school with my friends.

I am now going to an accessible school in Harrow which has lifts. This has made me very happy and I have a lot of new friends who have made me welcome. But I have still lost my old friends.

I wish that other disabled children get their choice of schools. (Anthony Ford aged 12, 1998 in Comic Relief 1999)

The battle that the Fords waged for Anthony made it possible for Zahrah to gain access to Hampstead school as the attitudes began to change, but this did not help Anthony who had to move.

Barriers of attitude, school organisation, curriculum, teaching, learning, communication and school environment each can exclude disabled pupils from being included. But where school staff are prepared to find solutions to these barriers then it does prove not only possible but beneficial for the school, its staff and pupils to include disabled pupils.

The Alliance recently launched 'Whose Voice is it Anyway' (Wilson and Jade 1999), a report into the views of young people on their education, and this was followed up with a conference in September 2000 into the sorts of support that young disabled people need to be included in mainstream. 'The Inclusion Assistant' (Alliance 2001) is a report and video of this consultation. The voice of young people is a powerful testimony of the effectiveness of inclusive education. This generation of young disabled people will not be invisible.

The Alliance has at the same time as supporting individual campaigns been seeking to both change the legal position and the attitude towards inclusion among politicians and educationalists both locally and nationally. The1993 Act had again made integration conditional upon a child's needs being able to be met, not interfering with other children and being an efficient use of resources. The Alliance and linked organisations had objected to this formulation in the consultation on this Bill. Soon after this at the Council for Disabled Children, which represented the main voice of the voluntary sector, we were able to persuade them to set up a working party on integration. Because the working party left enough time to listen to the experiences and thinking of disabled people and parents of disabled children who wanted inclusion we were able to recommend that these caveats should go and for those parents who wanted a mainstream place they should have a right to get one (Council for Disabled Children 1994). The Alliance adopted the scrapping of the three caveats as a short-term objective. We sponsored an early day motion signed by 37 MPs in 1996.

This meant that when the School Standards and Framework Bill was being debated and the CDC set up the Special Education Consortium in 1997 it was able to sponsor an amendment in the House of Lords to get rid of the caveats. Responding, the government in 1998 said they would listen to what the Disability Rights Task Force said on this issue and they agreed that the caveats should possibly be amended as they were often used by local authorities to prevent inclusion. Under the consultation on the Disability Rights in Education Bill in 2000 the government agreed to get rid of the appropriate educational provision clause but wanted to keep the other two: efficient use of resources and not interfering with the education of other children. The Special Education Consortium, representing over 200 organisations, adopted the scrapping of section 316 and the three caveats as a principled position.

The newly formed Disability Rights Commission which included Phillipa Russell of CDC and Jane Campbell of the National Independent Living Centre agreed at its first meeting, after some lobbying by the Alliance, to recommend scrapping the caveats. The majority of voluntary organisations, parents and disabled people's organisations supported the Alliance position in the consultation. The government at the time of writing in 'The Special Education and Disability Bill' has also removed the second caveat leaving only not interfering with the efficient education of other children.

Conclusion

Thanks to an extension of Parliament due to Foot and Mouth disease the Bill was enacted and two of the three caveats have been removed. We are now in a very different place to 1989. We have a Government Action Programme and Green Paper with an increase in inclusion at their heart. The Alliance even has a representative on the National Advisory Group on SEN. The teaching profession and National Union of Teachers are more accepting of inclusion. Many more local education authorities are developing inclusion and more than 156,000 disabled pupils are now attending mainstream schools. Another 100,000 in England remain segregated and depending on where you live the local policies are very different. Now we have to build and strengthen a network of inclusion campaigners and trainers in every locality to make inclusion a reality for the benefit of all. It would be foolish to think that everything will be plain sailing from now on, but inclusion involving the wholesale restructuring of education to meet the needs of all pupils in mainstream schools is at least a real possibility and a reality for thousands of disabled pupils in no small measure due to the efforts of the Alliance for Inclusive Education and its members. A small group of thoughtful committed citizens has changed their part of the world.

> ## Questions
>
> - How can re-thinking of a educational system's core beliefs and values lead to change when only a small but committed group of activists understand how oppressive the status quo position is?
> - In what ways can the voice of the excluded influence.

CHAPTER 12

Disability issues in the postmodern world

Mike Oliver

Introduction

As author of the concluding chapter, I have had the opportunity not given to the other authors, to read their chapters and hence to incorporate some of the issues they raise. However, what follows will be structured around issues that I wish to raise concerning the relationship between disability and social change in the world to which we are moving. These issues have been generated partly in response to my book *The Politics of Disablement*, which was published originally in 1990 and which is frequently cited by other authors in this volume. The book appeared to trigger an academic interest in disability studies that resulted in a publishing explosion throughout the 1990s to support more and more emerging courses in disability studies as well as stimulating a wider interest in disability issues from theoretical, political, cultural and experiential perspectives.

My central argument in that book (Oliver 1990) was that exclusion from the world of work is the most important factor in what happens to disabled people and the way we are treated by society. The coming of industrialism shook many groups and individuals out of the labour force and consequently they came to be seen as burdens on society in general and the taxpayer in particular. Hence, society had to do something about disabled people and it did, not being shy about developing a whole range of exclusionary practices in respect of disabled people. However it needed people to sanction and carry out these exclusionary practices and it found the increasingly powerful medical profession and the newly emerging ideology of individualism willing supporters.

This is obviously a very simplified version of a complex argument about exclusion, which I published more than ten years ago now. It has not been without its critics and revisionists of one kind or another. You pay too much attention to work and not enough to culture say some. Society's hatred of us is because we are classed as 'other'; not because we are unable to work say others. You fail to allow for the personal limitations that impairments bring with them say yet others. Pernicious social forces such as sexism, racism, homophobia and ageism are more important than work in our lives say yet more critics. And even if what you say is true, the coming of the welfare state and the development of community care will eventually ensure the inclusion of disabled people because they will be taken care of, so the final argument goes.

Both my book and the chapters in this volume are centrally concerned with the issue of social change and any differences between them are matters of emphasis and degree rather than fundamental disagreements. However my argument then and now is located within what has been called a Marxist, though I prefer the term materialist, framework. Not all of the authors herein would operate within the same framework and even those that do, might still see the issues before us in slightly different ways from me. In this final chapter, therefore, I shall attempt to interweave the arguments of the other authors with my own, focusing firstly on the production of disability under conditions of modernity before going on to consider some of the changes that are happening now with the occurence of what has variously been called the coming of postmodernity (Bauman 1992), high modernity (Giddens 1990) or late capitalism (Jamieson 1991).

The production of disability in modern societies

As I have already indicated, one of the criticisms frequently levelled at social analysis based upon Marxist or materialist theory is that it is over-deterministic and relies too heavily on the economic. I do not have the space here to deal with this common criticism but in respect of my own materialist analysis of the production of disability in modern societies (Oliver 1990), I do see the political and cultural as important forces in shaping this production process and indeed did discuss these issues in that book. Many of the contributors herein add to, rather than attempt to replace my explanation with their own and add significantly to our understanding of that process in so doing. Hughes, for example, shows how the capitalist mode of production was responsible for constituting disabled people as other because 'productivist culture had no place for impaired labour power. It was surplus to value'. Hence, he argues that disabled people were positioned as the opposite of the independent, productive individual; as dependent other.

In his analysis Hughes rightly argues that the disability movement has been the central player in the struggle for anti-discrimination legislation in the modern world but he warns against committing too much of the political struggle to material and structural issues. Instead, or as well as, he suggests that the disability movement must continue to embrace a cultural politics of identity and difference because 'the threads of economic, cultural and social life which have constituted disabled people as dependent are beginning to unravel'. This is certainly the case and I agree that disability politics must embrace the cultural as well as the economic and social. However it should not be forgotten that disabled people all over the world still constitute the poorest of the poor and for many the key issue remains survival rather than cultural representation.

In their analysis of disability politics in modern societies herein, Barnes and Mercer argue that traditional political institutions such as political parties and parliaments have largely failed disabled people both in economic and political terms. Not only have they failed to ensure a reasonable quality of life but they have also failed both to fully include us in the political process and to properly represent our issues and interests. As a consequence disability movements have grown up outside the state sphere and have forced disability issues onto the agenda from the outside. Despite chronic underfunding and sometimes overt and covert sabotage, these movements have been phenomenally successful and have forced governments to listen to the voices of disabled people. It is because of this success, Barnes and Mercer argue, that these movements currently run the risk of being incorporated in the political apparatus of the state.

The importance of the cultural is brought out in Sullivan's chapter herein and he also reminds us that the trajectory of disability movements is not the same in all modern societies. Thus he argues that the nature of disability politics in New Zealand has been shaped by the historical relationship between Maori, the tangata whenua (local people, indigenous) and Pakeha. Because of this New Zealand became a bi-cultural society in which partnership was the main approach to the resolution of problems of all kinds. Hence when in the 1970s the Disabled Persons Assembly (DPA) was formed, it entered into a politics of partnership and aimed to be as inclusive as possible allowing for a broad range of individual and group membership. The consequences of this were profound for the disability movement in New Zealand, argues Sullivan. By adopting a consensual politics of partnership rather than a confrontational politics of self-determination, disabled people failed to do the intellectual work necessary to define who they were and what their problems actually are.

This, of course, stands in marked contrast to the experience of disabled people in Britain who produced *The Fundamental Principles of Disability* (UPIAS 1976) and have since defined their problems within a conceptual framework that has come to be known as the social model of disability. Hahn, in his contribution, suggests that social models were developed in both Britain and the United States but that they developed in very different ways. In Britain the central theme of the social model was that of oppression leading to an economic or class-based interpretation of the problems that disabled people faced. In the USA, however, the central organising concept of disabled people was civil rights leading to a minority group interpretation of the problems that disabled people faced. However, both movements have pursued the road to civil rights through the passage of anti-discrimination legislation, which Hahn suggests is unlikely to lead to the full inclusion of disabled people in the United States or elsewhere.

Not all the authors in this volume however write about disability issues from within the boundaries of what I have called modern societies. Camilleri and Callus describe the experiences of disabled people in Malta and suggest that for much of the 20th century disabled people were locked away in cellars and barns and were kept out of sight because disability was regarded as a thing of shame. When eventually this shameful production of disability was challenged, the challenge came not from the state or disabled people themselves but from the Catholic Church. As well as attempting to provide charitable services to bring disabled people out of the cellars, the Church also tried to reconstruct disabled people as 'angels' rather than 'untouchables'. While this latter strategy met with some success, predictably it did little to ensure the inclusion of disabled people into Maltese society because people are perhaps even more suspicious of angels than untouchables.

Camilleri and Callus also chart the gradual involvement of the Maltese State in the production of disability, initially in the area of education, with the establishment of special schools. Vlachou-Balafouti charts a similar state involvement in Greece and argues that education is essential to the production of disability because it shapes both self and society. In other words education shapes the process whereby we come to know ourselves and others as well as being a reflection of the institutional arrangements that a society makes in order to respond to the needs of particular social groups. And (almost) using a social model analysis, she identifies the disabling barriers to an inclusive education system in Greece including 'unsupportive teachers, inflexible curricula, conflicting and contradictory educational aims, market ideology and medicalisation'.

Rieser, in his contribution, describes the way in which a specific movement for inclusion in education has developed in Britain and he charts its relationship to the disability movement *per se*. He further argues that the tactics of the Alliance for Inclusion, which have included equality training, challenging the media and political campaigning, have had some success and that we are in a very different place than 1989. Apsis writes from the perspective of a young disabled person and suggests that for inclusion to become a reality, we need to rethink what we value about education and why. What's more, central to this process of rethinking is the voice of young disabled people, which should be properly heard and valued.

The importance of the experiential is taken further by Thomas in her chapter. She argues that, under the influence of feminism, a number of disabled women writers have rejected the binary divide between the personal and social and insist on the way oppression is interconnected both within the private and public spheres of life. She rejects the position of some disability theorists, notably Finkelstein and myself, who argue that attempting to incorporate personal experiences of impairment into the social model of disability risks diluting our political struggles to overcome the barriers in society we face. She further argues that the incorporation of experience actually adds both to our theoretical understandings of disability as well as our political struggles for inclusion.

Rioux uses Canadian history to show how the political struggles for change in respect of disabled people have themselves changed and that they are now being shaped by issues of human rights and social justice rather than by those of social development and charitable aid. She sees these changes as wholly positive although she recognises that there is still a long way to go. Barton locates his analysis within what he sees as a growing disillusion with politics in modern societies and agues not only that disabled people need a politics of hope but that the experiences of disabled people also offer hope for politics. There are two reasons for his optimism; first the experiences of disabled people are so stark that they expose the stark realities of inequality, oppression and discrimination that still characterise modern societies, and secondly that through their own collective self-organisation, disabled people are rescuing the political process from inertia and apathy.

So far I have attempted to summarise what I see as the key issues emerging from the other contributors to this volume. In several of the chapters, there are points raised that I would dispute or disagree with but I have decided not to deal with these in any detail because all of the chapters add to our understandings of the production of disability under the conditions of modernity. However, social theorists are increasingly beginning to argue that the current changes that are occurring are so profound that we can no longer talk about our worlds using modernity as the central concept. Instead we need to reconceptualise this world as postmodernity and for the rest of this chapter I want to take their, and my, arguments further by considering the way disability is likely to be produced under the emerging conditions of postmodernity.

The production of disability under the changing conditions of postmodernity

There are a number of preliminary points that I need to make about this. To begin with there is the issue of terminology: different theorists use different terminology to refer to these

changes that are now occurring and while modernity/postmodernity have become the dominant descriptive terms, I prefer to think that we are entering the phase of late capitalism.
However, for the purposes of this chapter I will retain the dominant terminology although
there will inevitably be some slippage. In addition and just to say a bit more about my own position which I (still) locate as within Marxism, I don't agree with those Marxists who Daly (1999:
62) suggests 'see this perspective only a threat to Marxism and, indeed, the whole radical tradition'. Rather, like Laclau and Mouffe (1987), only by taking on the postmodern perspective do
I believe it is 'possible to reactivate the emancipatory potential of Marxism ... as part of a
broader project of radical democracy' (Daly 1999: 63).

It is also true that with the coming of the postmodern turn, we have seen changes to the
nature of theorising itself. The goal of objectivity has broken down in the face of criticisms
from a variety of disempowered and disenfranchised groups (Barnes and Mercer 1997; Clough
and Barton 1999) to the point where personal experience has sometimes become a standpoint
epistemology (Morris 1991). Again some of the authors in this volume stress the importance
of the experiential in the struggle for change and I shall return to this later. The overall
outcome of the nature of theory itself becoming increasingly contested has been that it has
often been denigrated from both sides because of its partiality: academics suggest that new
theory is often unrepresentative of the totality of experience and activists that it is usually irrelevant to the lives of most people. The solution to this dilemma according to Carol Thomas
(1999) is to combine structural analysis with writing oneself into the picture; in other words,
theory needs to eradicate the distinction between the personal and the political, as she argues
herein.

As I have already suggested most social theorists would agree that the kind of changes we
are experiencing as we move into the 21st century are profound and may even be as significant
for us and the changes in our lives as the replacement of feudalism by capitalism was for our
ancestors in a previous epoch. The fundamentals of this are well known: the move from a
fordist to a post-fordist mode of production; the coming of globalisation and the decline in
importance of the nation state; the increasing importance of fundamentalism and
consumerism to the process of identity formation; the rise of a global postmodern culture; the
increasing importance of new technology; and the speed-up of mass communication through
satellites and the internet, to name some of the most important ones.

It can be argued that as far as disabled people are concerned, the coming of postfordism
offers the real possibility that disabled people might be better integrated into the workforce
than they were under a fordist mode of production (Oliver 1995); especially with the potential
that new technology offers in opening up job opportunities (Roulstone 1998). However there
is little evidence yet to support such an argument; the unemployment rate among disabled
people has changed little in the past ten years and remains similar to that during the period of
fordism (Burchardt 2000), despite the fact that we have seen the introduction of anti-discrimination legislation in many parts of the world (Drake 1999). Recent evaluations of the Americans with Disabilities Act (1990) come to similar conclusions; little progress has been made in
getting disabled people into the labour force.

This pessimistic analysis does not merely condemn disabled people to continuing poverty in
the postmodern world but means the positioning of disabled people as dependent in modern
societies is unlikely to be changed under the conditions of postmodernity and makes Hughes'

call for the disability movement to develop a cultural politics of identity all the more pertinent and urgent. However, the consequences of the coming of postmodernity for disabled people are not solely dependent upon bottom-up politics but also the policy responses of the state (national or global) to what it perceives as problems. It is to this issue that I now propose to turn.

The economy and social and educational policy

There is no doubt that since the rise of modernity, social and educational policy has been shaped by capital's need for accumulation and profit although this is not an attempt to deny that political struggles against inequality and injustice have also played a part and are continuing so to do, as Rioux makes clear in her contribution herein. Nevertheless all social and educational policy can be seen (in part at least) as inextricably linked and intended to facilitate these two aims. The welfare state, in its broadest sense, has been part of this and has been seen and even dismissed by some as a failed project of modernity.

With the coming of postmodernity however, then it is likely that the relationship between the economy and social policy will change fundamentally. And according to some commentators, this is already happening:

> Social policy in such conditions is conceived less as a means to redistribute incomes and wealth, or to act as a band-aid for capitalism, and rather as a means of increasing individual opportunities by creating labour market flexibility in a global economy and expanding the non-inflationary growth rate of the British economy. (Driver and Martell 1999: 250)

This, of course, will affect the future of the welfare state. Giddens (1998), for example, suggests that the new welfare state must switch to being a 'risk-management' enterprise whose aim is to prevent problems from occurring rather than one which compensates afterwards. This would obviously involve a renegotiation of the relationship between the economy and social and educational policy; he suggests that the radically reformed welfare state would, in fact, be a 'social investment state in the positive welfare society' (Giddens 1998: 127).

Quite what he means by this is unclear but others have been more explicit:

> If the welfare state is to survive, it will have to restructure along several lines to meet the needs of the new consumer and the new economy – without forgetting to take care of those who little occupy the role of consumer: the elderly and the disabled for instance. Problem setting and solving upon the grounds of real, objective and expert needs are now crosscut with those set by the more subjective agendas of desires and wants. If it cannot respond by learning from and by co-operating with the other welfare sectors, the welfare state will become increasingly irrelevant, or be replaced by … the competition state. (Gibbins and Reimer 1999: 130–1)

The problem with this analysis however is that it continues to position disabled people in the way described by Hughes: as dependent, as non-consumers. There are two problems with this. To begin with, it is simply inaccurate to position either elderly or disabled people as non-consumers; pensions and benefits provide a substantial boost to the economy. For example, disabled people have more than a billion pounds to spend each year on personal mobility and Motability buys more new cars every year than any other organisation in Europe. Additionally, Gibbins and Reimer, like many other postmodernists, don't throw out the modern baby from the postmodern bath. If all knowledge is contested and relative under postmodern conditions, how can we base the postmodern welfare state on objective need? Elsewhere (Oliver 1996a) I have argued that this was one of the central reasons why the welfare state failed disabled people under the conditions of modernity.

They are right to point out, however, that the welfare state will change fundamentally in the postmodern society to which we are moving. Under modernity the main goals of policy were a healthy and compliant workforce and a social division of labour which reproduced this. Leaving aside the odd difficulty caused by the boom and bust trade cycle, by and large under modernity social policy delivered these goals very well. However it is becoming increasingly obvious that under the conditions of postmodernity with the rise of the global economy and higher productivity due to new technology, these conditions are changing fast. In sum, less people work to produce more goods and the goals of the postmodern state are not so much concerned with the supply of labour and social reproduction as with the demand for goods worldwide and the need to control the ever-increasing non-working population.

The precise implications for this are difficult to predict with any certainty, but in the next section I want to consider what will happen to the education of disabled people; a central concern of several of the other contributors to this volume.

The development of education policy in the postmodern world

As the nature of work changes in the postmodern world, it is inevitable that the relationship between work and education is changing to accommodate it. This is bound to have a major impact on education. As Lipsky and Gartner put it:

> Just as the regime of the production line influenced the shape of public education in the industrial era, the nature of post-industrial society and its work have consequences for the educational system of the twenty first century. (Lipsky and Gartner 1997: 250)

Under conditions of postmodernity, education no longer functions entirely to serve the needs of the capitalist nation state.

The reasons for this are becoming increasingly obvious. To begin with we are seeing the rise of the global economy in which both the size and power of multinational companies are beginning to supersede the nation state. As a consequence these multinationals have a presence in education systems with their sponsorship schemes buying books, computers and other equipment and funding research and scholarship. Additionally the global economy is increasingly being driven by consumption rather than production, making the rationale for these sponsorship schemes obvious; their corporate imagery penetrates deeper and deeper into ever younger minds. Finally, flexible labour markets are becoming increasingly internationalised, posing difficulties for national education systems. As more and more young people come to realise that their futures have been exported, they increasingly vote with their feet and abandon their schools for the shopping malls and the streets.

Given these far-reaching and fundamental changes which are now occurring in the economy, it is obvious that the relationship between it and education will also change fundamentally. But more importantly for our purposes here, if these changes are indeed occurring, then there is bound to be a considerable impact on the way education is provided for disabled people, notably through the mechanism of special education. Before going on to consider this in some detail we need to examine the evidence we already have for changes in the relationship between education and the economy that are beginning to occur.

One obvious change as we move away from the condition of modernity is that less people are working to support more people who don't. This is reproduced in education where the numbers of people studying full and part time are far greater than they have ever been. Additionally we see governments supporting a whole range of 'education for life' initiatives which acknowledge that the old relationship between education and the economy has broken down; schooling no longer ends when adolescents have been prepared for jobs for life.

> Governments need to emphasise 'life long education', developing education programmes that start from an individual's early years and continue on even late in life. (Giddens 1998: 125)

Further, with the marketisation of education, we have seen a move away from the ideology of 'education for personal growth' and onto education serving the needs of flexible international labour markets and the global economy. Finally, in recent years we have seen the development of sustained critiques of the normative criteria such as IQ testing on which education for modernity have been based.

But not all the trends are in the same direction. For example we see the education curriculum, in schools as well as further and higher education, being driven increasingly by other kinds of normative criteria such as standard assessment tests (SATS) of one kind or another. Additionally, despite the development of flexible learning systems, we continue to see paper chases to obtain educational qualifications for jobs even where such qualifications are not necessary because, as Jordan has recently pointed out:

> …it is a complete fallacy to suppose a correlation between high standards in education and technical training and high levels of economic participation. (Jordan 1998: 47)

Indeed many disabled people can testify to this, having taken training course after course to the point of being overeducated and underemployed. And finally of course, despite this and the effects of globalisation, national politicians still see votes for education as key to their election. Education has been the number one priority in two recent elections in Britain for the current government.

Educating disabled people within the contradictions of post-modernity

This apparently contradictory set of 'social facts' are relatively easy to explain. We are straddling the shift from one kind of society to another and under such circumstances we can expect to see a battle between conservative and radical forces. Indeed the German sociologist Karl Mannheim drew attention to this in a book tellingly entitled *Ideology and Utopia*. More recently other writers have turned to this and Jock Young has called the phenomenon 'the contradictions of late modernity'. Using a nautical metaphor, he explains:

> The movement into late modernity is like a ship which has broken from its moorings. Many of the crew try to return to the familiar sanctuary of the harbour but to their alarm the compass spins, the ship continues on its way and, looking back, the quay is no longer secure: at times it seems to be falling apart, its structure fading and disintegrating. The siren voices which forlornly, seriously, soberly try to convince them that going back is possible are mistaken. (Young 1999: 191)

So what does all this mean for special education and the education of disabled people under the changed conditions of postmodernity? If education is going to be re-created in the new society to which we are moving and going back is impossible, then it is also inevitable that special education will be transformed by that process of re-creation, indeed if it is to survive at all. Special education does not exist in some kind of privileged vacuum which will keep it immune from these changes because:

> There can be no disputing that the history of special education is inseparable from the history of regular education. (Richardson 1999: xv)

In fact, we can begin to see from the struggles already being waged over the role and future of special education that it will be transformed by some of the major social and economic forces I have outlined in this chapter as well as those discussed by Rieser, Aspis and Vlachou-Balafouti elsewhere in this volume. The way in which debates in special education have moved away from what used to be called the integration/segregation debate and onto what has come to be called the inclusion/exclusion debate is indicative of the fact that this debate, once narrowly confined to education is now about the possibility of the inclusive society (Oliver 1996a). And with the coming of the idea of the inclusive society, special education, which has excluded throughout its history, faces the possibility of its own demise.

Of course, it is possible to argue, as Roger Slee does, that this shift 'connotes a linguistic adjustment to present a politically correct façade to a changing world' (Slee 1998: 131). While this may be the case for many within special education, I would argue that the implications of this changing world are so profound that mere linguistic adjustment is a strategy which is bound to fail those special educators wishing to keep things as they are.

If Giddens is right, then the implications for special education are indeed profound. Up to now the special education paradigm has attempted to compensate individuals for their (presumed) intellectual, physical or behavioural deficits although, as I and others have already suggested, it has failed. Quite how it could reconstruct itself as a risk management enterprise is difficult to see and hence it is unlikely to be provided with the social investment to make a positive contribution to the welfare society. Hence, as I have already suggested, the future for special education is likely to be bleak. What this will mean for the education of disabled people under the conditions of postmodernity is not just dependent upon how the state responds to these changing conditions but also upon the ways in which disability movements respond as well. It is this to which we must finally return.

The politics of postmodernity

The contradictions of late modernity have been identified earlier as just as apparent in the arena of human agency as they are in other aspects of our worlds. As Barnes and Mercer describe herein, on the one hand we see the decline of traditional political institutions like monarchies, states and parties and yet on the other we see a plethora of disempowered and disenfranchised groups organising themselves into new social movements of all kinds. These movements often cross national boundaries, present broadly based critiques of existing economic, political and social institutions and arrangements and use a whole range of tactics to promote their ideas and goals.

These struggles have taken place within disability and we have seen the emergence of an increasingly powerful international disability movement (Driedger 1989), although as Hahn, Sullivan and Camilleri and Callus have reminded us, national contexts do influence the trajectory of these movements nationally. However it would be wrong to suggest, as some postmodernist theorising about new social movements does, that this means that movements like the disability movement are located solely around struggles over 'postmaterialist values'.

This can lead to the kind of absurd claims that have been made by theorists like Williams (1999) who suggests that the disability movement has 'written the body out' (p. 803) of all consideration. Quite how he comes to this conclusion when one of the central planks of the disability movement since Berkeley 1961 has been independent living is a mystery. Independent living is of course about nothing more or less than rescuing the body from the hands of medics, other professionals and welfare administrators. And of course, the struggle for independent living is in the first instance a struggle to rescue the disabled body from the hands of doctors and welfare administrators and not a struggle about conceptual or cultural representation.

That is not to deny the importance of such representations and as Hughes makes clear, struggles have and will continue to take place at the ideological or cultural level and promote celebrations rather than control of difference. The struggles so far have been allied to an increasingly thriving disability arts movement which has moved beyond 'art as therapy' and onto 'transformative identity politics' and beyond. Of course, the contradictions of late modernity cannot be ignored here either; with the emergence of the radical forces of celebration we have also seen the coming of the conservative forces of eradication. For disabled people the potential for celebration with the coming of postmodernity is, at least, tempered by the threats of genetic engineering, selective abortion, non-resuscitation policies, health care rationing and euthanasia.

The disability movement has also had an important influence on the development of social and educational policy. The three big ideas of the movement, the social model, civil rights and independent living, have not merely changed the social and legal framework within which policies are developed and services provided, but they have also impacted upon professional practice. And as a consequence of this, the material circumstances under which many disabled people now live out their lives have changed for the better. But, of course, whether they are changing fast enough and for enough disabled people remains a crucial issue (Burchardt 2000).

Education and social policy is not immune from the effects of these new social movements. It is not just being changed by the broader economic and social forces that are transforming all our lives but it is also being transformed by the dissenting voices of disabled people ourselves: we are writing ourselves into the picture of an inclusive postmodernity. With the rise of a powerful international disability movement, the critical voices of disabled people have begun to speak out against our decarceration in all areas of our lives and the institutions in which we have been placed under modernity; whether those institutions be residential homes, hospitals, villages, special schools or units. Hence political struggles have developed around our rights to go to the schools, colleges and universities of our choice as well as all other areas of economic and social life (Campbell and Oliver 1996).

In these increasingly intense struggles between conservative and radical forces, standing still is not an option for disabled people. If the forces of reaction emerge triumphant, society will not continue to fund special places for special people because the economic returns will not justify it and eradication will be the preferred option. If the forces of radicalism emerge triumphant, there will simply be no place for special facilities of any kind in the inclusive society.

Conclusions

At the beginning of this article I suggested that I was more comfortable with the term 'late capitalism' than 'postmodernity'. My reason for this is that my own intellectual background owes much to Marxist social theory. To put it bluntly, I was a Marxist before it was fashionable, while it was fashionable and I still think it has much to offer now it is no longer fashionable. One thing that it has to offer which postmodernism does not is an optimistic view of the future. While postmodern theorising tends to be suspicious about our abilities to shape the future and is perhaps pessimistic about the world to which we are moving, I am more optimistic about future possibilities and our abilities to make our own histories.

What all the contributors make clear in their own ways in this volume is that disabled people do not share the pessimism of much postmodern thinking. Under the changing conditions of modernity, we have forced our ideas and issues onto political agendas and have rung crucial changes out of many of our dominant social institutions. While there is some indication that disability movements across the world are beginning to experience some of the fragmentation that has characterised other social movements as we move into the postmodern world, I remain optimistic and expect the next epoch to be much more inclusive than the previous one. Martin Sullivan, in his chapter, quoted the words of Bob Dylan. Like Leonard Cohen, I remain convinced that 'Democracy is coming...', for disabled people at least.

Questions

- Can we expect to see major changes to economic and social policy in respect of disabled people in the future, and why or why not?
- Do disabled people have the power to transform their own lives?

References

1 in 8 Group (1996) Disability in the Media 1 in 8 Group 78, Mildmay Grove South, London N1 4PJ.

Abberley, P. (1987) 'The concept of oppression and the development of a social theory of disability', *Disability, Handicap and Society* 2, 5–20.

Abberley, P. (1989) 'Disabled people, normality and social work', in L. Barton (ed.) *Disability and Dependency*. Lewes: The Falmer Press.

Abberley, P. (1992) 'Counting us out: a discussion of the OPCS disability surveys', *Disability, Handicap and Society* 7(2):139–56.

Abberley, P. (1993) 'Disabled people and "Normality"', in J. Swain *et al.* (eds) *Disabling Barriers – Enabling Environments*. London: Sage.

Able Update (1999) The Magazine of DPA (New Zealand) Inc. Election '99. DPA, PO Box 27-524, Wellington 6035, New Zealand. 9(1), August.

ACT (2000) *School Life. Research on the views of children and young people about their education*. Preston: ACT. (Obtainable from ACT, (Northwest) Ltd., Preston Business Centre, Watling Street Road, Preston, Lancs, PR2 8DY.)

Ainscow, M. (1991) *Effective Schools for All*. London: David Fulton Publishers.

Ainscow, M. (1995) 'Special needs through school improvement: school improvement through special needs,' in C. Clark *et al.* (eds) *Toward Inclusive Schools*. London: David Fulton Publishers.

Ainscow, M. (1999) *Understanding the Development of Inclusive Schools*. London: Falmer Press.

Ainscow, M. *et al.* (1994) *Creating the Conditions for School Improvement*. London: David Fulton Publishers.

Ainscow, M. *et al.* (2000) *The Index for Inclusion*. Bristol: CSIE.

Allan, J. (1999) *Actively Seeking Inclusion: Pupils with Special Needs in Mainstream Schools*. London: Falmer Press.

Alliance (2001) *The Inclusion Assistant – A Consultant with Young Disabled People and their Parents*. By Alliance for Inclusive Education. Unit 2, 70 South Lambeth Road, London SW8 1RL.

Allman, P. (1999) *Revolutionary Social Transformation: Democratic Hopes, Political Possibilities and Critical Education*. London: Bergin and Garvey.

Andrews v Law Society of British Columbia (1989) 1 S.C.R. 143, 56 D.L.R. (4th)1.

Andrews, G. (1991) *Citizenship*. London: Lawrence and Wishart.

Anspach, R. (1979) 'From stigma to identity politics', *Social Science and Medicine,* 13A, 765–73.

Apple, M. (1986) *Teachers and Texts. A Political Economy of Class and Gender Relations in Education.* London: Routledge and Kegan Paul.

Armstrong, D. and Dolinski, R. (1999) 'What about Chantel? From inside out: an insider's experience of exclusion', *Internation Journal of Inclusive Education* 3(1): 27–36 (Special Issue: Competition, Selection and Inclusive Education).

Armstrong, D. *et al.* (2000) 'Introduction: what is this book about?', in F. Armstrong *et al.* (eds) *Inclusive Education: Policy, Contexts and Comparative Perspectives.* London: David Fulton Publishers.

Aronson, R. (1999) 'Hope after hope', *Social Research* 66(2), 471–94 (Special Issue).

Aspis, S. (2000) *Disabled Children with Learning Difficulties Fight for Inclusive Education.* London: Changing Perspectives.

Atkinson, D. *et al.* (eds) (2000) *Good Times, Bad Times: Women with Learning Difficulties Telling their Stories.* Kidderminster: BILD publications.

Awatere, D. (1984) *Maori Sovereignty.* Auckland, NZ: Broadsheet.

Bakhtin, M. (1984) *Rabelais and His World.* Bloomington: Indiana University Press.

Barnes, C. (1990) *Cabbage Syndrome: The Social Construction of Dependence.* Lewes: The Falmer Press.

Barnes, C. (1991) *Disabled People in Britain and Discrimination: A Case for Anti-discrimination Legislation.* London: Hurst and Co. in association with the British Council of Organizations of Disabled People.

Barnes, C. (1992) 'Qualitative research: valuable or irrelevant?', *Disability, Handicap and Society* 7(2), 115–24.

Barnes, C. (1995) *Making Our Own Choices: Independent Living, Personal Assistance and Disabled People.* Belper: British Council of Organizations of Disabled People.

Barnes, C. (1996) 'Theories of disability and the oppression of disabled people in western society', in L. Barton (ed.) *Disability and Society: Emerging Issues and Insights*, 43–60. London: Addison Wesley Longman.

Barnes, C. (1997) 'A Legacy of Oppression: A History of Disability in Western Cultures', in L. Barton and M. Oliver (eds) *Disability Studies: Past, Present and Future.* Leeds: The Disability Press.

Barnes, C. (1998) 'Review of *The Rejected Body* by Susan Wendell', *Disability and Society* 13(1), 145–6.

Barnes, C. and Mercer, G. (eds) (1996) *Exploring the Divide: Illness and Disability.* Leeds: The Disability Press.

Barnes, C. and Mercer, G. (eds) (1997) *Doing Disability Research.* Leeds: The Disability Press.

Barnes, C. *et al.* (1999) *Exploring Disability: A Sociological Introduction.* Cambridge: Polity Press.

Bartolo, P. A. (2000) 'The development of inclusive education for children with autism in Malta' in Mark G. Borg and Paul A. Bartolo (eds) *Autism: the Challenge of Inclusion.* Proceedings of the First Malta International Conference on Autism. Malta: The Eden Foundation.

Barton, L. (1993a) 'The struggle for citizenship: the case of disabled people', *Disability and Society* 8(3), 236–48.

Barton, L. (ed.) (1993b) *Disability and Dependency.* Lewes: The Falmer Press.

Barton, L. (2001) 'Disability and social justice', in A. Zoniou-Sideris and A. Vlachou (eds) *Policies and Practices in the Area of Special/Inclusive Education* (tentative title). Athens: Hellenic Grammata.

Barton, L. and Oliver, M. (eds) (1997) *Disability Studies: Past, Present and Future*. Leeds: The Disability Press.

Barton, L. and Slee, R. (1999) 'Competition, selection and inclusive education: some observations', *Internation Journal of Inclusive Education* 3(1), 3–12 (Special Issue: Competition, Selection and Inclusive Education).

Bauman, Z. (1992) *Intimations of Postmodernity*. London: Routledge.

Bauman, Z. (1993) *Postmodern Ethics*. Oxford: Blackwell.

Bauman, Z. (1995) *Life in Fragments: Essays in Postmodern Morality*. Oxford: Blackwell.

BCODP (1986) *Disabled Young People Living Independently*. London: British Council of Organizations of Disabled People.

BCODP (2001) Personal enquiry, 6 March.

Beatson, P. (1998) 'Managing disability. An interview with John Stott', *New Zealand Journal of Disability Studies* 3, 3–27.

Beatson, P. (2000) *The Disability Revolution in New Zealand. A Social Map*. Palmerston North, NZ: Massey University.

Begum, N. (1992) 'Disabled women and the feminist agenda', *Feminist Review* 40, 70–84.

bell hooks (2000) *All About Love: New Visions*. London: The Women's Press.

Beresford, P. and Campbell, J. (1994) 'Disabled people, service users, user involvement and representation', *Disability and Society* 9(3), 315–26 (Special Issue).

Berkowitz, E. D. (1987) *Disabled Policy: America's Program for the Handicapped*. New York: Cambridge University Press.

Bezzina, F. (1989) 'The reality – a chain of decisions', in F. Bezzina (ed.) *Lejn il- Futur (The Journey Ahead)*, proceedings of a national seminar held on the 27–28 May 1989. Malta: Kummissjoni Nazzjonali Handikappati.

Bezzina, F. (ed.) (1993) *Special Education in Malta: A National Policy*. Malta: Kummissjoni Nazzjonali Persuni b'Dizabilità.

Bezzina, F. (ed.) (1996) *Measures Taken to Ensure Equal Opportunities for Disabled Persons and their Families* (unpublished list). Malta: Kummissjoni Nazzjonali Persuni b'Dizabilità

Bezzina, F. (ed.) (1999) *National Disability Survey 1999*. Malta: Kummissjoni Nazzjonali Persuni b'Dizabilità.

Bezzina, F. and Camilleri, J. M. (eds) (1994) *Persons with Disability and Employment*. Malta: Kummissjoni Nazzjonali Persuni b'Dizabilità.

Bezzina, F., and Camilleri, J. M. (eds) (1996): *National Conference on Special Education in Malta: proceedings*. Malta: National Commission Persons with Disability. A verbal intervention by Mr S. Sciriha.

Bickenbach, J. E. *et al.* (1999) 'Models of disablement, universalism, and the international classification of impairments, disabilities, and handicaps', *Social Science and Medicine* 48, 1173–87.

Binney, J. (1989) 'The Maori and the signing of the Treaty of Waitangi', in D. Green (ed.) *Towards 2000: Seven Leading Historians Examine Significant Aspects of New Zealand History*. Wellington, NZ: GP Books.

Bishop, M. E. (ed.) (1995) *Religion and Disability: Essays in Scripture Theology and Ethics*. Franklin: Sheed and Ward.

Bordo, S. (1990) 'Feminism, postmodernism, and gender-scepticism', in L. J. Nicholson (ed.) *Feminism and Postmodernism.* London: Routledge.

Boswell, J. (1988) *The Kindness of Strangers.* New York: Pleneurn Press.

Bowe, F. (1978) *Handicapping America: Barriers to Disabled People.* New York: Harper and Row.

Brandt, E. N. Jr. and Pope, A. M. (1997) *Enabling America: Assessing the Role of Rehabilitation Science and Engineering.* Washington, DC: National Academy Press.

Branson, J. and Miller, D. (1989) 'Beyond integration policy: The deconstruction of disability', in L. Barton (ed.) *Integration: Myth or Reality?* London: The Falmer Press.

Briffa, M. and Camilleri, J. M. (eds) (1997) Equal Opportunities Persons with Disability: a White Paper. Proceedings of public discussions. Malta: Kummissjoni Nazzjonali Persuni b'Dizabilità.

Bristo, M. (2000) Letter of Transmittal, in NCD. *Promises to Keep: A Decade of Federal Enforcement of the Americans with Disabilities Act.* Washington DC: National Council on Disability.

British Columbia, L. A. (1897) 'Annual Report'. British Columbia, Legislative Assembly.

British Columbia Assembly. (1898) 'British Columbia Assembly, Annual Report'.

Brock, J. (1966) 'The right to live in the world: the disabled in the law of torts,' *California Law Review* 54, 841–64.

Brown v Topeka Board of Education (1954) 347 US 483.

Brown, O. (1985) 'To incite insight: gender and disability', *Race, Gender, Class* 2, 11–19.

Brown, S. E. *et al.* (eds) (1985) *With the Power of Each Breath: A Disabled Women's Anthology.* Pittsburgh, PA: Cleis Press.

Burchardt, T. (2000) *Enduring Economic Exclusion: Disabled People, Income and Work.* York: Joseph Rowntree Foundation.

Camilleri, J. M. (1999) 'Disability: a personal odyssey', *Disability and Society* 14(6), 845–53. London: Carfax.

Campbell, J. and Oliver, M. (1996) *Disability Politics. Understanding Our Past, Challenging Our Future.* London: Routledge.

Carrithers, M. *et al.* (eds) (1985) *The Category of the Person.* Cambridge: Cambridge University Press.

Casey, E. (1997) *The Fate of Place: A Philosophical History.* Los Angeles: University of California Press.

Cawson, A. (1982) *Corporatism and Welfare: Social Policy and State Intervention in Britain.* London: Heinemann.

Central Office of Statistics (1998) *Demographic Review of the Maltese Islands.* Malta: Central Office of Statistics.

Centre for Educational Research and Innovation (1986) *Young People with Handicaps: The Road to Adulthood.* Paris: OECD.

Chappell, A. L. (1997) 'From normalization to where?', in L. Barton and M. Oliver (eds) *Disability Studies: past, present and future.* Leeds: The Disability Press.

Charlton, J. I. (1998) *Nothing About Us Without Us: Disability Oppression and Empowerment.* Berkeley: University of California Press.

Christie, I. with Mensah-Coker, G. (1999) *An Inclusive Future: disability, social change and opportunities for greater inclusion by 2010.* London: Demos.

Clark v Clark (1982) O.R. (2nd) 383, 4, 4 C.H.H.R. D/1187 (CoCt).

Clark, C. *et al.*(1995) 'Dialectical analysis, special needs and schools as organizations', in C. Clark *et al.* (eds) *Towards Inclusive Schools?* London: David Fulton Publishers.

Clark, C. *et al.* (1999) 'Inclusive schools and schools as organizations', *Internation Journal of Inclusive Education* 3(1), 37–5. 1

Clark, C. *et al.* (eds) (1998) *Theorising Special Education.* London: Routledge.

Cleburne v Cleburne Living Center (1985) 473 US 432.

Clough, P. and Barton, L. (eds) *Articulating with Difficulty: Research Voices in Inclusive Education.* London: Paul Chapman Publishing.

Cohen, J. (1999) 'Changing paradigms of citizenship and the exclusiveness of the demos', *International Sociology* 14(3), 245–68.

Cole, T. (1989) *Apart or a Part?: Integration and the Growth of British Special Education*, Milton Keynes: Open University Press.

Coleridge, P. (1993) *Disability, Liberation and Development.* Oxford: Oxfam Publications.

Comic Relief (1999) 'The best lesson plans in the world ever'. Comic Relief, 5th Floor, 89 Albert Embankment, London SE1 7TP.

Comic Relief (2001) 'Young persons guide to changing the world, the universe'. London: Comic Relief.

Commission on Citizenship (1990) *House of Commons Commission on Citizenship.* London: HMSO.

Cooper, M. (1999) 'The Australian Disability Rights Movement Lives', *Disability and Society* 14(2), 217–26.

Coote, A. and Campbell, B. (1982) *Sweet Freedom: The Struggle for Women's Liberation.* London: Picador.

CORAD (1982) *Report of the Committee on Restrictions Against Disabled People.* London: HMSO.

Corbett, J. (1994) 'A proud label: exploring the relationship between disability politics and gay pride', *Disability and Society* 9(3), 343–57.

Corbett, J. (1998) 'Inclusivity and school culture: the case of special education', in J. Prosser (ed.) *School Culture.* London: Paul Chapman.

Corbett, J. (1999) 'Inclusive education and school culture', *Internation Journal of Inclusive Education* 3(1), 53–61.

Corker, M. (1998) *Deaf and Disabled, or Deafness Disabled?* Buckingham: Open University Press.

Corker, M. (1999) 'Differences, conflations and foundations: the limits to "accurate" theoretical representation of disabled people's experience?', *Disability and Society* 14(5), 627–42.

Corker, M. (2000) 'The U.K. Disability Discrimination Act: disabling language, justifying inequitable social participation', in L. P. Francis and A. Silvers (eds) *Americans with Disabilities: Exploring Implications of the Law for Individuals and Institutions*, 357–70. New York: Routledge.

Corker, M. and French, S. (1999) 'Reclaiming discourse in disability studies', in M. Corker (ed.) *Disability Discourse.* Buckingham, Philadelphia: Open University Press.

Council for Disabled Children (1994) 'Policy statement from the integration working party'. 8, Wakley Street, London EC1.

Crewe, N. and Zola, I. K. (1983) *Independent Living for Physically Disabled People.* London: Jossey Bass.

Crow, L. (1996) 'Including all of our lives: renewing the social model of disability', in C. Barnes and G. Mercer (eds) *Exploring the Divide: Illness and Disability*. Leeds: The Disability Press.

Crowther, J. and Shaw, M. (1997) 'Social movements and the education of desire', *Development Journal. An International Forum* 32(3), 266–79 (Special Issue).

CSIE (2000) *Index for Inclusion*. Bristol: CSIE.

Cuschieri, L. (1995) *Monseigneur Mikiel Azzopardi, 1910–1987*. Malta: Dar tal-Providenza.

Daly, G. (1999) 'Marxism and postmodernity', in A. Gamble *et al.* (eds) *Marxism and Social Science*. Basingstoke: Macmillan.

Davis, K. (1996) 'Disability and legislation: rights and equality', in G. Hales (ed.) *Beyond Disability: Towards an Enabling Society*. London: Sage.

Dean, C. (2001) 'The Age of Apathy', *Times Educational Supplement* 18, 6 May.

Deegan, M. J. and Brooks, N. (eds) (1985) *Women and Disability*. New Brunswick, NJ: Transaction Books.

Degener, T. (1995) 'Disabled persons and human rights: the legal framework', in T. D. A. Y. Koster-Dreese (ed.) *Human Rights and Disabled Persons: Essays and Relevant Human Rights Instruments*. The Netherlands: F. Martinus Nijhoff Publishers.

DeJong, G. (1983) 'Defining and implementing the independent living concept', in N. Crewe and I. K. Zola, *Independent Living for Physically Disabled People*. London: Jossey Bass.

Department of Social Science (1998) *Labour Force Survey*. London: DSS.

DEE (1999) 'Are you prepared for the Future? Inclusive Education'. Disability Equality in Education, Unit 4Q Leroy House, 436 Essex Road, London N1 3QP.

Department of Education and Science (1978) 'Special Educational Needs (The Warnock Report)'. London: HMSO.

Department of Information (1969) Act No. II of 1969 *Employment of Disabled Persons Act*. Malta: DOI.

Department of Information (2000) Act I of 2000. *The Equal Opportunities (Persons with Disability) Act*. Malta: DOI.

DES (1977) *DES Statistics 1977*. London: DES.

DfEE (1997 to 2000) *Secondary School Performance Tables*. (November), London: DFEE.

DfEE (1999) *SEN Statistical Bulletin*. London: DfEE.

DfEE (2000) 'Statistics of Education: Special Educational Needs Statistics January 2000' 09/00, London: DFEE.

Disability Rights Task Force (1999) *From Exclusion to Inclusion: a report of the civil rights task force on the civil rights of disabled people*. London: Department of Education and Science.

Drake, R. (1994) 'The exclusion of disabled people from positions of power in British voluntary organizations', *Disability and Society* 9(4), 461–89.

Drake, R. (1999) *Understanding Disability Policy*. Tavistock: Macmillan.

Driedger, D. (1989) *The Last Civil Rights Movement: Disabled Peoples International*. London: Hurst and Co.

Driedger, D. and Gray, S. (eds) (1992) *Imprinting our Image: An International Anthology by Women with Disabilities*. Charlottetown Canada: gynergy books.

Driver, S. and Martell, L. (1999) 'New Labour: Culture and Economy', in L. Ray and A. Sayer (eds) *Culture and Economy After the Cultural Turn*. London: Sage.

Drudy, S. and Lynch, K. (1993) *Schools and Society in Ireland*. Dublin: Gill and Macmillan.

Durie, M. (1994) *Whaiora. Maori Health Development*. Auckland: Oxford University Press.

Durie, M. (1998) *Te Mana, Te Kawanatanga. The Politics of Maori Self-Determination*. Auckland: Oxford University Press.

Dyson, R. (2000) *Making a World of Difference: Whakanui Oranga. The New Zealand Disability Strategy Discussion Document*. Wellington, New Zealand: Ministry of Health.

Eldridge v British Columbia (Ministry of Health) (1997) 3 S.C.R. 624.

Elias, N. (1978) *The Civilizing Process: Volume 1: The History of Manners*. Oxford: Basil Blackwell.

Elias, N. (1982) *The Civilizing Process: Volume 2: State Formation and Civilization*. Oxford: Basil Blackwell.

Enticott, J. and Graham, P. (1992) *Polls Apart: Disabled People and The 1992 General Election*. London: The Spastics Society.

Evans, M. and Lee, E. (eds) (2001) *Real Bodies*. Basingstoke: Macmillan.

Eve v Eve (1986) 2 S.C.R. 388, 31 D.L.R. (4th).

Fagan, T. and Lee, P. (1997) 'New social movements and social policy: a case study of the disability movement', in M. Lavalette and A. Pratt, *Social Policy: a conceptual and theoretical introduction*. London: Sage.

Farell, P. (1997) *Teaching People with Learning Difficulties: Strategies and Solutions*. London: Paul Chapman.

Fawcett, B. (2000) *Feminist Perspectives on Disability*. London: Prentice Hall.

Fine, M. and Asch, A. (eds) (1988) *Women With Disabilities: Essays in Psychology, Culture and Politics*. Philadelphia: Temple University Press.

Finger, A. (1990) *Past Due: A Story of Disability, Pregnancy and Birth*. London: The Women's Press.

Finkelstein. V. (1980) *Attitudes and Disabled People: Issues for Discussion*. New York: World Rehabilitation Fund.

Finkelstein, V. (1981) 'Disability and the helper/helped relationship: an historical view', in A. Brechin *et al.* (eds) *Handicap in a Social World*. Sevenoaks: Hodder and Stoughton.

Finkelstein, V. (1996a) 'Outside, Inside Out', *Coalition*, April, 30–36.

Finkelstein, V. (1996b) *Modelling Disability*. Paper presented at the 'Breaking The Moulds' conference, Dunfirmline, Scotland, 16–17 May 1996.

Finkelstein, V. (2000) 'Here we go again', *Coalition*, 12 August, (published by Greater Manchester Coalition of Disabled People).

Finkelstein, V. and French, S. (1993) 'Towards a psychology of disability', in J. Swain *et al.* (eds) *Disabling Barriers – Enabling Environments*. London: Sage.

Flying Pigs, Journal of the Alliance for Inclusive Education Unit 2 ,70 South Lambeth Road, London SW8 1RL.

Foucault, M. (1967) *Madness and Civilization*. London: Tavistock.

Foucault, M. (1977) *Discipline and Punish*. Harmondsworth: Penguin.

Foucault, M. (1979) *Discipline and Punish*. New York: Vintage.

Fougeyrollas, P. *et al.* (1998) 'Social consequences of long term impairments and disabilities: conceptual approach and assessment of handicap', *International Journal of Rehabilitation Research* 21, 127–41.

Fragoudaki, A. (unpublished paper) 'On Greek Education', submitted for a European Comenius Project on Teachers Training.

Fragoudaki, A. (1987) *Language and Ideology: A Sociological Approach of Greek Language*. Athens: Odysseus.

Franklin (1986) 'Franklin to Secretary of State PSA, NSA Vol. LXXXIII, 84085, Halifax, August 5, 1768', in S. C. Clark (ed.) *The Social Development of Canada: An Introductory Study with Select Documents*. New York: AMS Press.

Frederikou, A. and Folerou, F. (1991) *The Teachers of Primary Education*. Athens: Ypsilon.

Freire, P. (1970) *Pedagogy of the Oppressed*. New York: Continuum.

Freire, P. (1998) *Pedagogy of Hope. Reliving Pedagogy of the Oppressed*. New York: Continuum.

French, S. (1993) 'Disability, impairment or something in between?', in J. Swain *et al.* (eds) *Disabling Barriers – Enabling Environments*. London: Sage.

French, S. (1999) 'The wind gets in my way', in M. Corker and S. French (eds) *Disability Discourse*. Buckingham, Philadelphia: Open University Press.

Fulcher, G. (1989) *Disabling Policies? A Comparative Approach to Education Policy and Disability*. Lewes: The Falmer Press.

Fulcher, G. (1993) 'Schools and contests: a reframing of the effective school debate?', in R. Slee (ed.) *Is There a Desk With My Name On It? The Politics of Integration*. London: Falmer Press.

Fulcher, G. (2001) 'Policy and integration', in A. Zoniou-Sideris and A. Vlachou (eds) *Policies and Practices in the Area of Special/Inclusive Education* (tentative title). Athens: Hellenic Grammata.

Fullan, M. (1993) *Change Forces: Probing the Depths of Educational Reform*. Lewes: Falmer.

Funderburg, L. (1998) 'Loving thy neighborhood' , *The Nation*, 24.

Fuss, D. (1989) *Essentially Speaking: Feminism, Nature and Difference*. London: Routledge.

Galea-Curmi, E. *et al.* (1997) 'Common human needs: career educational and vocational guidance with students who have disabilities', in R.G. Sultana and J. M. Sammut (eds) *Careers Education and Guidance in Malta: issues and challenges*. Malta: Publishers Enterprises Group (PEG).

Gamble, A. (2000) *Politics and Fate*. Cambridge: Polity Press.

Geertz, C. (1993) *The Interpretation of Cultures*. London: Fontana.

Georgeson, S. (2000) *The Disabled Persons Assembly 1998 –1999: Success, Challenges and Lessons for the Disability Movement in New Zealand,* a Masters in Social Work thesis, School of Social Policy and Social Work, Massey University, New Zealand.

Gergen, K. and Davis, K. (eds) (1985) *The Social Construction of the Person*. New York: Springer Verlag.

Germon, P. (2000) 'Growing our movement', in *Coalition* August, 15–20 (published by Greater Manchester Coalition of Disabled People).

Gibbins, J. and Reimer, B. (1999) *The Politics of Postmodernity*. London: Sage.

Giddens, A. (1990) *The Contradictions of Modernity*. Cambridge: Polity Press.

Giddens, A. (1998) *The Third Way*. Cambridge: Polity Press.

Gleeson, B. (1999) *Geographies of Disability*. London: Routledge.

GMCDP (2000) 'Where have all the activists gone', in *Coalition* (Special Issue). Manchester: Greater Manchester Coalition of Disabled People, August.

Goffman, E. (1968) *Asylums*. Harmondsworth: Penguin.

Gooding, C. (1996) *Disability Discrimination Act 1995*. London: Blackstone Press.

Green. N. (1986) 'Halifax 24, 1766, Green to the Lords Commissioners of Trade and Plantations, PAC, NSA, vol LXXVII', in S. C. Clark (ed.) *The Social Development of Canada: An Introductory Study with Select Documents*, 223–4. New York: AMS Press.

Gregory, J. (1987) *Sex, Race and the Law*. London: Sage.

Groce, N. *et al.* (1998) 'Measuring the quality of life: rethinking the World Bank's disability adjusted life years', *International Rehabilitation Research Review* 4, 12–16.

Guinier, L. (1994) *The Tyranny of the Majority: Fundamental Fairness in Representative Democracy*. New York: The Free Press.

Hahn. H. (1982a) 'The need for deinstitutionalization: mental health', in G. E Caiden and H. Siedentopf (eds) *Strategies for Administrative Reform*, 71–84. Lexington, Massachusetts: D. C. Heath and Co.

Hahn, H. (1982b) 'Disability and rehabilitation policy: is paternalistic neglect really benign?', *Public Administration Review* 43, 385–9.

Hahn, H. (1983) 'Paternalism and public policy', *Society* 20, 36–46.

Hahn, H. (1984a) 'Reconceptualizing disability: a political science perspective', *Rehabilitation Literature* 48, 362–5, 374.

Hahn, H. (1984b) *The Issue of Equality: European Perceptions of Employment Policy for Disabled Persons*. New York: World Rehabilitation Fund.

Hahn, H. (1985a) 'Changing perceptions of disability and the future of rehabilitation', in L. G. Perlman and G. F. Austin (eds) *Societal Influences on Rehabilitation Planning: A Blueprint for the Twenty-first Century*, 53–64. Alexandria, Virginia: National Rehabilitation Association.

Hahn, H. (1985b) 'Disability and the problem of discrimination', *American Behavioral Scientist* 28(3), 293–318.

Hahn, H. (1985c) 'Toward a politics of disability: definitions, disciplines, and policies', *The Social Science Journal* 22(4), 87–105.

Hahn, H. (1986a) 'Disability and the urban environment: a perspective on Los Angeles', *Society and Space* 4, 273–88.

Hahn, H. (1986b) 'Public support for rehabilitation: the analysis of U.S. disability policy', *Disability, Handicap, and Society* 1(2), 121–37.

Hahn, H. (1987a) 'Adapting the environment to people with disabilities: constitutional issues in Canada', *International Journal of Rehabilitation Research* 10(4), 363–72.

Hahn, H, (1987b) 'Advertising the acceptably employable image: disability and capitalism', *Policy Studies Journal* 15(3), 551–7

Hahn, H. (1987c) 'Civil rights for disabled Americans: the foundations of a political agenda', in A. Gartner and T. Joe (eds) *Images of Disability/Disabling Images*, 181–203. New York: Praeger.

Hahn, H. (1987d) 'Public policy and disabled infants: a socio-political perspective', *Issues in Law and Medicine* 3(1), 3–27.

Hahn, H. (1988a) 'Can disability be beautiful?', *Social Policy* 18(3), 26–32.

Hahn, H. (1988b) 'Disability and the reproduction of body images: the dynamics of human appearances', in J. R. Wolch and M. Dear (eds) *The Power of Geography: How Territory Shapes Social Life*, 370–88. London: Allen and Unwin.

Hahn, H. (1988c) 'The politics of physical differences: disability and discrimination', *Journal of Social Issues* 44, 39–43.

Hahn, H. (1989) 'The politics of special education', in D. K. Lipsky and A. Gartner (eds) *Beyond Separate Education: Quality Education for All*, 225–41. Baltimore, Maryland: Paul H. Brookes Co.

Hahn, H. (1990) 'Theories and values: ethics and contrasting perspectives on disability', in B. Duncan and D. E. Woods (eds) *Ethical Issues in Disability and Rehabilitation*, 101–4. New York: Rehabilitation International.

Hahn, H. (1991) 'Alternative views of empowerment: social services and civil rights', *Journal of Rehabilitation* 57(4), 17–19.

Hahn, H. (1993a) 'Equality and the environment: the interpretation of "reasonable accommodation" in the Americans with Disabilities Act', *Journal of Rehabilitation Administration* 17, 101–6.

Hahn, H. (1993b) 'The political implications of disability definitions and data', *Journal of Disability Policy Studies* 4(2), 41–52.

Hahn, H. (1993c) 'The potential impact of disability studies on political science (and vice-versa)', *Policy Studies Journal* 21(4), 740–51.

Hahn, H. (1994a) 'Feminist perspectives, disability, sexuality, and law: new issues and agendas', *Southern California Review of Law and Women's Studies* 4(1), 97–144.

Hahn, H. (1994b) 'The minority group model of disability: implications for medical sociology', in R. Weitz and J. J. Kronenfeld (eds) *Research in the Sociology of Health Care* 11, 3–24. Greenwich, Connecticut: JAI Press.

Hahn, H. (1995) 'The appearance of physical differences: a new agenda for political research', *Journal of Health and Human Resource Administration* 17(4), 391–415.

Hahn, H. (1996) 'Antidiscrimination laws and social research on disability: the minority group perspective', *Behavioral Sciences and the Law* 14, 1–19.

Hahn, H. (1997a) 'An agenda for citizens with disabilities: pursuing identity and empowerment', *Journal of Vocational Rehabilitation* 9, 31–7.

Hahn, H. (1997b) 'New trends in disability studies: implications for educational policy', in D. K. Kirsky and A. Gartner (eds) *Inclusion and School Reform: Transforming America's Classrooms*, 315–28. Baltimore, Maryland: Paul H. Brookes Co.

Hahn, H. (1998) 'Advocacy and educators with disabilities: emerging issues and opportunities', in R. J. Anderson *et al.* (eds) *Enhancing Diversity: Educators with Disabilities*, 225–36. Washington, DC: Gallaudet University Press.

Hahn, H. (2000a) 'Accommodation and the ADA: unreasonable bias or biased reasoning?', *Berkeley Journal of Employment and Labor Law* 21(1), 166–92.

Hahn, H. (2000b) 'Disputing the doctrine of benign neglect: a challenge to the disparate treatment of Americans with disabilities', in L. P. Francis and A. Silvers (eds) *Americans with Disabilities: Exploring Implications of the Law for Individuals and Institutions*, 269–74. New York: Routledge.

Hahn, H. and Beaulaurier (2001) 'Attitudes Toward Disabilities: A Research Note on Activists with Disabilities' *Journal of Disability Policy Studies,* 12(1), 40–46.

Haraway, D. (1991) *Simians, Cyborgs, and Women: the Reinvention of Nature*. London: Free Association Books.

Harding, S. (1991) *Whose Science, Whose Knowledge? Thinking from Women's Lives*. Milton Keynes: Open University Press.

Hargreaves, A. (1994) *Changing Teachers, Changing Times*. London: Cassell.

Hearn, K. (1988) 'Oi! What about us?', in B. Cant and S. Hemmings (eds) *Radical Records: Thirty Years of Lesbian and Gay History*. London: Routledge.

Hearn, K. (1991) 'Disabled lesbians and gays are here to stay', T. Kaufman and P. Lincoln (eds) *High Risk Lives: Lesbian and Gay Politics after the Clause*. Bridport: Prison Press.

Heller, E. (1959) *The Disinherited Mind*. New York: Meridian.

Helman, C. (1994) *Culture Health and Medicine* (3rd edn). Oxford: Butterworth Heinemann.

Hevey, D. (1997) *The Creatures Time Forgot: Photography and Disability Imagery*. London: Routledge.

Hill Collins, P. (1990) *Black Feminist Thought: Knowledge, Consciousness, and the Politics of Empowerment*. London: Routledge.

Hillyer, B. (1993) *Feminism and Disability*. Norman and London: University of Oklahoma Press.

HMSO (1974) Statistics of Education 1973 Vol 1. London: HMSO.

HMSO (1978) Special Educational Needs Report of the Committee of Enquiry into the Education of Handicapped Children and Young People (Warnock) Cmnd 7212. London: HMSO.

Holbrook, T. M. and Percy, S. L. (1992) 'Exploring variations in state laws providing protection for persons with disabilities', *Western Political Quarterly* 45, 201–20.

Hollinger, R. (1994) *Postmodernism and the Social Sciences*. London: Sage.

HRH The Prince Philip (1990) *Duke of Edinburgh Handbook*. Kensington, London (2nd edn).

Hughes, B. (1996) 'Nietzsche: philosophizing with the body', *Body and Society* 2(1), 31–44.

Hughes, B. (1999) 'The constitution of impairment: modernity and the aesthetic of oppression', *Disability & Society* 14(2), 155–72.

Hughes, B. (2000) 'Medicine and the aesthetic invalidation of disabled people', *Disability & Society* 15(4), 555–68.

Hughes, B. and Paterson, K. (1997) 'The social model of disability and the disappearing body: towards a sociology of impairment', *Disability & Society* 12(3), 325–40.

Humphrey, J. (1999) 'Disabled people and the politics of difference', *Disability & Society* 14(2), 173–88.

Humphries, S. and Gordon, P. (1992) *Out of Sight: The Experience of Disability 1900–1950*. London: Northcote House.

Hurst, R. (2000) 'To revise or not to revise', *Disability and Society* 15(7), 1083–7.

ICIDH, C. S. F. (1981) 'The handicap creation process', *ICIDH International Network* 4(1–2).

ILEA(1985) Educational Opportunities for All (The Fish Report). London: ILEA.

Integration Alliance (1989) 'Integration Now: Conference Report', Unit 2, 70 South Lambeth Road, London SW8 1RL.

Illich, I. (1975) *Medical Nemesis: The Expropriation of Health*. London: Marion Boyars.

Illich, I. *et al.* (1977) *Disabling Professions*. London: Marion Boyars.

Imrie, R. (2000) 'Disabling environments and the geography of access policies and practices', *Disability & Society* 15(1), 5–24.

Inclusion and Special Education 2000. Report presented to 'NMC on its way' a conference on the implementation of the National Minimum Curriculum held at the University of Malta in June 2000.

Isaacs, P. (1996) 'Disability and the education of persons', in C. Christensen and F. Rizvi (eds) *Disability and the Dilemmas of Education and Justice*. Buckingham: Open University Press.

ISEC (2000) *International Special Education Congress, Manchester Proceedings on CD-ROM*, Inclusive Technology inclusive.co.uk.

Jamieson, F. (1991) *Postmodernism, or the Cultural logic of Late Capitalism*. London: Verso.

Jigsaw Partnerships (1995) *Disabled and Proud. Pastime Image Posters*. Clitheroe: Jigsaw Partnerships.

Johnson, R. A. (1999) 'Mobilizing the disabled', in J. Freeman and V. Johnson (eds) *Waves of Protest: Social Movements Since the Sixties*, 25-45. Lanham, Maryland: Rowman and Littlefield.

Johnson, T. (1993) 'Expertise and the state', in M. Gane and T. Johnson (eds) *Foucault's New Domains*. London: Routledge.

Jones, M. and Marks, L. A. B. (1999) *Disability, Divers-ability and Legal Change*. International Studies in Human Rights. London: Martinus Nijhoff Publishers.

Jordan, B. (1998) *The New Politics of Welfare*. London: Sage.

Jordan, L. and Goodey, C. (1996) *Human Rights and Social Change: The Newham Story*. CSIE Bristol 1, Redland Close, Elm Lane, Redland, Bristol BS6 6UE.

Kingi, J. and Bray, A. (2000) *Maori Concepts of Disability*. Dunedin, NZ: Donald Beasley Institute Inc.

Kinsella, P. (1998) reported in the minutes of a meeting of the Parliamentary Select Committee on Social Affairs held on Tuesday 10 December 1998. Malta Government Printing Press: Malta.

Kokaska, C. J. *et al.* (1984) 'Disabled people in the Bible', *Rehabilitation Literature* 45(1–2), 20–21.

Kottaridi, Y. *et al.* (1998/1) *Disabled Children and Their Families in Mediterranean Countries: A Preliminary Study in Greece*. Athens: Institute of Social Policy.

Krieger, L. (2000) 'Afterword: socio-legal backlash', *Berkeley Journal of Employment and Labor Law* 21(1), 476–520.

Laclau, E. and Mouffe, C. (1987) 'Postmarxism without apologies', *New Left Review* 166, 79–106.

Lakey, J. (1994) *Caring about Independence: Disabled People and the Independent Living Fund*. London: Policy Studies Institute.

Lane, H. (1992) *The Mask of Benevolence: Disabling the Deaf Communit*. New York: Vintage.

LaPlant, M. P. *et al.* (1997) 'Disability and employment', in *Disability Abstracts*, No. 10, 30 (January) University of California: Disability Statistics Centre, http://dsc.uesf.edu./abs/ab11txt.htm.

Lawton, D. (1997) 'Values and education: a curriculum for the 21st century', *Values and the Curriculum Conference*, University of London Institute of Education.

Lazarus, R. S. (1999) 'Hope: a coping resource against despair', *Social Research* 66(2), 653–78 (Special Issue).

Lepofsky, D. (1997) 'A report card on the *Charter's* guarantee of equality to persons with disabilities after 10 years – what progress? what prospects?', *National Journal of Constitutional Law* 7(3), 263–431.

Lepofsky, D. and Bickenbach, J. (1985) 'Equality rights and the physically handicapped', in A. Bayefsky and M. Eberts (eds) *Equality Rights and the Canadian Charter of Rights and Freedoms*, 323–76, Toronto: Carswell.

Levine, E. L. and Wexler, E. M. (1981) *P. L. 94–142: An Act of Congress*. New York: Macmillan.

Lipsky, D. and Gartner, A. (1997) *Inclusion and School Reform: Transforming America's Classrooms.* Baltimore: Paul H. Brookes.

Lister, R. (1990) *The Exclusive Society: Citizenship and the Poor.* London: Child Poverty Action Group.

Lloyd, M. (1992) 'Does she boil eggs? Towards a feminist model of disability', *Disability, Handicap & Society* 7(3), 207-21.

Lloyd, T. (1993) *The Charity Business: The New Philanthropists.* London: John Murray.

Lukes, S. (1973) *Individualism.* Oxford: Blackwell.

McDonnell, P. (2001) 'Deep structures in special education', in A. Zoniou-Sideris and A. Vlachou (eds) *Policies and Practices in the Area of Special/Inclusive Education* (tentative title). Athens: Hellenic Grammata.

McKnight, J. (1977) 'Professionalized service and disabling help', in I. Illich *et al.* (eds) *Disabling Professions.* London: Marion Boyars.

Macpherson, C. (1962) *The Political Theory of Possessive Individualism: Hobbes to Locke.* Oxford: Oxford University Press.

Management Systems Unit (1999) *Residential Services for Persons with Disabilities.* Unpublished report commissioned by the National Commission Persons with Disability. Malta.

Marconis, J. J. and Plummer, K. (1998) *Sociology: a global introduction.* London: Prentice Hall, Europe.

Marris, V. (1996) *Lives Worth Living: Women's Experience of Chronic Illness.* London: Pandora, Harper Collins.

Marshall, T. H. (1950) *Citizenship and Social Change.* Cambridge: Cambridge University Press.

Marshall, T. H. (1964) *Class, Citizenship and Social Development.* New York: Doubleday.

Marx, K. (1979) 'The symbolic power of money', in M. Solomon (ed.) *Marxism and Art: Essay Classic and Contemporary,* 44–6. Detroit, Michigan: Wayne State University Press.

Marx, G. and McAdam, D. (1994) *Collective Behaviour and Social Movements.* Englewood Cliffs: Prentice Hall.

Mason, M. (1992) 'A nineteen-parent family', in J. Morris (ed.) *Alone Together: Voices of Single Mothers.* London: The Women's Press.

Mason, M. (1997) Overhead used in a presentation at the Council for Disabled Children in London.

Mason, M. (2000) *Incurably Human.* London: Working Press.

Mason, M. and Rieser, R. (1994) *Altogether Better.* London: Comic Relief.

Matthews, G. W. (ed.) (1983) *Voices from the Shadows: Women with Disabilities Speak Out.* Ontario Canada: Women's Educational Press.

Mauss, M. (1938) 'Une categorie de L'esprit humaine: la notion de personne, celle de "moi"'. *Journal of the Royal Anthropological Institute* 68, 263–81.

Meager. N. *et al.* (1999) *Monitoring the Disability Discrimination Act (DDA) 1995: Department for Education and Employment, Research Report 119.* London: Institute for Employment Studies.

Mello, J. A. (1995) *AIDS and the law of workplace discrimination.* Boulder: Colorado.

Meltzer, H. *et al.* (1989) *Disability in the UK.* London: HMSO.

Miller, N. (1991) *Getting Personal: Feminist Occasions and Other Autobiographical Acts.* London: Routledge.

Miller, P. J. (2000) Paper presented at the Society for Disability Studies, Sheraton Hotel, Chicago, 29 June.

Mills, C. W. (1963) *The Sociological Imagination*. Harmondsworth: Penguin.

Minow, M. (1990) *Making All the Difference: Inclusion, Exclusion and American Law*. Ithaca: Cornell University Press.

Morris, J. (1989) *Able Lives: Women's Experience of Paralysis*. London: The Women's Press.

Morris, J. (1991) *Pride Against Prejudice: Transforming Attitudes to Disability*. London: The Women's Press.

Morris, J. (1992a) *Disabled Lives. Many Voices. One Message*. London: BBC.

Morris, J. (ed.) (1992b) *Alone Together: Voices of Single Mothers*. London: The Women's Press.

Morris, J. (1992c) 'Personal and political: a feminist perspective on researching physical disability', *Disability, Handicap and Society* 7(2), 157–66.

Morris, J. (1993a) *Community Care or Independent Living?* York: Joseph Rowntree Foundation.

Morris, J. (1993b) *Independent Lives? Community Care and Disabled People*. London: Macmillan.

Morris, J. (1995) 'Creating a space for absent voices: disabled women's experience of receiving assistance with daily living activities', *Feminist Review* 51 (autumn), 68–93.

Morris, J. (ed.) (1996) *Encounters With Strangers: Feminism and Disability*. London: The Women's Press.

Mosoff, J. and Grant, I. (1999) *Intellectual Disability and the Supreme Court*. Toronto: Canadian Association for Community Living.

Munford, R. and Sullivan, M. (1997) 'Social theories of disability: the insurrection of subjugated knowledges', in P. O'Brien and R. Murray, *Human Services. Towards Partnership and Support*. Palmerston North, NZ: Dunmore Press.

Myrdahl, G. (1940) *American Dilemma*. New York: Macmillan.

National Commission Persons With Disability (1993) *Special Education in Malta: A National Policy*. Malta: Kummissjoni Nazzjonali Persuni b'Dizabilità.

National Commission Persons With Disability (1995) *Persons with Disability and Employment: A National Policy*. Malta: Kummissjoni Nazzjonali Persuni b'Dizabilità.

National Commission Persons with Disability (1999) *National Disability Survey*. Malta: Kummissjoni Nazzjonali Persuni b'Dizabilità.

National Commission Persons With Disability (2000a) *Disability Issues – a course outline*. Malta: Kummissjoni Nazzjonali Persuni b'Dizabilità.

National Commission Persons With Disability (2000b): *PEKTUR Programme – prospectus*. Malta: Kummissjoni Nazzjonali Persuni b'Dizabilità.

National Minimum Curriculum (2000). Malta: Government Printing Press.

NCD (2000) *Promises to Keep: A Decade of Federal Enforcement of the Americans with Disabilities Act*. Washington, DC: National Council on Disability.

Newbold, G. (1995) *Quest for Equity: A History of Blindness Advocacy in New Zealand*. Palmerston North, NZ: Dunmore Press.

OFSTED (2000) *Evaluating Educational Inclusion*. London: OFSTED.

Oliver, M. (1986) 'Social policy and disability: some theoretical issues', *Disability, Handicap and Society* 1(1), 5–17.

Oliver, M. (1990) *The Politics of Disablement*. Basingstoke: Macmillan.

Oliver, M. (1995) 'Disability, empowerment and the inclusive society', in G. Zarb (ed.) *Removing Disabling Barriers*. London: Policy Studies Institute.

Oliver, M. (1996a) *Understanding Disability: From Theory to Practice*. London: Macmillan.

Oliver, M. (1996b) 'Defining impairment and disability: issues at stake', in C. Barnes and G. Mercer (eds) *Exploring the Divide: Illness and Disability*. Leeds: The Disability Press.

Oliver, M. (1997) 'The disability movement is a new social movement', *Community Development Journal. An International Forum* 32(3), 244–51 (Special Issue).

Oliver, M. and Barnes, C. (1998) *Disabled People and Social Policy: From Exclusion to Inclusion*. London: Longman.

Oliver, M. and Zarb, G. (1997) 'The politics of disability: a new approach', in L. Barton and M. Oliver (eds) *Disability Studies: Past, Present and Future*. Leeds: The Disability Press.

O'Neil, J. (1986) 'The disciplinary society', *British Journal of Sociology* 37(1), 42–60.

Pare, A., trans. by Pallister, L. (1982) *On Monsters and Marvels*. Chicago, Illinois: University of Chicago Press.

Paterson, K. and Hughes, B. (1999) 'Disability studies and phenomenology: the carnal politics of everyday life', *Disability and Society* 14(5), 597–610.

Paterson, K. and Hughes, B. (2000) 'The disabled body', in P. Hancock *et al.* (eds) *The Body, Culture and Society: An Introduction*. Buckingham: Open University Press.

Pearpoint, J. *et al.* (1992) *Strategies to Make Inclusion Work*. Toronto: Inclusion Press.

Pennhurst v Halderman (1981) 451 US 1.

Pennsylvania Association of Retarded Citizens (PARC) v Commonwealth of Pennsylvania (1971), 334 F. Supp. 1257.

Percy, S. L. (1989) *Disability. Civil Rights and Public Policy: The Politics of Implementation*. Tuscaloosa. Alabama: University of Alabama Press.

Perkins, Smith and Cohen Ltd. (1999) *Developments in Employment Law, Summer 1999: Court Trilogy Sharply Focuses Definitions of Disability*, http://www.psychoston.com/pubempsu99dis.html

Pointon, A. (1999) 'New images of disability in the civil rights campaign', in B. Franklin (ed.) *Social Policy, the Media and Misrepresentation*. London: Routledge.

Probyn, E. (1993) *Sexing the Self: Gendered Positions in Cultural Studies*. London: Routledge.

QCA (2000) Curriculum 2000 Appendix on General Inclusion Statement, p. 1. London: QCA.

Rae, A. (2000) 'Debate or divisiveness', *Coalition* August, 5–8 (published by Greater Manchester Coalition of Disabled People).

Rappaport, I. (1987) 'Terms of empowerment/exemplars of prevention: toward a theory for community psychology', *American Journal of Community Psychology* 15(2), 1–14.

Ratima, M. *et al.* (1995) *He Anga Whakamana. A framework for the delivery of disability support services for Maori*. Wellington, NZ: Core Services Committee, Ministry of Health.

Regan v Taxation with Representation of Washington (1983) 461 US 540.

Richardson, J. (1999) *Common, Delinquent and Special: The Institutional Shape of Special Education*. London and New York: Falmer Press.

Riddell, S. *et al.* (1993) 'The significance of employment as a goal for young people with recorded special educational needs', in *British Journal of Education and Work* 6(2), 57–72.

Rieser, R. (1989) Disability and the School Curriculum, Curriculum Equality Discussion Paper, London: ILEA.

Rieser, R. (1994) 'Insider perspective: the voice of a disabled teacher', in L. Barton (ed.) *Course Reader M.Ed in Inclusive Education*. Sheffield: University of Sheffield.

Rieser, R. (ed.)(1995) 'Invisible Children: Report of the Joint Conference On Children, Images and Disability', Save The Children,17 Grove Lane, London SE5 8RD.

Rieser, R. (2000) 'Disability discrimination, the final frontier: disablement, history and liberation', Ch 7 and 'Special educational needs or inclusive education: the challenge of disability discrimination in schooling', in M. Cole (ed.) *Education Equality and Human Rights*. London: Routledge/Falmer.

Rieser, R. and Mason, M. (1990/1992) *Disability Equality in the Classroom: A Human Rights Issue*, DEE, Unit 4Q, Leroy House, 436 Essex Road, London N1 3QP.

Rioux, M. H. (1994) 'Towards a concept of equality of well-being: overcoming the social and legal construction of inequality', *Canadian Journal of Law and Jurisprudence* VII(1), 127–47.

Rioux, M. H. (1997) 'Disability: the place of judgment in a world of fact', *Journal of Intellectual Disability Research* 41(3), 102–11.

Rioux, M. and Frazee, C. (1999) 'The Canadian framework for disability equality rights', in M. Jones and L. A. Marks (eds) *Disability, Divers-ability and Society*, 171–88. Great Britain: Kluwer Law International.

Robertson. A. and Minkler, M. (1994) 'New health promotion movement: a critical examination', *Health Education Quarterly* 21(3), 295–312.

Rose, N. (1989) *Governing the Soul: The Shaping of the Private Self*. London: Routledge.

Rose, R. (1999) 'Children's rights and adult responsibilities', in D. Matheson and I. Grosvenor (eds) *An Introduction to the Study of Education*. London: David Fulton Publishers.

Roth, W. (1983) 'Disability as a social construct', *Society* 20(3) 56–61.

Roulstone, A. (1998) *Enabling Technology: Disabled People, Work and the New Technology*. Buckingham: Open University Press.

Rowbotham, S. (1972) *Women, Resistance and Revolution*. Harmondsworth: Penguin.

Rowley v Hendrik Hudson Central District Board of Education (1982) 458 US 176.

Sayce, L. (2000) *From Psychiatric Patient to Citizen: Overcoming Discrimination and Exclusion*. Basingstoke: Macmillan.

Russell, M. (1998) *Beyond Ramps: Disability at the End of the Social Contract*. Monroe, Maine: Common Courage Press.

Scarry, E. (1985) *The Body in Pain: The Making and Unmaking of the World*. New York: Oxford University Press.

Schofield, A. N. (1955) *Parliamentary Elections*. London: Shaw and Sons.

Schwartz, D. B. (1997) *Who Cares? Rediscovering Community*. Boulder, Colorado: Westview Press.

Scotch, R. K. (1984) *From Good Will to Civil Rights: Transforming Federal Disability Policy*. Philadelphia, Pennsylvania: Temple University Press.

Scotch, R. (1989) 'Politics and policy in the history of the disability rights movement', *Milbank Memorial Quarterly* 62(2:2), 380–401.

Scott, A. (1990) *Ideology and New Social Movements*. London: Unwin Hymen.

Sebba, J. and Sachdev, D. (1997) *What Works in Inclusive Education*. Ilford, Essex: Barnardos.

Sen, A. (1999) *Development as Freedom*. Oxford: Oxford University Press.

Shakespeare, T. (1993) 'Disabled people's self-organisation: a new social movement?', *Disability and Society* 8(3), 249–64.

Shakespeare, T. (1999) 'Losing the plot? Discourses of disability and genetics', *Sociology of Health and Illness* 21(5), 669–88.

Shakespeare, T. (2000) 'Disabled Sexuality: Towards Rights and Recognition', *Bent*, July. http://www.bentvoices.org/culturecrash/shakespeare.htm

Shakespeare, T. *et al.* (1996) *The sexual politics of disability: untold desires.* London: Cassell.

Shakespeare, T. and Watson, N. (2000) *The Social Model of Disability: an Outdated Ideology.* Unpublished paper.

Shapiro, J. P. (1993) *No Pity: People with Disabilities Forging a New Civil Rights Movement.* New York: Times Books.

Sharp, A. (1992) 'The Treaty, the tribunal and the law: recognising Maori rights in New Zealand', in H. Gold (ed.) *New Zealand Politics in Perspective,* (3rd edn). Auckland, New Zealand: Longman Paul Limited.

Shaw, R. (1996) *The Activists Handbook.* Berkeley, California: University of California Press.

Simon, R. (1987) 'Empowerment as a Pedagogy of Possibility', *Language Arts* 64(4), 370–83.

Skeggs, B. (ed.) (1995) *Feminist Cultural Theory: Process and Production.* Manchester: Manchester University Press.

Skeggs, B. (1997) *Formations of Class and Gender.* London: Sage.

Slee, R. (1995) *Changing Theories and Practices of Discipline.* London: Falmer Press.

Slee, R. (1998) 'The politics of theorising special education' in C. Clark *et al., Theorising Special Education.* London: Routledge.

Southeastern Community College v Davis (1979) 442 US 397.

Stacey, J. (1995) 'The lost audience: methodology, cinema history and feminist film criticsm', in B. Skeggs (ed.) *Feminist Cultural Theory: Process and Production.* Manchester: Manchester University Press.

Stacey, J. (1997) 'Feminist Theory: capital F, capital T', in V. Robinson and D. Richardson (eds) *Introducing Women's Studies* (2nd edn). London: Macmillan.

Stanley, L. (ed.) (1990) *Feminist Praxis: Research, Theory and Espistemology in Feminist Research.* London: Routledge.

Stanley, L. and Wise, S. (1983) *Breaking Out: Feminist Consciousness and Feminist Research.* London: Routledge and Kegan Paul.

Stone, E. (ed.) (1999) *Disability and Development.* Leeds: The Disability Press.

Stuart, O. (1992) 'Race and disability: just a double oppression?', in *Disability, Handicap & Society* 7(2), 177–88.

Stuart, O. (1993) 'Double oppression: an appropriate starting point', in J. Swain *et al.* (eds) *Disabling Barriers – Enabling Environments.* London: Sage.

Sullivan, M. (1991) 'From personal tragedy to social oppression: the medical and social theories of disability', in *New Zealand Journal of Industrial Relations* 16, 255–72.

Sullivan, M. (1999) 'Does it say what we mean, do we mean what it says, do we know what it says? Assessing disability policy in tertiary institutions from a social model perspective'. Keynote address *DisAbility in Education – Maximising Everybody's Potential.* Conference proceedings (computer disc), University of Otago, Dunedin, New Zealand.

Swann, W (1989) *Integration Statistics: LEA's Reveal Local Variations.* London: Centre for Studies on Integration in Education.

Taylor, V. (1997) 'The trajectory of national liberation and social movements: the South

African experience', *Community Development Journal. An International Forum* 32(3), 252–65 (Special Issue).

The Times (Malta) (2000) 'Cospicua council objects to Church plans for battered men and women', 19 February.

Thomas, C. (1997) 'The baby and the bath water: disabled women and motherhood in social context', *Sociology of Health and Illness* 19(5), 622–43.

Thomas, C. (1999) *Female Forms: Experiencing and Understanding Disability*. Buckingham: Open University Press.

Tilstone, C. and Rose, R. (2001) 'Policy to practice: inclusion through education in the UK', in A. Zoniou-Sideris and A. Vlachou (eds) *Policies and Practices in the Area of Special/Inclusive Education* (tentative title). Athens: Hellenik Grammata.

Tomlinson, S. (1982) *A Sociology of Special Education*. London: Routledge and Kegan Paul.

Tomlinson, S. (1985) 'The expansion of special education', *Oxford Review of Education* 11(2), 157–65.

Tomlinson, S. (1988) 'Why Johny can't read: critical theory and special education', *European Journal of Special Needs Education* 3, 45–58.

Touraine, A. (1981) *The Voice and the Eye: An Analysis of Social Movements*. Cambridge: Cambridge University Press.

Traustadottir, R. and Johnson, K. (eds) (2000) *Women with Intellectual Disabilities: Finding a Place in the World*. London: Jessica Kingsley Publishers.

Troyna, B. and Vincent, C. (1996) 'The ideology of expertism: the framing of special education and racial equality policies in the local state', in C. Christensen and F. Rizvi (eds) *Disability and the Dilemmas of Education and Justice*. Buckingham: Open University Press.

Tsiakalos, G. (1999) *Human Dignity and Social Exclusion: The European Politis in Education*. Athens: Hellenic Grammata.

Turner, B. S. (1996) *The Body and Society* (2nd edn). London: Sage.

Turpin v R. (1989) 1 S.C.R. 1296.

United Nations (1988) *World Programme of Action Concerning Disabled Persons*. Geneva: United Nations.

United Nations (1993) *Standard Rules on the Equalization of Opportunities for People with Disabilities*. New York: The United Nations.

UPIAS (1996) *Fundamental Principles of Disability*. London: Union of the Physically Impaired Against Segregation

Ustun, T. B. *et al.* (1998) 'A reply to David Pfeiffer "the ICIDH and the need for its revision"', *Disability and Society* 13(5), 829–31.

Vernon, A. (1996a) 'A stranger in many camps: the experience of disabled black and ethnic minority women', in J. Morris (ed.) *Encounters With Strangers: Feminism and Disability*. London: The Women's Press.

Vernon, A. (1996b) 'Fighting two different battles: unity is preferable to enmity', in *Disability & Society* 11(2), 285–90.

Vernon, A. (1998) 'Multiple oppression and the disabled people's movement', in T. Shakespeare (ed.) *The Disability Reader: Social Science Perspectives*. London: Cassell.

Vernon, A. (1999) 'The dialectics of multiple identities and the disabled people's movement', *Disability and Society* 14(3), 385–98.

Vlachou, A. (1997) *Struggles for Inclusive Education.* Buckingham: Open University Press.

Vlachou, A. (1999) 'Equality and full participation for all? School practices and special education-integration in Greece', in F. Armstrong and L. Barton (eds) *Disability, Human Rights and Education: Cross Cultural Perspectives.* Buckingham: Open University Press.

Vlachou, A. (2000) 'Greek policy-practices in the area of special/inclusive education', in F. Armstrong *et al.* (eds) *Inclusive Education: Policy, Contexts and Comparative Perspectives.* London: David Fulton Publishers.

Walker, R. (1990) *Ka Whawhi Tonu Matou Struggle Without End.* Auckland, NZ: Penguin Books.

Walker, R. (1993) 'Maori people: their political development', in H. Gold (ed.) *New Zealand Politics in Perspective,* (3rd edn). Auckland, New Zealand: Longman Paul Limited.

Wendell, S. (1996) *The Rejected Body. Feminist Philosophical Reflections on Disability.* London: Routledge.

Wexler, P. (1992) *Becoming Somebody: Toward a Social Psychology of School.* Lewes: The Falmer Press.

Whitelocke, B. M. (1766) *Notes Upon the King's Writs for Choosing Members of Parliament.* London: Morton (Volume 1).

Wilkinson, M. (1999) 'Lots of carrot and a bit of stick', *Disability Now,* 12 November.

Williams, S. (1977) Speech of Secretary of State for Education and Science at the opening of Inkersall Green Special School at Staverly Derbyshire on 21 January 1977 quoted in HMSO 1978, Warnock Report, para 8.6, p.122.

Williams, S. (1999) 'Is anybody there? Critical realism, chronic illness and the disability debate', *Sociology of Health and Illness* 21(6), 797–819.

Wilson, C. and Jade, R. (1999) 'Whose Voice is it Anyway: Talking to young Disabled People at School', Alliance for Inclusive Education, Unit 2, 70 South Lambeth Road, London SW8 1RL.

Woods, P. (1981) 'Strategies, commitment and identity: making and breaking the teacher', in L. Barton and S. Walker (eds) *Schools, Teachers and Teaching.* Lewes: The Falmer Press.

World Health Organization (1980) *International Classification of Impairments. Disabilities, and Handicaps.* Geneva: World Health Organization.

Young and Powerful (1998a) Letter in *Flying Pigs* 3, 11 (summer). The Journal for the Alliance of Inclusive Education, Unit 2, 70 South Lambeth road, Vauxhall, London SW8 1RL.

Young and Powerful (1998b) 'Proposals to the Department for Education and Employment on developing inclusive education', *Flying Pigs* (autumn), 8–9.

Young, I. (1990) *Justice and the Politics of Difference.* Princeton, NJ: Princeton University Press.

Young, I. (2000) *Inclusion and Democracy.* Oxford: Oxford University Press.

Young, J. (1999) *The Exclusive Society.* London: Sage.

Youngberg v. Romeo (457 US 307, 1982).

Zola, I. K. (1983) 'Developing new self-images and interdependence', in N. Crewe and I. K. Zola (eds), *Independent Living for Physically Disabled People.* London: Jossey Bass.

Zola, I. K. (1989) 'Toward a necessary universalizing of disability policy', *The Milbank Quarterly* 67, 401–12.

Index